D0205874

White, Male and Middle-class

For Stuart, Becky and Jess

WHITE, MALE AND MIDDLE-CLASS

Explorations in Feminism and History

Catherine Hall

Routledge
New York

First published in the U.S.A. and Canada in 1992 by
Routledge, Chapman & Hall, Inc.
29 West 35th Street
New York, NY 10001

First published by Polity Press
in association with Blackwell Publishers.

ISBN 0 415 90662 8 (Cloth)
ISBN 0 0415 90663 6 (paperback)

Cataloging in Publication Data is available
from the Library of Congress

Typeset in 10½ on 12 pt Times by Times Graphics, Singapore
Printed in Great Britain by T. J. Press Ltd., Padstow, Cornwall

This book is printed on acid-free paper.

Contents

Part III Race, Ethnicity and Difference

Acknowledgements

'The History of the Housewife' first appeared in *The Politics of Housework* edited by Ellen Malos, London, 1980, and is published by kind permission of Allison & Busby. 'The Early Formation of Victorian Domestic Ideology' first appeared in *Fit Work for Women* edited by Sandra Burman, London, 1979, and is published by kind permission of Croom Helm. 'Gender Divisions and Class Formation in the Birmingham Middle Class, 1780–1850' first appeared in *People's History and Socialist Theory* edited by Raphael Samuel and is published by kind permission of Routledge & Kegan Paul. 'The Butcher, the Baker, the Candlestick-maker: the shop and the family in the Industrial Revolution' first appeared in *The Changing Experience of Women* edited by Elizabeth Whitelegg, Madeleine Arnot, Else Bartels, Veronica Beechey, Lynda Birke, Susan Himmelweit, Diana Leonard, Sonja Ruehl and Mary Anne Speakman, Oxford, 1982, and is published by kind permission of Martin Robertson. A version of 'The Tale of Samuel and Jemima: gender and working-class culture in early-nineteenth-century England' first appeared in *Popular Culture and Social Relations* edited by Tony Bennett, Colin Mercer and Janet Woollacott, Milton Keynes, 1986, and is published by kind permission of Open University Press. 'Private Persons versus Public Someones: class, gender and politics in England, 1780–1850' first appeared in *Language, Gender and Childhood* edited by Carolyn Steedman, Cathy Urwin and Valerie Walkerdine, London, 1985, and is published by kind permission of Routledge & Kegan Paul. 'Strains on the "Firm of Wife, Children and Friends": middle-class women and employment in early-nineteenth-century England' first appeared in *Women's Work and the Family Economy in Historical Perspective* edited by Pat Hudson and W. R. Lee, Manchester, 1990, and is published by kind permission of Manchester University Press. 'Missionary Stories: gender and ethnicity in England in the 1830s and 1840s' was first published in *Cultural Studies* edited by Lawrence Grossberg, Cary Nelson and Paula Treichler, New York and London, 1992, and is reprinted by kind permission of Routledge, Chapman & Hall. A version of 'Competing Masculinities' first appeared as 'The Economy of Intellectual Prestige: Thomas Carlyle, John Stuart Mill and the case of Governor Eyre' in *Cultural Critique*, no. 12, Spring 1989.

I am grateful to David Held at Polity Press for proposing this collection. The Economic and Social Research Council supported the joint research project of Leonore Davidoff and myself, between 1978 and 1982 and are now (1990–92) supporting my research on 'Race, Ethnicity and the English Middle Class 1832–68'. I am deeply grateful for that support.

Many people have helped me over the years with this work – in classes, workshops, seminars and conferences, libraries and archives – I thank them all. The discussions I have had with the women's history classes at the Birmingham Midland Institute in the 1970s, the students and staff of the Cultural Studies Department at the Polytechnic of East London since 1983, the collectives of *Feminist Review* and *Gender and History*, and varied feminist reading groups, have all helped me to shape the questions addressed in these essays. I could not have survived without the collectivity of feminist historians in Britain. David Albury, Michèle Barrett, Veronica Beechey, Moira Ferguson, Cora Kaplan, Keith McClelland, Jokhim Meikle and Bill Schwarz have all listened to me, discussed with me and kept me going. Lata Mani gave me helpful comments on chapter 10. Sally Alexander and Leonore Davidoff have both been critical and supportive in ways that have been vital to me, as has the love and encouragement of my sister, Margaret Rustin, and my mother, Gladys Barrett: these essays would not have been written without them. Stuart, Becky and Jess have lived with this work over the years and I dedicate this book to them.

1 Feminism and Feminist History

As a feminist historian writing in the 1990s I cannot be naïve either about memory, which feminist historians and theorists have done so much to explore, or about telling stories, which post-structuralism has helped us to think about when reading or writing history. My narrative, which concerns the ways in which I have engaged with feminism and history over the last twenty years, and the ways in which the essays in this book reflect the historical specificity of certain moments in that process, is necessarily partial, full of absences and silences, marked by its attempt to tell a coherent story, to make sense of tensions and contradictions which cannot in life be so neatly resolved. This, with all its particularities, is my story.

Historians construct stories, stories which necessarily have a narrative shape but in which the tensions between the teller, the tropes of the discourse (the beginning, the middle, the end), and what are understood to have been the events, are consciously worked on. But history, for me, is not just another fiction. Historical research is always premissed on a relation between past and present, is always about investigating the past through the concerns of the present, and always to do with interpretation. Historians attempt to interpret past realities and the meanings which they were given through language (for there is never only one real meaning, or one set of meanings), realities which can only be reached through forms of representation, which can only be read textually (in the widest sense of the term), which can never be grasped in an unmediated way. The stories which they construct, from laborious archival work ordered by conceptual frameworks, are grounded through an attempted comprehensiveness in relation to evidence, a commitment to look at countervailing accounts, an effort to test interpretations against others, the practices of good scholarship.

Some of this I learned as a student, some of it through feminism, some through working in cultural studies. The meaning of being an historian over the last twenty years, of trying to do certain kinds of historical work, has significantly changed. Feminism has made an important contribution to these changes. This introduction and the essays which follow are part of the story of that dynamic relation between feminism and history.

I have always loved history. I loved, as a child, being taken to places on family outings, whether castles, abbeys, battlefields, or royal palaces, walking round the walls of York, climbing on Hadrian's Wall, going down the shaft in Leeds City Museum's reconstructed coal-mine, having days out – outings that are intimately connected in my memory with those rare occasions when we were allowed to have fish and chips. Such trips were much encouraged by my mother, a first-generation grammar school girl who made it to Oxford to read history and had her budding historical career cut short by marrying a minister and becoming a minister's wife.

I loved reading historical novels too – especially by Rosemary Sutcliff – imaginatively living in another world. In my adolescence, I turned to those which combined exciting hints of sexual adventure with their historical drama: the many volumes of Jean Plaidy collected weekly from the local library, and *Katharine*, about the mistress of John of Gaunt, which we owned and I must have read at least a dozen times. I can still remember reading the exciting bits of *Gone With the Wind* (impervious to its racism), tucked behind the sofa in the house of family friends in Lancashire. Those memories of *Gone With the Wind* are mixed up with the sherry trifle which was a feature of those visits, a forbidden treat since alcohol was unknown in our temperance household, and over which there was a conspiracy of silence, combined with suppressed giggles when my father commented on how good the trifle was!

History lessons at my school, Leeds Girls' High School, were the only classes which I really enjoyed and which inspired me to try and find out things for myself. What a disappointment, having promised the class a radical reinterpretation of Sulamein the Magnificent, which would prove that he was not nearly as bad as had always been made out, that I could find no evidence in our school library to support this claim and had to rely entirely on vigorous assertion in defence of my claim! My favourite history teacher, Miss Braddy as she was then, is fixed in my memory as she was when we were doing A-levels, the Tudors and Stuarts, and she introduced us to Christopher Hill's *The Century of Revolution*, just published, as our set text. An unlikely choice in a very conventional girls' grammar school but one that set me off on a long love-affair with the British Marxist historians.

It wasn't surprising, then, that I too ended up reading history at university. History always seemed the only choice, and that seemed to lead straight on to research, although on an unlikely topic – the English medieval aristocracy. That was because of Rodney Hilton's teaching at Birmingham, which opened up to me a whole new and exciting world, a different and imagined feudal world, in which men made their own history and it was therefore vital for historians to grasp 'the political and social consciousness of the various classes'.[1] Hilton had been a member of the Communist Party Historians' Group, that group which had decided to challenge British historiography and construct a new body of Marxist history that would both connect with popular politics and engage with the academic establishment. Rodney Hilton, Christopher Hill, Edward Thompson and Eric Hobsbawm, together with the other members of the group, called for a major reassessment of English cultural and political history and a communism which would combine elements of Marxism with popular radical English traditions.[2]

By the early 1960s, when I went to university, a substantial body of that work had already appeared and the Cold War freeze-out which had marginalized much of what had been done in the 1940s and 1950s was beginning to melt. The medieval England to which Hilton introduced me was theorized in ways that made sense to me – class struggle, popular resistance, a whole social formation; these were concepts at the heart of his writing and teaching. For a young woman bred on radical nonconformity and the *New Statesman*, growing up in Leeds as a Young Socialist and an activist in YCND, connected to the tail-end of the New Left as it entered popular politics through the peace movement in the early 1960s, this was a heady brew. My marriage in 1964 to a Jamaican intellectual active in New Left politics, whom I had first encountered on an Aldermaston march, strengthened this nexus of political and personal connections and gave me confidence to pursue my own project.

Hilton's radical political agenda, twinned with his deep love for the activity of historical research, was an inspiring combination and one which led me to think that I could overcome the practical difficulties associated with my bad Latin – and even worse palaeographic skills – and become a medieval historian. Being a research student, however, turned out to be an alienating and disappointing life. The excitement of intensive teaching was over, now I was expected to get on with it alone and sustain my own project; weeks in the Public Record Office with undecipherable manuscripts, visits to dusty episcopal archives – what was this to do with class struggle and popular resistance? The model of the lone researcher seemed to be the only available paradigm, despite the collective discussions of the Communist Party historians.

Then came 1968 – which signified for me not only the months of student activism, the demands for a new curriculum, the insistence that the history syllabus should include discussion of theory and historiography (totally neglected in the majority of courses), but also the familiar discomfort, not yet recognized for what it was, of being a woman active in left politics. This was much intensified by the fact that I was by now many months pregnant with my first child and while other students revelled in the excitement of occupying the Great Hall at Birmingham University I found it too uncomfortable to sleep on the floor and had to go home – hardly a properly revolutionary experience! In December 1968 my baby was born and I soon found that the life of a mother did not fit well with that of a researcher. The printed Pipe Rolls were difficult to focus on in the few hours that Becky slept; questions which had seemed fascinating, such as the construction of aristocratic hegemony in the West Midlands, lost their edge for me in the midst of a totally new life dominated by the unfamiliar demands of a baby – by milk, nappies and a twenty-four-hour day. Gradually it became clear that finding a new way to survive was the most pressing issue – and a women's group seemed to provide the answer.

The first Women's Liberation Group met in Birmingham in February 1970. Many of us were young mothers with children who had started talking informally about the things that felt wrong with our lives, especially our isolation. We set up what became a consciousness-raising group, though I don't think we thought of it as such at the time, and began to talk about what it meant to be a woman. Most of us had some kind of history in left politics, and a university education. Some of us attended the first women's movement conference at the end of February 1970. We read Juliet Mitchell's *The Longest Revolution* and Sheila Rowbotham's 'Women's Liberation and the New Politics', thought about why we wanted to exclude men from our group, and began to wonder about organizing campaigns on women's issues in Birmingham. Being active in a women's group, which rapidly evolved into other groups, and starting to organize collective childcare, seemed much more satisfying and immediate than doing historical research. In 1971 my second child was born and motherhood seemed to combine more comfortably with political activism than the Public Record Office.

I can distinctly remember one of my first encounters with feminist history, though some of the details may be wrong as I can no longer find the evidence. It was through reading an article by three American feminists who offered a reinterpretation of Victorian womanhood. The article was an eye-opener and I remember presenting a version of it to a women's study group I was in. When our children were a little older and we had organized a more effective system of childcare, I began to think again about doing historical work, but this time focused on women. My fascination with what it had meant for me to become a housewife and mother, and the ways in which I and my sisters had developed a politics from that perspective, informed my first experiments in this new area of historical research. The politics of housework which we had begun to elaborate questioned the division of labour in the home, challenged the ways in which hidden reproductive work was being done by women, and demanded a different future for them. 'The History of the Housewife' – chapter 2 of this book – first given as a paper to a Ruskin History Workshop in London and later published in a shortened version in *Spare Rib*, reflected the combination of those new concerns with the older agenda inherited from the Marxist historians.

Feminist history as first conceptualized in the early 1970s was about the recovery of women's history. We needed to fill out the enormous gaps in our historical knowledge which were a direct result of the male domination of historical work. How had women lived in the past, what had they experienced, what kinds of work had they done, in what patterns of family life had they been involved, what records had they made? How could we find out?

Thus, in that first crucial text for British feminist history *Hidden from History* (1973), Sheila Rowbotham wrote in her preface that, while working on her book, she kept asking herself:

> In what conditions have women produced and reproduced their lives, both through their labour and through procreation; how has the free expression of this activity been distorted and blocked by the circumstances of society?[3]

A year earlier Anna Davin had written in her essay 'Women and History' that feminists had to reject what had passed for history and begin anew. 'In a class society,' she argued, 'history has meant the history of the rulers, and in a male dominated society the history of men.'[4] The socialist and utopian rhetoric of such writing was characteristic of this first generation of feminist historians. Our socialism was heavily infused with humanism, redolent with the conviction that we too could make history, albeit not in conditions of our own making. We were convinced of the possibility of a socialist feminist politics and a socialist feminist history. We might not have wanted a marriage between Marxism and feminism, given the elaboration of our critique of marriage, but we certainly wanted a working partnership.

'The History of the Housewife', the first version of which was written in 1973, has the hallmarks of this early attempt to link the new language of feminism with a reworked Marxism. It was concerned to recover a lost history and give value and meaning to the activities of women which had not been legitimated in traditional historical writing. Implicitly it challenged the grand narratives of Marxism (long before post-modernism emerged on the scene), which told the story of the transition from feudalism to capitalism and from manufacture to modern industry without any reference to women. That challenge could in part be met by recovering older traditions of feminist history-writing – such as Alice Clark's investigation of the impact of the transition from feudalism to capitalism on women's work (an aspect of the transition never mentioned in the many discussions about it amongst men that I had heard over the years), and Ivy Pinchbeck's study of women's work and the Industrial Revolution.[5]

The working concepts I made use of included the sexual division of labour (a reworking of the Marxist emphasis on the social division of labour); the insistence on the family as a site for the provision of the social relations of production (connected to the Althusserian concept of ideological state apparatuses, or ISAs);

the stress on housework as the invisible support for the generation of surplus value (the beginnings of the debate over whether housework was, or was not, productive which eventually ground to a halt as the inadequacy of an attempted application of Marxism to a different set of problems became apparent); and the notion of a 'dominant ideology' which oppressed women. Other concerns of this essay are the separation of home from work and the break that this represented for women, and the family as a unit of consumption. The Althusserian concept of 'relative autonomy' – the relative autonomy of the family, for example, from forms of social determination – is also in play as a way of theorizing uneven developments and explaining the different temporalities of production and reproduction.

This first phase of feminist history-writing in the 1970s was also marked by an ambition, a conviction that it was possible to aim for a broad historical sweep, to rethink historical epochs, to construct new temporalities. In the early days of the women's movement it seemed appropriate to generalize, to use secondary sources, to deal with long historical periods. Those heady days have now been replaced by more cautious approaches and more careful investigations. We soon began to feel the need for more detailed work, a more nuanced and dense grasp of particular historical moments. This shift in emphasis was connected with the gradual move away from thinking primarily about feminist history as part of a political movement towards thinking about it as an academic subject. The professionalization of feminist history (however limited it has been in Britain) has both advantages and disadvantages, for it was our political certainties which gave us the strength to make the assertions that we did. It would be a pity if the loss of those certainties, and the ever more complex understanding of the ways in which gender difference interacts with other axes of power, were to prevent us in the future from moving from the particular to the more general.

During the 1970s women's history gradually became a subject in its own right. Adult education provided a facilitating framework for the development of new kinds of courses and new areas of study and had an excellent radical pedigree. Both Raymond Williams's *Culture and Society* and E. P. Thompson's *The Making of the English Working Class* were written while their authors were working in adult education.[6] Cora Kaplan has evoked the excitement of teaching women's writing in these arenas in the 1970s, for adult education classes provided an ideal opportunity to feed ideas into collective practice and be sure of a critical response with a political inflection.[7] We met in those classes because of a movement, we collectively developed our new objects of study and new forms of analysis, and our manifesto that 'Women's history – and therefore people's history – has yet to be written, and to write it is part of our present struggle'.[8] All this was a far cry from the individualist mode of historical research.

In Birmingham the Extra-Mural Department was happy to cooperate with the establishment of a regular yearly slot in its programme. This started off as 'Women in Society' in 1974, boasting one section on history; became, in 1975, 'Women in History' (aiming to cover the medieval, early modern and modern); and in succeeding years increasingly narrowed its focus as articles and books slowly became available and the research which made new teaching possible was set in motion. In the late 1970s a feminist history research group was set up, also under the aegis of the Extra-Mural Department, which developed a collective research project, gave collective papers and published an article.[9] Similar courses and groups were being established around the country, utilizing the WEA and extra-mural facilities when appropriate or relying on independent networks. These varied groups were all concerned with the work of historical reconstruction, the recovery of a past, which was so vital if we were to believe in a future for ourselves. That work focused on putting women back into the historical picture, recognizing and celebrating women's achievements which had been lost through the male domination of historical writing.[10]

While feminist critics reread the canon with the objective of finding a female self and a speaking voice for women, feminist historians set about discovering what women had done in the workplace, in the home, as mothers, daughters, wives and lovers, what political movements they had been involved with, what forms of struggle they had engaged in, what battles they had won and what they had lost, how men had managed to maintain their power over women for so long. At that time woman/women was not a contested category. Rather it seemed clear to us that women, 'our sex', were those who were oppressed by men, those who must demand power and agency for themselves and make history. Such a formulation inevitably masked a multitude of problems for, as Ann Snitow points out, the tension 'between needing to act as women and needing an identity not overdetermined by our gender . . . is at the core of what feminism is'.[11]

By 1975 I had decided that I had no future as a medievalist and that I should turn to the nineteenth century. I went to Essex University to do an MA, the only university in the country where it was possible to study women's history as part of a postgraduate course. While there I pursued my interest in domestic ideology (conceptualized as a coherent ideology) particularly in relation to the early-nineteenth-century middle class. Chapter 3, 'The Early Formation of Victorian Domestic Ideology', was originally written as my MA dissertation. In that work I began to explore the ways in which women had themselves been implicated in the construction of a new bourgeois culture in the late eighteenth and early nineteenth centuries. Far from a 'dominant ideology' having been imposed on women by men, women ideologues, particularly the redoubtable Hannah More, had played a vital part in defining and articulating the boundaries of a new domesticated morality. Here was a woman indeed making history, but not in the conditions of her own making. Hannah More was a great anti-Jacobin propagandist, but consideration of the tensions between her forms of political conservatism and the radicalism of her claims for women's sphere (albeit a radicalism very different from that of her despised antagonist Mary Wollstonecraft) was to be highly relevant in what were to become the Thatcher years. Furthermore, an appraisal of More and Wollstonecraft highlighted the tensions between issues of equality and difference, a central and necessarily unresolved conflict for feminism.[12]

'The Early Formation' was written in the shadow of E. P. Thompson's *The Making of the English Working Class*, a text on which many feminist historians cut their teeth. For, slicing across our preoccupation with women was a constant preoccupation with class questions. British feminism and British feminist history developed in dialogue with the Labour movement and class politics. Political identities and political discourses in Britain have been vitally associated with class identities and the language of class has, since the early nineteenth century, provided a dominant discourse of politics, closely intertwined with the language of radicalism and socialism. The language of class was the language which was used to articulate what was different about capitalism and modernity and thus has occupied a key position in nineteenth- and twentieth-century society. Feminism in Britain in the late 1960s and early 1970s was rooted in an engagement and dialogue with those languages of class, of radicalism and of socialism, and indeed with the political movements associated with them. By the mid-1970s a distinctive radical feminist voice had emerged, with its own historical agenda, challenging and fertilizing socialist feminism and transforming the feminist agenda with its insistence, particularly, on questions about the control of women's sexuality and male violence.[13] In the first years of the new women's movement, however, the dialogue with socialism was pre-eminent.

Feminist history in Britain developed in a quite specific relation to this engagement with socialism and with class politics. The first national conference of the women's liberation movement was held at Ruskin College, Oxford, the trade union college where Raphael Samuel, one of the founder members of the New Left, of the History Workshop movement and *History Workshop Journal*, teaches history. It was the result of a demand from a group of women. It began as a history workshop and grew into a national conference. At the same time the early history workshops took up questions about women's history and became a place where budding feminist historians could meet, where our double marginality – from the historical establishment and from the heartlands of labour history – acted as a stimulus rather than silencing us. *History Workshop Journal* was from its inception both a space and a site of struggle for feminist historians. Sally Alexander and Anna Davin's feminist editorial in the first issue of the journal summed up the preoccupations of the mid-1970s:

> By bringing women into the foreground of historical enquiry our knowledge of production, of working class politics and culture, of class struggle, of the welfare state, will be transformed. Men and women do inhabit different worlds, with boundaries which have been defined (and from time to time re-arranged) for them by the capitalist mode of production as it has made use of and strengthened the sexual division of labour and patriarchal authority. It is relationships like that between the two worlds, between the sexual division of labour and class struggle, home and work, or the private sector and the public, the social relations between men and women which form the substance of feminist history, and will enrich all socialist history.[14]

Here class struggle, the capitalist mode of production, the sexual division of labour, patriarchy and public and private provided the conceptual framework for a distinctively socialist feminist approach. That approach was the result of long and hard work, of many collective discussions, of unsuccessful as well as successful attempts to rework concepts. What now appears a seamless development was an uneven and difficult process, with tiny theoretical gains being won at great, if sometimes exciting, cost.

British feminist history was fed and watered by the tradition of British Marxist historiography – many of us were taught by those historians, inspired by their example and their influence, their commitment to the possibility of a political project in the rewriting of histories, their attempts to recover the heroic stories of peasants, or humble seventeenth-century Puritans, or the working class, their determination to hold together the use of empirical evidence and a powerful theoretical framework, their success in terms of their readership and their capacity to make a difference. We learned from them how to construct historical narratives in terms of class struggle. But the engagement with that historiography, the challenge that it presented in terms of the things that were not said and were not explored, the refusal to consider seriously the woman question, the conviction that class was gender blind – only slowly and tentatively articulated by us – also moved us to reject our fathers and to attempt to do a different kind of work, write different histories, inspired by a different set of political imperatives.[15]

The exploration of class, particularly as a cultural formation, has remained, however, at the heart of my work and the essays in Part II of this book represent the effort to understand the complex interplay of gender and class. Many of them were written while I was working with Leonore Davidoff, for in 1978 we began a joint research project on the place of gender in the formation of the English middle class, published in 1987 as *Family Fortunes: Men and Women of the English Middle Class, 1780–1850.*[16] The preoccupations with gender and class reflected both the feminist politics of the mid-1970s and the historiographical concerns of that period. The early optimism of the women's movement of the late 1960s and early 1970s, the euphoric sensation that our new understanding of the sexual division of labour, the organization of the family and the power relations between men and women meant that society could be transformed, that the world could be turned upside down by our new view of it and by willing it, organizing it to be so, was giving way to a more sober conviction that the kinds of social change which we sought were going to be very difficult to achieve, not least because of the changes involved for ourselves and in ourselves. The utopian moment was over – the long haul had begun.

One response to this was the turn to psychoanalysis, heralded by Juliet Mitchell's *Psychoanalysis and Feminism*, and the recognition that feminine subjectivity presents serious problems for feminists, that out wants and desires might be more contradictory than we had realized, that our psyches might be more resistant to change than our social selves.[17] Another response was linked to the socialist-feminist dialogue with radical feminism, for the socialist perspective kept the question of a different future for women and men on the agenda. This inspired the attempt to come to terms with the extent to which women's oppression could only be understood as part of a whole social process in which men are implicated quite as much as women. Thus the move away from an exclusive focus on women and the beginnings of a feminist interest in men and the construction of masculinities. Significantly, Michèle Barrett's chapter on sexuality and subjectivity in her influential book *Women's Oppression Today* (1980) was 'Femininity, Masculinity and Sexual Practice', an indicator of a new emphasis but one which has been strongly criticized and regarded as possibly dangerous by some feminists, in its return to that ever central object of study, men.[18]

From its inception, the project on which Leonore Davidoff and I worked together, and which resulted in both *Family Fortunes* and the essays on gender and class published here, was concerned with women *and* men. We wanted not just to put the women back into a history from which they had been left out, but to rewrite that history so that proper recognition would be given to the ways in which gender, as a key axis of power in society, provides a crucial understanding of how any society is structured and organized.[19] What was the specific relation of women to class structures and how should women's class position be defined? How was class *gendered*, to use the word which began to be increasingly utilized by feminists as a way of thinking about the social relations between the sexes and the ways in which men's power over women provides a fundamental form of social, economic and political power?[20] How was it different to be a man or a woman belonging to a particular social class? Do men and women have different class identities? Are their forms of class consciousness and class solidarity the same? Since in classical Marxism class is defined as a relation to the means of production, what were the implications of this for women? Was women's labour in the home unproductive? Were women engaged in class struggles in the same ways as men? Did women have an identity as women which cut across forms of class belonging? These were the kinds of questions which raged amongst feminists in the 1970s, which provoked some fascinating and important debates (as well as some dead ends), and which made us determined to explore the meaning of class for both men and women, in the conviction that a class formation could not possibly be understood by looking at only men or only women, that masculinities and femininities are always defined in relation to each other and that they only make full sense when placed in a whole social, economic and cultural world.

Our central preoccupations were, then, class and gender. The concept of gender emerged from years of consciousness-raising. Work had to be done to discover a new analytic term, a concept which was strong enough to counter class without being reducible to sex. Gender was understood relationally: manliness, to use the nineteenth-century term, is what is not feminine, femininity the opposite of manliness, 'the rugged lofty pine and graceful slender vine' of the anonymous poem in a commonplace book, or in the words of the popular poet Ann Taylor Gilbert, writing on the differences between men and women in 1807:

> Man's proudest glory is his head,
> A Woman's is her heart.[21]

We only establish the differences between men and women by discursively constructing 'the other', as we might now put it. Furthermore, those definitions are not fixed in essence but are constantly changing as they are contested and reworked. Masculinities and femininities are thus historically specific and we can trace the changes over time in the definitions which have been in play and in power. What it means to be a man or a woman is not given at birth, but constructed in culture and constructed through difference.

Other developments in feminist theory and history were also crucial to the definition of our project and, in particular, there were important influences from the United States. The debates over class had never had the pertinence there that they had had in Britain, since class is a highly contested category in the USA and socialist politics have occupied a much less central position there. In the United States the dominant paradigm was set by the emphasis on individual rights, on equality and on sisterhood. One of the first and most evocative slogans to come from the American women's movement was that impassioned cry, 'Sisterhood is powerful'. Women together, organized and with a collective identity and collective demands, could be politically effective. The refusal of the status of victim – people who have things done to them, who cannot be agents in their own liberation – was empowering in terms of both public campaigns and private struggles. American feminist historians began to explore the myriad sources of modern feminism and the specificity of women's culture.

The recognition, within the women's movement, of women's potential for power and agency in the world was reflected in the writing on 'women's culture'. Nancy Cott, for example, in *The Bonds of Womanhood* (1977), looked at the ways in which middle-class American women in the early nineteenth century increasingly occupied a separate sphere from men, in which they began to spend more time together and to recognize mutual interests. Women gradually began to combine, both in the family and outside it through friendship, to protect those mutual interests, moving from gossip over teacups to semi-formal organizations such as maternal associations and missionary ventures, often using the church as a base.[22] Mary Ryan, in her *Cradle of the Middle Class*, developed this argument in the context of a community study of the middle class, and looked at the ways in which women's organizations were able to challenge the boundaries between public and private.[23] Other writers began to explore the ways in which these mutual interests provided, on the one hand, a basis for a heightened awareness of the particularity of women's identity and needs and, on the other, could bring them into more direct conflict with men through moral reform attacks on the 'double standard' and temperance. In some instances this opened the way for explicitly feminist concerns. Carroll Smith Rosenberg's article, 'The female world of love and ritual', was undoubtedly the most influential piece of historical writing on women's culture, with its celebration of women's agency, its demonstration of the strength of their homosocial relationships, and the pleasure women had in their 'alternative world'. It mirrored the pleasure feminists had in the world which they were creating and stressed a commonality of culture which was symptomatic of this first phase of feminism but neglected the differences and power relations between women, rooted both in class and ethnicity, which dominated feminist politics in the 1980s.[24]

'Sisterhood is powerful' recognized the power which collectivities of women could have, whether in friendship groups and through gossip (who is excluded, who is included) or in informal or formal organizations. The perception of the extent of women's power and influence was in part based on the recognition of the multiplicity of sites of power, which was certainly understood by feminists in the 1970s as they challenged male power and asserted themselves in the home, in the kitchen and bedroom, against their men, with their children, in workplaces and political organizations. Feminism placed the issue of power on the political agenda, just as the black power movement did in the United States. Foucault's knowledge/power couplet, his *theorization* of the multiplicity of power relations, his challenge to orthodox Marxist conceptions of power as residing in 'the ruling class' or 'the state', may now be to the fore in the minds of students schooled in post-structuralist thought, but the political preconditions for the take-up of such ideas in Britain were in part to do with feminism.

The recognition of the multiplicity of sites of power between men and women was linked to the concept that 'the personal is political' – one of the key breakthroughs of the early women's movement – the understanding that *sexual politics*, the politics of power relations between men and women, is part of everyday personal life. Thus, the question of who does the washing-up, who changes the nappies, who sweeps the floor, who does the shopping, who feels it is their fault when things go wrong in a family or household, is not just to do with individual difficulties between couples but is part of a social organization of power. Men's power over women is not only at play in the public arenas of education or employment, but in the most private recesses of our experience, in our feelings about ourselves as daughters, mothers, wives and lovers. Such a perception, which now seems entirely common sense, emerged from the consciousness-raising groups of women in the United States and Britain. No theorist can be said to have discovered it, it was a genuinely collective naming of a problem which in the 1950s had had 'no name'. As such, it posed a fundamental challenge to the seemingly 'natural' relations between the sexes.

Feminist politics in the 1970s was inevitably very preoccupied with the place of the family, attempting to understand the extent to which women's oppression, to use the language of the 1970s, was rooted in the family.[25] The recognition of the myth of the happy nuclear family, often starting with women's experience of motherhood and childcare, the beginnings of work on representations of the family, the gradual discovery of the extent of violence within the family, the understanding that 'there is nothing wrong with thinking that there's a great deal wrong with the family', the realization of the particularities of the Western nuclear family and the discovery of possible alternatives, the attempt to create and live with such alternatives – all this was part of the feminist politics of the family in the 1970s.[26] It was clear that the family was one of the keys to it all – the place where boys first learned to be boys and girls to be girls, the place where sexuality was tied to reproduction, where women were trapped in the dual burdens of motherhood and low-paid work, where men could be patriarchs, monarchs of all they surveyed, even if their territory was very modest and their subjects few. The family was central to social organization and central to the power relations between the sexes. As such, the neglect by historians of the institution of the family and its place in the social and political world was quite extraordinary.

Feminist historians in the 1970s drew on this common body of feminist theory and practice; the desire to understand the connections between sexual politics and class politics, the recognition of women's agency, 'sisterhood is powerful', the conviction that power relations between the sexes were at the heart of the social and psychic order, 'the personal is political', and the knowledge that the institution of the family was not only central to women's subordination but also to economic, political and social life. The women's movement can also be said to have inspired the work on the middle class which Leonore Davidoff and I launched into. Whereas much of the early British feminist history investigated the lives of working-class women, inspired by the example of socialist history, the recovery of 'history from below', and the absence from that of any adequate work on women, we drew on the feminist injunction that you should always start with yourself and what you know and experience. For most feminists in the 1970s, 'experience' was still a central category, and so we began to investigate the institution into which we were both born, and which we had in our turn reproduced, the middle-class family. Ten years ago there was a striking absence of historical work on the middle class, let alone the middle-class family. In deciding to work on the middle class we were undoubtedly driven in part to discover what seemed to be the moment of formation of that particular family form which has remained hegemonic into the late twentieth century.[27]

Our preoccupations were still, however, in part centred on male theory (not only Marx but Gramsci for his work on civil society and the construction of hegemony, and Weber for his rich and suggestive analysis of the relations between particular religious forms and the development of capitalism), on male historiography, on male power, and indeed on the relational aspects of the historical specificities of masculinities and femininities. From this rich brew, nineteenth-century middle-class men emerged as a central object of study; fascinating in their conviction of their own power, their sense of themselves as making history, their future. At the end of 1978 I spent three months in the Birmingham Reference Library reading *Aris's Birmingham Gazette* between the 1780s and 1840s. I became increasingly desperate about the virtual absence of women from any page of these papers until I finally realized – one of those realizations that is so obvious once you have made it – that the newspaper was contributing to the construction of a new middle-class male public sphere by the very items that were chosen to be reported, whether philanthropic meetings, civic processions or significant funerals. Men moved to the centre of the story – not to displace women, but in order to be able to make sense of the particular articulations of masculinity or femininity within the middle class. To be a middle-class man was to be a somebody, a public person, while the essence of middle-class femininity was being constructed as private and domestic. Such oppositions acquired their meanings ideologically, but that ideology had material effects of the most immediate and concrete kind.

The essays in Part II are all concerned with the complex interplay between gender and class. What were the distinctive patterns of domesticity associated with the English nineteenth-century middle class? What was the relation between prescribed ideologies and lived practices? What were the particular masculine and feminine identities constructed within the middle class? What tensions were there between class and gender identities, and how might these contradictions have contributed to the development of feminism? What kind of impact had middle-class notions of proper relations between men and women had on working-class people? What access could historical specificity give us to the particularities of the gender/class dynamic?

While many nineteenth-century middle-class men may have tried to speak for their wives, as James Luckcock, the Birmingham jeweller, did so memorably in the poem he wrote about himself on his wife's behalf, entitled 'My Husband' (quoted chapter 4), a careful use of a variety of sources made it possible to rethink the ways in which middle-class men had selectively thought about and recorded their world, many of those categories being preserved in the writings of middle-class male historians. In our study, both male and middle class were subjected to the feminist lens – whiteness, for me however, was a more resistant category.

While white feminist theorists, critics and historians were struggling over the meanings of gender, black feminists were issuing a different challenge. This happened first in the United States where black women questioned the white and ethnocentric concerns of American feminism as it had emerged in the late 1960s and 1970s. The concept of sisterhood came under fire as black women insisted on the importance of recognizing difference and diversity and argued that the white feminist version of sisterhood was exclusive to white women, who only accepted sisters on their own terms.[28] These issues became vital to feminist politics in Britain as black women challenged white feminists in campaigns, at meetings and at conferences. The formation of autonomous black women's groups in the late 1970s, particularly the Organization of Women of African and Asian descent, which attempted to bring together black women from a number of different backgrounds and perspectives, was a critical moment for feminism.[29] Black feminists argued that a white, Eurocentric, Western feminism had attempted to establish itself as the only legitimate feminism, that this feminism did not speak to the experiences of black women, and that there was little recognition of the ways in which the gains of white women were made at the expense of black women.

In 1982 Hazel Carby, in her critique of white feminist theory in Britain, was also scathing about the new forms of history. When white feminists, she argued, 'write their herstory and call it the story of women but ignore our lives and deny their relation to us, that is the moment in which they are acting within the relations of racism and writing *his*story'.[30] Valerie Amos and Pratibha Parmar took up this emphasis on the 'herstory' which had developed in Britain and the amnesia on questions of race from which it suffered:

> The 'herstory' which white women use to trace the roots of women's oppression or to justify some form of political practice is an imperial history rooted in the prejudices of colonial and neo-colonial periods, a 'herstory' which suffers the same form of historical amnesia of white male historians, by ignoring the fundamental ways in which white women have benefitted from the oppression of Black people.[31]

Feminist theory and practice, these black feminists were insisting, must entail an understanding of imperialism and a critical engagement with, and challenge to, racism.

In the United States black women started to write their own story, both fictionally and in more conventional historical forms.[32] Black feminist historians were faced with the double problem that African-American history was well developed but failed to address questions of gender, while women's history failed to address questions of race.[33] The 'double consciousness' of the black American man had been written about by Dubois most eloquently in the early twentieth century: 'One ever feels his twoness – an American, a Negro; two souls, two thoughts, two unreconciled strivings; two warring ideals in one dark body, whose dogged strength alone keeps it from being torn asunder.'[34] This 'double consciousness' had to be extended to include the dynamic of gender. In Britain the problems in constructing a black feminist history have been different from those in the USA since there is a much less well developed black historiography as a base for building and critique. The black and Asian population in Britain occupies a very different position from the black population in the United States, since it was only in the 1950s that large numbers of Afro-Caribbean and Asian peoples came into Britain. Not until the 1960s and 1970s did a black identity haltingly emerge, articulating the particular dreams and desires of 'immigrants', constructing solidarities and allegiances between different ethnic communities. The identity of the 'black Briton' remains uncertain and contested, the dream of 'going home' still a living reality for many.[35]

As Delia Jarrett Macaulay has recently described, her writing of black women's history was connected with the emergence of a black feminist identity, which has its own history in relation to the black power movement. That moment was associated with the late 1970s, the space which the Greater London Council (GLC) opened up in London for women and ethnic minorities, the move to establish a black caucus in the Labour Party, and the ways in which these political events intersected with the powerful impact of black women's writing. The International Conference on the History of Blacks in Britain which Macaulay attended in London in 1981 was hardly affected by the contemporary black presence; the only paper presented which related to women was about the Hottentot Venus.[36] Peter Fryer's vital book *Staying Power* was published in 1984 but its history of blacks in Britain had almost nothing to say about women.[37] The absence of a black women's history became a problem with a name.

The conditions for the development of such a history were, however, hardly propitious. In the 1980s the entry of black and Asian women into the higher education system was extremely limited, coinciding with the period when history departments were drastically cut back, funding for historical research decimated, adult education threatened. What work has been done by black feminist historians has once again come from the margins – teachers, librarians, activists, who have been determined to begin to write their own histories.[38]

But black women, as we have seen, presented a challenge to white women as well as developing their own historical project. White women must find out for themselves how different racisms, each with their contingent historical conditions, arising from the colonial and imperial ventures of the last five centuries, have been and continue to be central to British history and an understanding of British society. It was not the task of black women to teach white women this, any more than it was the task of women of teach men; oppressors should learn about their own forms of oppression. The understanding of difference is a task for all of us. As Audre Lorde wrote:

> Women of today are still being called upon to stretch across the gap of male ignorance, and to educate men as to our existence and our needs. This is an old and primary tool of all oppressors to keep the oppressed occupied with the master's concerns. Now we hear that it is the task of black and third world women to educate white women, in the face of tremendous resistance, as to our existence, our differences, our relative roles in our joint survival. This is a diversion of energies and a tragic repetition of racist patriarchal thought.[39]

Racism, imperialism, colonialism – these are issues for white women in Britain because they have shaped *our* histories, structured our stories, formed our identities. The 'Empire' is not just out there, it is inside us too. As Barbara Smith wrote in 1982:

> White women don't work on racism to do a favour for someone else, solely to benefit Third World women. You have to comprehend how racism distorts and lessens your own lives as white women – that racism affects your chances for survival, too, and that it is very definitely your issue. Until you understand this no fundamental change will come about.[40]

Yet as Vron Ware pointed out in 1990, 'a history of British women and "race" has been largely unexplored' and we have a 'white-washed' feminist history, one that has largely failed to explore the ways in which racism and the experience of black women are relevant to the history of white women, one which denies women's involvement in the Empire, and the crucial role which gender has played in 'organizing ideas of "race" and "civilization" throughout history'.[41] For white men and women experience their gender, their class, their sexual identities through the lens of race just as black men and women do. The difference is that while black has been a signifier of subjection, white has been a signifer of dominance, and the dominant rarely reflect on their dominance in the ways that the subjected reflect on their subjection.[42]

The obtuseness of British feminist historians on questions of race (including myself, despite my Jamaican husband and mixed-race children) only makes sense in the context of the political agenda which we constructed and the ways in which it was built on British amnesia.[43] The 'we' at that point becomes pertinent in an inescapable way. The collectivity of sisterhood in the 1970s and early 1980s was always subject to challenge – from working-class women, from lesbians in opposition to the heterosexism of the women's movement, from older women feeling their different experiences marginalized. The most powerful voice dominating the collectivity was the voice of middle-class, white women in their twenties and thirties. It took the angry black voice demanding, 'What exactly do you mean when you say WE?' – which must have been heard at countless tense meetings and encounters, insisting that white women must recognize the specificities and limitations of their own experience and the existence of difference – to disrupt that collectivity.[44]

The political imperatives of the first phase of the women's movement were the imperatives of gender. The political identities we constructed, and which constructed us, were defined primarily in relation to the axes of gender and class. In the process of constructing identities, that is, 'the process of representing symbolically the sense of belonging which draws people together into an "imagined community" and at the same time defines who does *not* belong or is excluded from it', we effectively excluded not only black women but those parts of ourselves which were identified in racial or ethnic terms.[45] Our 'Englishness', our 'whiteness', seemed irrelevant to our political project. It was only when this collective forgetting was challenged that parts of the self which had been repressed were articulated into more prominent forms of consciousness; another version of what happened when 'black' became a powerful political identity for people who had not previously conceptualized themselves in that way. Thus Michèle Barrett and Mary McIntosh, in their highly contested but nevertheless vital contribution to the white feminist 'critique from within', insisted that white women must pay serious attention to their own practices and ideas if we were to be able to unpick the ways in which the processes of domination had continued to be invisible.[46] It was this disaggregation of the unquestioned 'we', this gradual break-up of any universalizing category 'woman', that created the political conditions for the rethinking of that category and an attempt to redefine the feminist project so that the acceptance of difference was at its heart.

Developments in feminist theory had prepared the way for such a rethinking. The turn to psychoanalysis, and more specifically the feminist rereading of Freud through Lacan as a way of explaining the constitution of female subjectivity in and through language, had raised productive, if difficult, questions for feminist history.[47] In 1984 Sally Alexander took the bull by the horns and wrote a piece in *History Workshop Journal*, previously the bastion of socialist and socialist-feminist emphasis on class as the primary form of political identification, problematizing 'the absence of the sexually differentiated subject in marxism'. She argued that in order to place subjectivity and sexual difference at the heart of her historical work she had turned to 'the psychoanalytic account of the unconscious and sexuality' and that subjectivity was best understood through a process of differentiation, division and splitting in the individual, which is never finished or complete.[48] That notion of the formation of subjectivity as an ever-unfinished process, one that inevitably involves psychic conflict and antagonism, and one that is fundamentally unstable, but always has historical conditions of existence, has been particularly helpful in thinking about the specificity of subjectivities. For if, as Cora Kaplan argues,

> social life is ordered through psychic structures that to some extent organize its meanings, that psychic life in turn is only ever lived through specific social histories and political and economic possibilities.[49]

So Alex Owen, for example, has explored how in the nineteenth-century spiritualist movement in England, women were able to challenge the norms of femininity. For mediumship provided an expression of the instability of gendered identity, moments when the hidden and repressed components of the psyche could be brought to light, the seemingly unified and coherent self disrupted.[50] From a different kind of engagement with psychoanalysis Carolyn Steedman used memories, stories, fragments and dreams to reconstitute female working-class subjectivity, to insist on its psychic components, and think about how 'class and gender, and their articulations, are the bits and pieces from which psychological selfhood is made' and decisively add another nail to the coffin of an unreflecting masculinist narrative of the working class.[51]

The feminist rereading of Lacan has taken the insights of Saussurean linguistics (in terms of the ways in which language constructs meaning) in one direction. Other feminist theorists have also taken up the new tools of post-structuralism; the emphasis following Saussure on the ways in which language constructs rather than reflects meaning, the Foucauldian notion of discourse which allowed the old split between the material and the ideological to be abandoned in favour of a concept which embraced both ideas and practices, the attention to difference and binary oppositions explored in the work of Derrida.[52] Feminist historians in Britain have been relatively slow in taking up these approaches but the publication of books by Denise Riley and Joan Scott marked a watershed. *'Am I that name?' Feminism and the Category of 'Women' in History* and *Gender and the Politics of History* both insist that post-structuralism has opened up the possibility of forms of analysis which can transform feminist theory, feminist history, and feminist practice, and that there can be a history post post-structuralism.[53]

The two books share a central commitment to the critique of essentialism: in Riley's words,

> . . . 'women' is historically, discursively constructed, and always relatively to other categories which themselves change; 'women' is a volatile collectivity in which female persons can be very differently positioned, so that the apparent continuity of the subject of 'women' isn't to be relied on, while for the individual, 'being a woman' is also inconstant, and can't provide an ontological foundation.[54]

or in Scott's,

> The story is no longer about the things that have happened to women and men and how they have related to them; instead it is

> about how the subjective and collective meanings of women and men as categories of identity have been constructed.[55]

This common starting point, the insistence that we only have access to 'the real' through representation, and that it is language which constructs meaning rather than reflecting it, is at the heart of both projects.

This refusal of 'the real' has had profound repercussions within feminist history. It is difficult for British historians, even feminist historians, to do theoretical work since our training is so embedded in empiricism – a theory which is rarely recognized as such. There is tremendous resistance within the discipline to thinking theoretically. For Scott, the demand to theorize is combined with a challenge to do historical work differently and to reconstruct the project of history so that 'the story is no longer about the things that happened to women and men' but about how those categories of meaning have been constructed. There has been very strong opposition to this rethinking of categories, not only because of the resistance to theory but also because of the humanist refusal of a vocabulary concerned with discourse and not people. For the argument, according to Scott, is about what history is and how it should be written – the established frameworks of feminist history are found lacking, whether recovering lost histories, arranging more or less unhappy marriages between Marxism and feminism, or utilizing psychoanalytic thought; only post-structuralism and deconstruction can provide a way forward.

Historians' efforts to reconstruct a 'real' past and tackle questions of determination and causation are abandoned in favour of a focus on knowledge and power – how power is discursively constructed, how politics is about the contestation over meaning. By knowledge, following Foucault, Scott means the understandings of human relations produced by different cultures. Those meanings become contested politically and are the means by which relations of domination and subordination are constructed. Gender, for Scott, means knowledge about sexual difference and, therefore, the ways in which sexual difference is organized. Gender provides a system of meaning that constructs differences between men and women, for those meanings can only be constructed oppositionally and will always involve exclusion, repression, the silencing of competing definitions.[56]

The most sustained *political* critique of essentialism, I have argued, was developed by black women. 'Difference' became an issue for Western feminism because of the challenge to ethnocentrism, to the assumption that one group of women could speak for another. That challenge, coterminous with the development of critiques both of the unified subject and of the possibility of fixed meanings being attached to the categories 'man' or 'woman', has contributed to the necessity for feminist historians to assess our practices, uncomfortable though this may be. For the development of a politics of difference depends on a real capacity to de-centre.

This means de-centring our history-writing too. Part III of this book represents my first attempts to take up questions of race, ethnicity and difference, to work at the demolition of the categories of metropolis and periphery, and understand the ways in which the margins are determining of the centre. As Chandra Talpade Mohanty has argued:

> it is only in so far as 'Woman/Women' and 'the East' are defined as *Others*, or as peripheral, that (western) Man/Humanism can represent him/itself as the centre. It is not the centre that determines the periphery, but the periphery that, in its boundedness, determines the centre.[57]

The last two essays in the book are part of a larger project on the construction of English middle-class gendered national identities in the mid-nineteenth century. In this research I am exploring the shifting and contingent relations of gender, class, race and ethnicity between the 1830s and the 1860s.[58] In using the term 'race' I am well aware that it is a constructed category, but nevertheless it is one which we cannot manage without.[59] In the nineteenth century the word 'race' covered the terrain now also referred to by the term 'ethnicity' and was increasingly seen as a crucial dividing line between peoples. As a scientific category, 'race' is highly problematic and racial theories have been subjected to a sustained critique. However, in the last century the category of race was commonly in use and it still has some analytic force in describing relations between black and white populations, since racisms, based on these supposed racial categories, are only too present in contemporary society. Ethnicity, on the other hand, is a broader concept which allows us to distinguish Englishness more in terms of a cultural identity, with its own ethnocentric roots and perspectives. Englishness is not rooted in racially specific categories, however hard nineteenth-century writers tried to establish them, but signified an identification with an 'imagined community'. The Englishness of a particular class, the middle class in the nineteenth century I argue, was able to represent itself as 'Britishness' by its marginalization and subordination of other ethnicities – those of the Scots, the Irish, the Welsh, or indeed colonized peoples within the Empire who were also British subjects.

Englishness is not a fixed identity but a series of contesting identities, a terrain of struggle as to what it means to be English. Different groups competed for the domination of this space and the political and cultural power which followed from such domination. Englishness is defined through the creation of an imagined community: who is 'one of us', to evoke the language of Thatcher in the Britain of the 1980s, is quite as important in that definition as who is excluded. For the imagined community is built on a series of assumptions about 'others' which define the nature of Englishness itself. The 'others' whose history I am exploring are the black and white populations of Jamaica in the mid-nineteenth century. How were these peoples imagined between the heady days of emancipation in 1834 and the devastating events at Morant Bay in 1865 which resulted in the brutal punishment and deaths of many blacks, at the hands of a British Governor and British soldiers? What different images were offered by planters and philanthropists? How did middle-class English knowledge, perceptions, fantasies and dreams about these peoples shape their sense of themselves, both as white and as English? What was the place of the Empire, and more particularly Jamaica and the other West Indian islands, within English popular consciousness? What did the English know and how did they know it? What changes occurred in these decades which prefigure the new forms of popular imperialism in the late nineteenth century? How did the respectable middle-class orthodoxy of emancipation, the conviction that blacks were men and brothers, women and sisters, become the new racism of the late 1860s, confident in its assumption that blacks were a different species, born to be mastered?

A study of a local middle class sheds light on some of these questions. Take this example. In the 1830s Birmingham was a town which, despite its prosperous trade with slavers and West Indian planters in all the requisites of the slave trade and plantation economies from guns to fetters, prided itself on its identification with anti-slavery.[60] Two anti-slavery societies were formed there in the mid 1820s; one, the Female Society for the Relief of British Negro Slaves, was established in 1825 by a group of evangelical women in the area; the other, the Birmingham Anti-Slavery Society, was formed a year later by the middle-class fathers, husbands, sons, brothers and friends of the women, some of the most prominent merchants, professionals and clergymen in the town.[61] The two societies pledged themselves to join the struggle against slavery in the British colonies.

The men used their established public position to disseminate information and counter the propaganda of the West India lobby (who coordinated planter interests), to alert the town to the horrors of slavery through public meetings and the use of the local press, to petition MPs and Parliament in the interests of amelioration and abolition, to pressure Birmingham manufacturers not to produce slave fetters and shackles, to cooperate with the national anti-slavery society in countrywide efforts. Their society was typical of the burgeoning voluntary associations of middle-class men which were so crucial to *their* struggle for recognition and power.[62] The women used informal networks to inform their particular public of the distinctive horrors of female slavery; they organized meetings in their own homes (the homes always recorded in the minutes in their husbands' names), produced albums and workbags, sold anti-slavery pamphlets and books such as *The History of Mary Prince*, risked derision by visiting house to house in Birmingham in an effort to dissuade women from buying slave-grown sugar, raised money to free particular victims whose stories had become known through anti-slavery channels, organized what became in effect a national women's anti-slavery network.[63] The Female Society was to prove considerably more radical than its male counterpart and spearheaded the struggle for immediate abolition.[64] Thus the women tested and extended the limits of their sphere of femininity and constructed political identities for themselves on a different terrain to that of the men.

The activities of each society were gender specific, the men utilizing the machinery of the expanding civic world, the women operating at a more informal level. The concerns of the two societies were articulated in gendered rhetoric; furthermore, that rhetoric expressed what it should mean to be English. The men were preoccupied with the 'great national crime' of slavery and saw it as their task to remedy it. So, a resolution of 1832 argued:

> That considering freedom to be the birthright of every human being and that every person as the condition of his allegiance to the Crown of this empire is entitled to the full enjoyment of the civil rights and immunities of a free born subject this meeting deems no man a fit representative of Britons who does not hold these to be sacred and inviolable principles.[65]

No man was to be returned to the House of Commons who did not support these principles. Thus middle-class men who had just won representation conceptualized their imagined community – a world of freeborn Englishmen. Birmingham men must take on the national guilt, work on behalf of slaves, represent those who were helpless dependants just as they represented their womenfolk, their servants, their employees, organize themselves for the task to be done: the winning of freedom for the 'negroes', as they called them, the 'injured sons and daughters of Africa'.[66]

The women, unlike the men who took on a powerful paternalist role, were more inclined to identify with the female slaves, though that identification was always edged with ambivalence, the ambivalence of difference. 'Remember those in bonds, as bound with them; and them that suffer adversity as being yourselves also in the body' was their watchword.[67] 'The women of England', they argued, 'did not know the use they might be'. Their strength lay in their 'very weakness and feebleness', for God has chosen 'the weak things of the world, and the things that are despised, and the things that are not, to bring to nought the things that are'.[68] As dependants themselves, they pleaded for the even more helpless and silent female slaves, 'who have none in the land of their captivity to plead for them':

> that their sighs and groans reach us by no audible sounds – that their lacerated bodies are unexposed to our view – that they can stretch out to us no imploring hands, utter no piercing cries for deliverance – that all is silent, enduring, uncomplaining, woe – the generous minds of Britons would feel that such mute and unseen wretchedness possessed an irresistible claim to their sympathy and assistance.[69]

So women's dependence increased their influence on behalf of those who were weaker than themselves; thus they marked their difference. The Female Society aimed 'to awaken in the bosom of English women some sympathy for the weakest and most succourless of the human race, the female colonial slaves of Great Britain'.[70] While the ladies of Birmingham appealed to the gentlemen to take up the cause in Parliament, their imagined slaves, woeful victims, addressed their more fortunate sisters:

> Natives of a land of glory,
> Daughters of the good and brave,
> Hear the injured Negro's story,
> Hear and help the *kneeling slave.*

Think, how nought but death can sever
Your lov'd children from your hold,
Still alive – but lost for ever –
Ours are parted, bought and sold![71]

While James Luckcock wrote poetry in the voice of his wife, anonymous English women abolitionists wrote it in the voice of the slave.[72]

Between the late 1820s and 1833, when the emancipation of slaves in the British colonies passed the Imperial Parliament and was in effect forced upon the unwilling representative assemblies of the West Indian islands, the Birmingham anti-slavery societies were active in their different ways in mobilizing public opinion on the subject of slavery. But the triumph of 1833 was short-lived. It soon became clear that apprenticeship – the intermediate system of enforced labour which, together with £20 million in compensation, marked the concessions won by the planters – was slavery in another guise. Shocked by the failure of the national society to take a lead on this, the citizens of Birmingham decided that they must act. At a great public meeting held in 1835 at the Town Hall, that newly built symbol of municipal middle-class power which towered over the centre of the town, they resolved on 'the most vigorous and decisive measures for awakening the Country from its delusion' as to the real status of apprenticeship. 'The people of England were slumbering, and required to be awakened', argued the Revd Thomas Swan, a prominent Birmingham Baptist. 'In this highly favoured country', he continued,

> the friends of the negro were still to be found . . . he rejoiced in being able to tell the people of this country that the people of Birmingham would not be silent; – they would cry aloud, – their voice would be echoed throughout the kingdom, until having careered through the remotest corners of the earth, its thunders would burst the fetters of the slaves.

Swan's call was endorsed by John Angell James, the most distinguished of the town's Nonconformist ministers, a founder member of the Anti-Slavery Society and author of the celebrated *Anxious Enquirer after Salvation*, which ranked with *The Pilgrim's Progress* in many Christian homes. James 'congratulated his fellow-townsmen on the honours, of which they may be almost proud, of being the first town in the Empire that had raised its public and indignant voice against the present state of our negro fellow-subjects', and appealed to Birmingham men to enjoy their liberty and put it to good use. The speech which brought the most cheers and laughter was that of the Revd William Marsh, 'Millenarian Marsh' as he was popularly known, whose evangelical church was regularly packed for inspiration, blood and thunder. Marsh 'gloried in the name of Briton', but he was very concerned about the £20 million of taxpayers' money that had gone to the planters under false pretences. 'He stood', he argued,

> in the presence of John Bull – an honest and right-feeling animal – he is no longer a bull, but a man; and a good natured one when properly treated; and who would give more money to benefit mankind than all the rest of the world put together; but he did not like to be cheated. John Bull had therefore a right to say to the Planters – 'What has become of my money? . . .'[73]

The evocations of English manhood in these speeches were to do with honest men of action, men who could lead the country, who appreciated the unique rights and liberties associated with their freedoms, who were generous enough to appeal for those less fortunate than themselves. 'The people of this country', it was concluded, 'have but to express what they feel to extirpate the abomination in an instant'.[74] This was power indeed.

The campaign over apprenticeship between 1835–8 was effectively led from Birmingham, with the longtime activist Joseph Sturge in the forefront.[75] Before the campaign had been won in Parliament, however, the Jamaica House of Assembly itself abandoned the system and the slaves were fully emancipated on 1st August 1838. A two-day celebration was held in Birmingham to mark this historic moment. First there was a special children's event in the Town Hall from which a procession went to lay the foundation stone of the new Negro Emancipation School. In the evening a great meeting was held, again in the Town Hall, and the following morning a grand breakfast concluded the proceedings. The events were marked by a profound feeling of satisfaction, in part totally appropriate given the importance of the public campaign in Britain in forcing the planters to act, in part a little too redolent of self-satisfaction, as Sturge himself noted with concern. A series of significant public figures congratulated the men of Birmingham, in particular, for the sterling work they had done. George Thompson, the radical lecturer and publicist of anti-slavery, affirmed, amidst much cheering, that 'under God, he would say the men of Birmingham had led the way'. Sir Eardley Wilmot, a distinguished local MP who was in the chair for the evening meeting, when the Town Hall was jammed full with the great and the good of Birmingham society as well as a large number of ladies, introduced the proceedings by saying that they were gathered together 'to congratulate themselves' on the end of apprenticeship. Edward Baines, the Leeds MP and newspaper editor, argued that it was the people of England who had achieved the ending of slavery, 'and foremost among those would on all occasions be ranked the people of the spirited and independent town of Birmingham. (Cheers)' Charles Lushington, from the famous anti-slavery family, followed him, saying,

> It had long been his wish to visit their flourishing town, the inhabitants of which were justly distinguished for their industrial enterprise, their general intelligence, their enlightened philanthropy, and that ardent attachment to civil and religious liberty, which had evinced itself in so many acts of enlightened liberality and vigorous patriotism, for the results of which . . . the empire at large had most abundant cause to be eminently grateful. (Much cheering)

Benjamin Hawes MP waxed lyrical on the town's contribution to liberty in the heroic moment of 1832 (when huge reform demonstrations in Birmingham had, according to the Birmingham myth, made sure of the Reform Act)[76] and the continuation of its great traditions in 1838:

> This town was distinguished by its vast industrial resources, but it possessed higher claims to their respect; and he felt bound to say, as a member of Parliament, that he owed the honour of his seat to the great moral courage it had displayed in a moment of imminent national peril. He trusted it would long continue to maintain its standing in the moral as well as the political world, and that the great influence which it justly exercised on the feeling of the country would be long found enlisted on the side of those who fought for justice, and through justice for liberty, and through liberty for the enjoyment of the principles of their common Christianity . . .[77]

Thus Birmingham celebrated emancipation.

In the discourse on anti-slavery it was the British movement which had achieved emancipation; England meant, or could mean if they worked at it, freedom. In the Town Hall Joseph Sturge quoted a favourite English poet to immense cheering and applause:

> Slaves cannot breathe in England. If their lungs
> Inhale our air, that moment they are free.
> They touch our country and their shackles fall!
> That's noble and bespeaks a nation proud
> And jealous of the blessing. Spread it, then,
> And let it circulate through every vein
> Of all your empire, that when Britain's power
> Is felt, mankind may feel her mercy too.[78]

For the emancipationists, the air of England was conducive to liberty and they had won this round with the planters – an alternative definition of England, associated with a different rhetoric of mastery over others, had been defeated. But in both visions it was white power which was at stake. Any question of black agency was extremely muted for the abolitionists, only there as a threat as to what might have happened if action had not been taken. Blacks could not have taken action for themselves because they were victims, children who needed the care and protection of their older brothers and sisters, fathers and mothers in the abolitionist movement. The ending of slavery meant the beginning of adulthood, an adulthood which was imagined in ethnocentric terms. Today, as Lushington put it, the negro 'had put on the decorous array of manliness and independence', he was no longer a thing, a chattel, he was now a man. For manliness was defined by independence: a man who did not own himself or his property could not be a man. Those new men, as his brother went on to say, showed every sign of behaving as they should, as England wanted them to. He had great hopes for the negro character:

> There were none more ready to learn – none more obedient, more peaceable, or more docile; there were none more anxious to acquire knowledge, whether religious or otherwise, or better disposed to keep the laws of the land in peace and good-will towards their fellow creatures.[79]

This was music to the ears of the abolitionists – negroes must turn out to be men in their own fantasized image, men like themselves but with a proper sense of white superiority.

Such a conception of manhood carried with it its own laws of sexual difference – women were dependants, to be cherished and supported, protected and covered in law by their husbands and fathers. This was the foundation stone of bourgeois culture. When John Scoble, the secretary of the national Anti-Slavery Society, evoked the end of that system of concubinage and promiscuity so intimately twinned with slavery, he was greeted with loud and continuous cheering from his Birmingham audience. 'Yesterday', he was reported as saying,

> his fellow-Christians and fellow-men, to the number of many thousands, were held the property of other men; today they were their own property – *husbands could embrace their wives as their own property*, and slavery, with all its gloomy and revolting features, was at an end he trusted for ever. [author's italics] [80]

My unpicking of this event is not to discredit the struggle for anti-slavery but rather to explore the ways in which that discourse was rooted not only in the systems of economic thought of the period (an issue which was first taken up by Eric Williams in his classic work, *Capitalism and Slavery*) but also in an historically specific set of ideas and practices about gender, race, class and ethnicity. For in the struggles which took place over the definitions of empire in the nineteenth century, English men and women were constructing identities which drew on, challenged and constituted hierarchies of power formed through the axes of gender, race and class. As Stuart Hall has noted, the double legacy of slavery and emancipation still shapes what Britain has meant in the Caribbean and what the Caribbean means here.[81] Until we understand that history, the ways we (meaning the British) were implicated then, the strategies we were pursuing, for us as well as for them, we have little chance of constructing identities now which recognize and welcome difference but will persist in constructing 'others' as the exotic, the barbaric, those who cannot quite manage to be like 'us'.

The two final essays explore these issues: chapter 9 is concerned with the part played by a group of Baptist missionaries in Jamaica in articulating a discourse of 'the poor negro' which was extremely powerful in the England of the 1830s and 1840s; chapter 10 looking at the competing notions of English masculinity represented in the debate between Thomas Carlyle and John Stuart Mill over the events at Morant Bay and the conduct of Governor Eyre.

Feminist history, in my understanding of it, has moved a long way. Its object of study is no longer only women, if indeed it ever was, but its forms of analysis are distinctively feminist. It takes gender as one, but not the only, crucial axis of power. Its characteristics are as much to do with its form as its content – its divisions and differences (which have scarcely been represented here but which have provided a vital impetus), its engagement with politics, its sense of a constituency beyond the academic, its self-reflectivity, its commitment.[82]

The professional development of feminist history has been horribly skewed by the refusal of the British historical establishment to recognize it. David Cannadine, for example, who has escaped to the United States because of his despair at the failure of historians in Britain to seize the initiative, re-establish the place of historians as 'public teachers who deserve both public attention and public funding' and challenge the decimation of the profession in the Thatcher years, did not even see fit to mention feminism in his consideration of a possible future for British history.[83] A recent survey has shown that although nearly equal proportions of men and women read history as a first degree in British universities, only 17 per cent of lecturing jobs in a sample 53 universities were held by women, while only 12.7 per cent of senior lecturers were women, 6.6 per cent of readers and 3 out of 134 professors.[84] And this only concerns women, never mind those who define themselves as feminists. There is a striking contrast here with sociology, where feminists have been able to gain a firm place within the establishment and have had considerable impact on the transformation of the core syllabus. The contrast with the state of the discipline in the USA is even more remarkable, for there feminists have had a major impact on the pattern of expansion and development in the 1980s: women's history courses abound, women professors multiply, though for the most part, it must be said, in departments of women's history. There is a somewhat healthier situation in British polytechnics than in British universities, where the more receptive attitude to innovation in the curriculum in the 1980s allowed feminist historians to gain a few footholds. An assessment of the intellectual impact of feminist history, furthermore, would require a consideration of other relatively new and interdisciplinary subject areas such as cultural studies and women's studies. For the most part, however, in all sectors of higher education we remain on the margins.[85]

But the margins can be a very productive terrain – a space from which both to challenge establishments and develop our own perspectives, build our own organizations, confirm our own collectivities. The hopes for feminist history in the 1990s cannot be the same as they were in the 1970s for we are living in a very different political world, and some of the harsh lessons we have learned about both exclusivity and marginality must inform our practice in the future. The dream remains – a kind of history that excites and engages, that retains its critical edge, is open to new voices, and always in a dynamic relation to the political world in which we live.

NOTES

1 Rodney Hilton (ed.), *The Transition from Feudalism to Capitalism* (New Left Books, London, 1976), p. 157.
2 Bill Schwarz, 'The "people" in history: the Communist Party historians' group, 1946–56', in Centre for Contemporary Cultural Studies (eds), *Making Histories: Studies in History-Writing and Politics* (Hutchinson, London, 1982); Raphael Samuel, 'The Lost World of British Communism', *New Left Review*, no. 154, 1985.
3 Sheila Rowbotham, *Hidden from History. 300 Years of Women's Oppression and the Fight Against It* (Pluto, London, 1973), Preface, p. x.
4 Anna Davin, 'Women and History', in Micheline Wandor (ed.), *The Body Politic. Writings from the Women's Liberation Movement in Britain 1969–72* (Stage 1, London, 1972), p. 216.
5 Alice Clark, *Working Life of Women in the Seventeenth Century* (Routledge & Kegan Paul, London, 1982); Ivy Pinchbeck, *Women Workers in the Industrial Revolution, 1750–1850* (Virago, London, 1981).
6 Raymond Williams, *Culture and Society 1780–1950* (Chatto & Windus, London, 1958); E. P. Thompson, *The Making of the English Working Class* (Gollancz, London, 1963). Both volumes were subsequently published in paperback by Penguin.
7 Cora Kaplan, *Sea Changes. Culture and Feminism* (Verso, London, 1986), p. 9.
8 Davin, 'Women and History', p. 215.
9 Birmingham Feminist History Group, 'Feminism as Femininity in the 1950s', *Feminist Review*, no. 3, 1979.
10 This obviously connected to the efforts by Marxist historians to recover 'history from below'. See the Preface to E. P. Thompson's *The Making of the English Working Class* (Penguin, Harmondsworth, 1968).
11 Ann Snitow, 'A Gender Diary', in Marianne Hirsch and Evelyn Fox Keller (eds), *Conflicts in Feminism* (Routledge, London, 1990), p. 9.
12 'The difference dilemma' is named by Martha Minow who refuses the binary opposition of equality and difference. For a helpful essay on this, see Joan W. Scott, 'Deconstructing Equality-Versus-Difference: Or, the Uses of Poststructuralist Theory for Feminism', in Hirsch and Keller (eds), *Conflicts in Feminism*.
13 London Feminist History Group, *The Sexual Dynamics of History. Men's Power, Women's Resistance* (Pluto, London, 1983); Sheila

Jeffreys, *The Spinster and Her Enemies. Feminism and Sexuality 1880–1930* (Pandora, London, 1985).

14 Sally Alexander and Anna Davin, 'Feminist History', *History Workshop Journal*, no. 1, Spring 1976. For the journal as a site of struggle in labour history, see the response to Eric Hobsbawm from Sally Alexander, Anna Davin and Eve Hostettler, 'Labouring Women', *History Workshop Journal*, no. 8, Autumn 1989.

15 Barbara Taylor's *Eve and the New Jerusalem. Socialism and Feminism in the Nineteenth Century* (Virago, London, 1983), with its powerful critique of the limitations of Marxism's refusal of the utopian dimension of socialism, remains one of the most brilliant texts to come out of this political moment.

16 Leonore Davidoff and Catherine Hall, *Family Fortunes: Men and Women of the English Middle Class, 1780–1850* (Hutchinson and Chicago University Press, London and Chicago, 1987).

17 Juliet Mitchell, *Psychoanalysis and Feminism* (Allen & Unwin, London, 1975).

18 Michèle Barrett, *Women's Oppression Today* (Verso, London, 1980).

19 This commitment to the rewriting of history has been characteristic of feminist history in its second phase. See Anna Davin, 'Redressing the Balance or Transforming the Art? The British Experience', in S. Jay Kleinberg (ed.), *Retrieving Women's History. Changing Perceptions of the Role of Women in Politics and Society* (Berg/Unesco, Oxford, 1988).

20 Joan W. Scott's influential essay 'Gender: a useful category of historical analysis' first appeared in the *American Historical Review* in 1986. It subsequently appeared in *Gender and the Politics of History* (Columbia University Press, New York, 1988). For a more recent statement on the use of 'gender', see the editorial, 'Why Gender and History?', *Gender and History*, vol. 1, no. 1, Spring 1989.

21 Anon., from the commonplace book of Mary Young, Walthamstow, Essex, 1828, quoted in Davidoff and Hall, *Family Fortunes*, p. 397; Ann Taylor Gilbert, 'Remonstrance', Davidoff and Hall, *Family Fortunes*, App. 1, p. 457.

22 Nancy Cott, *The Bonds of Womanhood. 'Woman's Sphere' in New England, 1780–1835* (Yale University Press, New Haven, 1977).

23 Mary P. Ryan, *Cradle of the Middle Class. The Family in Oneida County, New York, 1790–1865* (Cambridge University Press, Cambridge, 1981).

24 Carroll Smith Rosenberg, 'The Female World of Love and Ritual: relations between women in nineteenth century America', *Signs*, no. 1, 1975.

25 Rosalind Delmar discusses the use of different languages at different moments within feminism to define the nature of the problem; see 'What is Feminism?' in Juliet Mitchell and Ann Oakley (eds), *What is Feminism?* (Blackwell, Oxford, 1986).

26 Micheline Wandor, 'The Conditions of Illusion', in Sandra Allen, Lee Sanders and Jan Wallis (eds), *Conditions of Illusion: Papers from the Women's Movement* (Feminist Books, Leeds, 1974), p. 206.
27 See particularly Margaret Hunt, *The Culture of Capitalism: The English Middling Classes, 1660–1800* (University of California Press, Stanford, 1992).
28 See, for example, Bell Hooks, *Ain't I a Woman? Black Women and Feminism* (Pluto, London, 1982).
29 Brixton Black Women's Group, 'Black Women Organizing', *Feminist Review*, no. 17, Autumn 1984.
30 Hazel V. Carby, 'White Women Listen! Black feminism and the boundaries of sisterhood', in Centre for Contemporary Cultural Studies (eds), *The Empire Strikes Back. Race and Racism in 70s Britain* (Hutchinson, London, 1982), p. 223.
31 Valerie Amos and Pratibha Parmar, 'Challenging Imperial Feminism', *Feminist Review*, no. 17, Autumn 1984, p. 5.
32 The most powerful piece of imaginative historical writing on American slavery for me is Toni Morrison's *Beloved* (Alfred A. Knopf, New York, 1987).
33 Evelyn Brooks Higginbotham, 'Beyond the Sound of Silence: Afro-American Women's History', *Gender and History*, vol. 1, no. 1, Spring 1989.
34 Quoted in Higginbotham, 'Beyond the Sound of Silence', p. 56.
35 Stuart Hall, 'Minimal Selves', *Identity*, ICA Documents 6, London, 1987; 'New Ethnicities', *Black Film, British Cinema*, ICA Documents 7, London, 1988.
36 Delia Jarrett Macaulay, 'Black Women's History'. Paper presented at the Women's History Conference, London, June 1991.
37 Peter Fryer, *Staying Power. The History of Black People in Britain* (Pluto, London, 1984).
38 See, for example, Ziggi Alexander and Audrey Deejee (eds), *Wonderful Adventures of Mrs Seacole in Many Lands* (Falling Wall Press, Bristol, 1984); Rozina Visram, *Ayahs, Lascars and Princes: Indians in Britain 1700–1947* (Pluto, London, 1986); Sylvia L. Collicott, *Connections: Haringey – Local – National – World Links* (London Borough of Haringey, London, 1986). For a very helpful introduction to black women's history in Britain, see Ziggy Alexander, 'Let it Lie Upon the Table: The Status of Black Women's Biography in the UK', *Gender and History*, vol. 2, no. 1, Spring 1990.
39 Quoted in Trinh T. Minh-ha, 'Difference: "A Special Third World Women Issue" ', *Feminist Review*, no. 25, Spring 1987, p. 10.
40 Quoted in Kum-Kum Bhavnani and Margaret Coulson, 'Transforming Socialist-Feminism: The Challenge of Racism', *Feminist Review*, no. 23, Summer 1986, p. 91.
41 Vron Ware, 'The Good, the Bad and the Foolhardy: Moving the Frontiers of British Women's History', in Flemming Rogilds, *Every*

Cloud has a Silver Lining. Lectures on Everyday Life, Cultural Production and Race, Studies in Cultural Sociology no. 28 (Akademisk Forlag, Copenhagen, 1990), pp. 111–13.

42 Avtar Brah, 'Difference, Diversity, Differentiation', in James Donald and Ali Rattansi (eds), *Race, Culture and Identity* (Sage, London, 1992).

43 There have been notable exceptions to this blindness. See, for example, Anna Davin, 'Imperialism and Motherhood', *History Workshop Journal*, no. 5, Spring 1978. More recently, see Moira Ferguson (ed.), *The History of Mary Prince a West Indian Slave Related by Herself* (Pandora, London, 1987); Clare Midgeley, 'Women and the Anti-Slavery Movement 1780s–1860s', University of Kent PhD, 1989.

44 The actual quotation is from Carby, 'White Women Listen!', p. 233.

45 Stuart Hall, Introduction to Stuart Hall and Bram Gieben (eds), *Formations of Modernity* (Polity, Cambridge, 1991). The concept of 'imagined community' is drawn from Benedict Anderson, *Imagined Communities. Reflections on the Origin and Spread of Nationalism* (Verso, London, 1983).

46 Michèle Barrett and Mary McIntosh, 'Ethnocentrism and Socialist-Feminist Theory', *Feminist Review*, no. 20, Summer 1985.

47 Juliet Mitchell and Jacqueline Rose (eds), *Feminine Sexuality: Jacques Lacan and the école freudienne*, trans. Jacqueline Rose (Macmillan, London, 1982); Jacqueline Rose, *Sexuality in the Field of Vision* (Verso, London, 1986).

48 Sally Alexander, 'Women, Class and Sexual Differences in the 1830s and 1840s: Some reflections on the writing of a feminist history', *History Workshop Journal*, no. 17, Spring 1984, pp. 132–3. For a more recent account of the relation between psychoanalysis and feminist history, see Sally Alexander, 'Feminist History', *History Workshop Journal*, no. 32, Autumn 1991.

49 Kaplan, *Sea Changes*, p. 4.

50 Alex Owen, *The Darkened Room. Women, Power and Spiritualism in late Victorian England* (Virago, London, 1989).

51 Carolyn Steedman, *Landscape for a Good Woman: A Story of Two Lives* (Virago, London, 1986), p. 7.

52 Scott, 'Deconstructing Equality-Versus-Difference'.

53 For a longer discussion of these two books, see my review in *Gender and History*, vol. 3, no. 2, Summer 1991.

54 Denise Riley, *'Am I That Name?' Feminism and the Category of 'Women' in History* (Macmillan, Basingstoke, 1989), pp. 1–2.

55 Joan W. Scott, *Gender and the Politics of History* (Columbia University Press, New York, 1988), p. 6.

56 For a discussion of some of the strengths and weaknesses of post-structuralist and deconstructionist accounts of the nineteenth century as compared with other forms of feminist history-writing, see

Judith Newton, 'Family Fortunes: "New History" and "New Historicism" ', *Radical History Review*, no. 43, 1989.

57 Chandra Talpade Mohanty, 'Under Western Eyes: Feminist Scholarship and Colonial Discourses', *Feminist Review*, no. 30, Autumn 1988, p. 81.

58 I am grateful to the Economic and Social Research Council who are supporting this research with a grant between August 1990 and 1992.

59 On 'race' as a category, see Paul Gilroy, *'There Ain't No Black in the Union Jack'. The Cultural Politics of Race and Nation* (Hutchinson, London, 1987), especially chs 1 and 2. For a discussion of some of the problems about using this category and an argument for 'ethnic' as an alternative, see Floya Anthias and Nira Yuval-Davis, 'Contextualising Feminism – Gender, Ethnic and Class Divisions', *Feminist Review*, no. 15, Winter 1983.

60 The British slave trade was abolished in 1807 but the Birmingham trade in slave guns did not decline until after the middle of the nineteenth century. Fryer, *Staying Power*, App. F, 'Birmingham, The Metal Industries and The Slave Trade'.

61 Birmingham Anti-Slavery Society, Minute Book 1826–37, Birmingham Reference Library, no. 152006; Ladies' Society for the Relief of Negro Slaves, Minute Book 1825–1852, Birmingham Reference Library, no. 302206; Female Society for Birmingham, West Bromwich, Wednesbury, Walsall and their respective neighbourhoods, *First Report* (Richard Peart, Birmingham, 1826); *Second Report* (Hudson, Birmingham, 1827). For discussions of the Female Society, see Midgeley, 'Women and the Anti-Slavery Movement'; Felly Nkweto Simmonds, 'The Role of the Birmingham Female Society for the Relief of British Female Slaves in supporting the education of women in the West Indies and Africa', Paper delivered at the Berkshire Conference of Women Historians, June 1990; Alex Tyrrell, 'A House Divided Against Itself: The British Abolitionists Revisited', *Journal of Caribbean History*, vol. 22, nos 1 and 2, 1988.

62 On the construction of the male public sphere and its place in class formation, see Davidoff and Hall, *Family Fortunes*, especially ch. 10; Robert J. Morris, *Class, Sect and Party: The Making of the British Middle Class, 1820–1850* (Manchester University Press, Manchester, 1990).

63 Female Society for Birmingham for the Relief of British Negro Slaves, Album, Birmingham Reference Library, no. 361221. On women's relation to the public, see Mary P. Ryan, *Women in Public. Between Banners and Ballots, 1825–1880* (Johns Hopkins University Press, Baltimore, 1990).

64 Ladies' Society for the Relief of Negro Slaves, Minute Book, 8 April 1830.

65 Birmingham Anti-Slavery Society, Minute Book, 27 July 1832.

66 Birmingham Anti-Slavery Society, Minute Book, 5 July 1837.
67 Female Society for ... the Relief of British Female Slaves, *First Report*, cover.
68 Female Society for ... the Relief of British Female Slaves, *Third Report* (Hudson, Birmingham, 1828), p. 26.
69 Female Society for ... the Relief of British Female Slaves, *First Report*, pp. 4–5.
70 Female Society for ... the Relief of British Female Slaves, *Third Report*, p. 11.
71 Female Society for ... the Relief of British Female Slaves, *Third Report*, cover.
72 For an analysis of British women's writing about slavery, see Moira Ferguson, *Subject To Others: British Women Writers and Colonial Slavery 1630–1834* (Routledge, New York, 1992).
73 Birmingham Anti-Slavery Society, *Report of the Proceedings of the great Anti-Slavery Meeting held at the Town Hall Birmingham* (Hudson, Birmingham, 1835), pp. 1, 15, 16, 17.
74 Birmingham Anti-Slavery Society, *Report of the Proceedings at Birmingham on the First and Second of August in Commemoration of the Abolition of Negro Apprenticeship in the British Colonies* (Tyler, Birmingham, 1838), p. 24.
75 For an account of the particular part played by Sturge, see Alex Tyrell, *Joseph Sturge and the Moral Radical Party in Early Victorian Britain* (Christopher Helm, London, 1987).
76 On the myth of Birmingham's making of the Reform Act, see Carlos Flick, *The Birmingham Political Union and the Movements for Reform in Britain 1830–39* (Archon Books, Conn., 1978).
77 Birmingham Anti-Slavery Society, *Report of the Proceedings*, pp. 26, 17, 35, 63.
78 Birmingham Anti-Slavery Society, *Report of the Proceedings*, p. 27.
79 Birmingham Anti-Slavery Society, *Report of the Proceedings*, pp. 35, 39.
80 Birmingham Anti-Slavery Society, *Report of the Proceedings*, p. 16.
81 Stuart Hall, 'Iron in the Soul', *Redemption Song*, BBC 2, 30 June 1991.
82 For an essay which explores the specificity of feminist theory, see Teresa de Lauretis, 'Upping the Anti (sic) in Feminist Theory', in Hirsch and Fox Keller (eds), *Conflicts in Feminism*, p. 258.
83 David Cannadine, 'British History: Past, Present – and Future?', *Past and Present*, no. 116, August 1987, p. 188.
84 *Times Higher Education Supplement*, 7 June 91.
85 For a discussion of the current state of feminist history, see Jane Rendall, 'Women's History, Feminist History, Gender History in Britain', in Karen Offen and Ruth Roach Pierson (eds), *Writing Women's History: International Perspectives* (Macmillan, Basingstoke, 1991).

PART I

The Beginnings

2 The History of the Housewife

Housewives have rarely thought of themselves as having a history – and historians have not thought of the housewife as worthy of academic study. The history of women in the home – of the changing nature of marriage, childcare and domestic labour, for example – is an area which badly needs exploration.

Every society has rules about which activities are suitable for which sex but these rules are not constant – the sexual division of labour is not a rigid division. The activities of men and women are always patterned, and the patterning always reveals relations of domination and subordination in relation to the major productive spheres. But the actual patterns of male and female activities within any one society at any one stage in the development in its mode of production differs. Women may do no heavy work in one society and only heavy work in another. The way in which the sexual division of labour is defined and decided will depend on both the real relations of sexuality, reproduction and work and the attitudes and beliefs about them. The sexual division of labour is not a given in nature but a constant in history.

Being a housewife, then, is a condition which is socially defined and its definition changes at different historical moments. When we talk about a housewife now we mean a woman whose work is to maintain and organize a household and look after her husband and children – we think of washing, cooking, cleaning and the full-time care of pre-school children. That work is unpaid: the woman is paid through her husband who is supposed to receive enough to support himself and his family. If, as Marx suggested, wages represent only the reward for necessary labour time – that is, what is necessary for the worker to reproduce the conditions of his own labour – then in modern capitalism the housewife has become one of those hidden conditions, and thus the invisible support for the generation of surplus value. Around this real, objective, but heavily disguised role the ideological definitions and supporting definitions have clustered. Since the 'real' labour of the world consists of public work, being a housewife now is seen as a job with little, if any, status; women often say when asked what they do, 'Oh, I'm only a housewife', or, 'I'm just a housewife'. It has not always has such a limited or despised status.

To be a housewife in fourteenth-century England meant something very different to what it does today, when it has been decisively separated from the productive and industrial sphere. It still involved domestic work and the care of children, and it was still unpaid: but for a large proportion of women it would also involve many other kinds of work besides – brewing, baking, looking after a dairy, keeping the poultry and so on. Part of the reason for that was the fact that the family itself, both among the peasants, and in the towns, was a productive unit.

The family means, in this context, father, mother, often unmarried brothers and sisters, possibly grandparents, children, servants and – in an urban situation – apprentices. In this family, the labour power of each individual member is only a definite portion of the labour power of the family. Women were, therefore, themselves centrally related to production, and not only through their husbands. The pre-industrial family was a self-sufficient economic unit and consequently domestic work had a much wider definition than it does now. It might well involve brewing, dairy work, the care of poultry and pigs, the production of vegetables and fruit, the spinning of flax and wool and also medical care – nursing and doctoring. These areas were roughly defined as 'women's work': but there is much more flexibility in the drawing of lines around women's work and men's work – work was done on the basis of task-orientation rather than by way of a rigid and formalized division of labour.

There were some jobs which were always specifically connected with one sex. The higher manorial officers were always men and the dairymaid, for example, was always a woman. A thirteenth-century manual on 'The Duties of Manorial Officers' gives us an account of the dairymaid's work:

> The dairymaid ought to be faithful and of good repute, and keep herself clean, and ought to know her business and all that belongs to it. She ought not to allow any under-dairymaid or another to take or carry away milk, or butter, or cream, by which the cheese shall be less and the dairy impoverished. And she ought to know well how to make cheese and salt cheese, and she ought to save and keep the vessels of the dairy that it need not be necessary to buy new ones every year.[1]

The two most powerful medieval theories about women were the creations of the Church and the aristocracy. The Church's view of women was heavily influenced by St Paul and saw women as the creation of the Devil and as both inferior and evil. Marriage was an institution set up to contain the unavoidable sin of sexuality; as Our Lord put it in a vision to Margery Kempe, the fifteenth-century mystic, 'for though the state of maidenhood be more perfect and more holy than the state of widowhood, and the state of widowhood more perfect than the state of wedlock, yet, daughter, I love thee as well as any maiden in the world'.[2] The aristocracy, on the other hand, developed the counter-doctrine of the superiority of women. This was connected with the cult of the Virgin Mary, the adoration of the Virgin in Heaven and the lady on earth. Though the two theories were at different poles, in one sense both combined to give women an other-worldly role – they were seen as in no way central to political or economic life. This split between the wicked and the divine, the prostitute and the saint, represents an ideological split and projection by men which has recurred in many forms. Women provided either an explanation for evil or a haven of good. Neither view had much to do with reality. In Chrétien de Troyes's romance *Lancelot*, the hero gets into Queen Guinevere's bedroom but Lancelot 'holds her more dear than the relic of any saint' and 'when he leaves the room he bows and acts precisely as if he were before a shrine'.[3] Neither of these theories was taken at face value outside the Church and the aristocracy; but what was clearly already accepted was that women were secondary and inferior.

Because of the need for their labour, women in the village were in a better position than aristocratic women, in the sense that they were involved in productive relations. What this means, in fact, is that they were free to be exploited in an equal way with men. The feudal economy was based on the ownership of land, which was the major source of power, by a relatively small number: the land was worked by both free and unfree peasants. Few received money wages – the unfree worked on the lord's land in return for renting some of the lord's land. Every peasant was subject to a lord and in a hierarchical society every lord was subject to another who was ultimately subject to the king. Supposedly there was a system of rights and obligations at each level but at the bottom of the ladder the obligations which the lord owed to the peasant were absolutely minimal whereas his rights were extensive.

Peasant women were able to hold land, though the normal assumption was that heads of households would be male – the position of widows in particular has long been recognized as of importance, both because of their longevity and their established rights. Manorial records, as Rodney Hilton has shown, do record a substantial number of women holding land – even as minors.[4] It seems that unmarried women with holdings would usually quickly marry – the labour of the man was as important to the woman as vice versa. However, their right to hold land was only because the holdings were small and would not affect the distribution of power on the feudal estate. Aristocratic women, with few exceptions, could not hold land since land was the key to the feudal economy and once the property rights of a family or aristocratic line came into question women were simply a marriageable commodity. It is clear that peasant women did do heavy work on the land, and there is evidence that at some points they got equal pay. The question as to whether women labourers were paid the same as their male counterparts seems to have something to do with job definition and bargaining power. Female domestic servants were low-paid, for example, because they were subject to non-economic compulsion since they tended to live in the lord's household and could have all kinds of personal pressure put on them. But it would be wrong to associate the respect given to women's labour with a society free from discrimination. Distinctions were of course made in the law, education, the Church, and in political and property rights between men and women. Peasant women could not assume the limited rights to property which men had – their rights were much less clear and would probably depend on the customs of a particular locality.

Women were, furthermore, subject to particular kinds of exploitation by the feudal lord. At Pattingham in Staffordshire in April 1369, Juliana, the daughter of Roger Baroun, was 'deflowered' by a Welshman and had to pay a five-shilling fine to the lord of the manor. A woman who was not a virgin had less monetary value to her feudal lord since a well-to-do peasant might refuse to marry her and consequently the cut of the marriage settlement which the lord got would be less. In 1388 Agnes, the daughter of Juliana Prynce, had to pay ten shillings to the lord of the manor to be able to marry and go as a free woman with her goods.[5]

But abstract theories about the proper role of women were not allowed to stand in the way of meeting familial and social needs. Peasant women were able to play a relatively independent role in day-to-day economic life – they were open to the same kind of exploitation by the feudal lord as were men, whereas at other times the appropriation of women's labour has been effected in a more indirect way. This means that women were likely to organize themselves politically in the same way as men. In Halesowen in Worcestershire in 1386, 'A certain John atte Lythe and Thomas Puttewey, serfs, by the advice, procurement and maintenance of a certain Agnes, wife of John Saddler, assembled an illegal conventicle of unknown rebels against the abbot . . . saying openly that they did not wish any more to be considered as serfs of the abbot and would not do any of the previously owed services.'[6]

The social, political and ideological dominance of the male was clear, however, at the local level. Women were not the heads of tithings, they didn't sit on local juries, they didn't fill the office of constable or reeve. Women with a legal title to a holding could often be obliged to marry and they had to suffer a regular barrage from the Church about their evil influence. Women played a variety of economic roles within the village – they were not all housewives, and 'housewife' had a much wider definition than it does now. They were not all housewives because there was a much smaller number of households to the population and there might be several women living in a household whose jobs were as domestic servants or labourers. Peasant women might, according to their age and marital status, be doing a variety of different jobs. They might be doing specifically women's work, such as spinning and carding or helping in the dairy; they might be doing work which was not rigidly defined as men's or women's – in the fields – ploughing or harvesting; their work might centre around their own household – cooking, brewery and caring for children or as domestic servants either in the lord's house or in the house of a richer peasant.

Housewife in fourteenth-century England tended to mean the coordinator and organizer of an establishment and of a centre of production. The condition of being wedded to a house was a more substantive one than it is now because the fourteenth-century house had a different function and meaning to the twentieth-century equivalent. It did imply a status which was, however, considerably limited by the current ideology on the position of women. This reminds us that the ideological forms do not merely reflect the economic but have a life and relative autonomy of their own which can even serve in certain instances to limit and restrict the economic sphere. The economic and ideological demands on women in the village were to a considerable degree in contradiction to each other.

The situation was very similar in the towns – being a housewife was recognized as a particular job but it involved a wide range of domestic activity. Generally there were no frontiers between professional or business life and private life. These activities all tended to go on in the same living/working area. The household was the centre both of domestic activity and mercantile activity. This integration of work and home contributed to the fact that it was not necessary to regard the socialization of children as one of the most important functions of the family. Children were not seen as a special group – once they were past infancy they were absorbed into the adult household and were educated by the process of life and work going on around them. Domestic service and apprenticeship were two of the major ways of educating and these applied to boys and girls alike (though the evidence as to girls being formally apprenticed is unclear, they certainly were apprenticed and trained informally).

In a feudal society the notion of service was central to the relations between lord and master, parents and children, lover and mistress. Transmission of a way of life from one generation to another was ensured by the everyday participation of children in adult life. In the towns, as in the villages, women were engaged in a wide range of economic activities connected with the family as a unit of production. Women figure in guild records as barbers, furriers, carpenters, saddlers, joiners, and in many other trades. There are relatively few trades which explicitly exclude women. All the female members of a merchant's household would be engaged in some form of economic activity – the housewife herself might spend a good deal of her energies organizing other men and women to fulfil the necessary domestic tasks so that she would be free to engage in mercantile activities. Women in smaller-scale households might take up one of the entrepreneurial activities which were often associated with women because they were extensions of domestic activity – Margery Kempe, who was the daughter of one of King's Lynn's leading citizens, describes how 'she now bethought herself a new housewifery' and went in for milling – this was after the failure of her brewing enterprise which she ascribes to God's disapproval of her involvement in such activities: 'Then for pure covetousness, and to maintain her pride, she began to brew, and was one of the greatest brewers in the town of N. for 3 years or 4, till she lost much money . . . For, though she had ever such good servants, cunning in brewing, yet it would never succeed with them.'[7]

But the degree to which it was considered the duty of the good wife to look after her husband should not be underestimated. 'The Goodman of Paris', a late-fourteenth-century text, instructs the wife:

> Wherefore love your husband's person carefully, and I pray you keep him in clean linen, for that is your business, and because the trouble and care of outside affairs lieth with men, so must husbands take heed, and go and come, and journey hither and thither, in rain and wind, in snow and hail, now drenched, now dry, now sweating, now shivering, ill-fed, ill-lodged, ill-warmed and ill-bedded. And naught harmeth him, because he is upheld by the hope that he hath of the care which his wife will take of him on his return, and of the ease, the joys and the pleasures which she will do him, or cause to be done to him, in her presence, to be unshod before a good fire, to have his feet washed and fresh shoes and hose, to be given good food and drink, to be well served and well looked after, well bedded in white sheets and nightcaps, well covered with good furs, and assuaged with other joys and desports, privities, loves and secrets whereof I am silent. And the next day fresh shirts and garments . . . Wherefore, dear sister, I beseech you thus to bewitch and bewitch again your husband that shall be, and beware of roofless house and smoky fire, and scold him not, but be unto him gentle and amiable and peaceable. Have a care that in winter he have a good fire and smokeless and let him rest well and be well covered between your breasts, and thus be with him . . . And thus shall you preserve and keep your husband from all discomforts and give him all the comforts whereof you can bethink you, and serve him and have him served in your house, and you shall look to him for outside things, for if he be good he will take even more pains and labour therein than you wish, and by doing what I have said, you will cause him ever to miss you and have his heart with you and your loving service and he will shun all other houses, all other women, all other services and households.[8]

The position of aristocratic women in the fourteenth century was much more rigidly circumscribed and narrowly defined than that of their lower-class sisters and this was paradoxically because they could not be housewives. Their position was much more determined by ideological considerations than by economic ones because their husbands and fathers were wealthy enough to free them from the economic necessity of engaging in domestic activity with all its ramifications. There are cases of widows who were heavily involved with estate management, or of queens who were actively involved politically, but in general most upper-class women were almost entirely without political or juridical rights and they spent their lives under the perpetual wardship of a father, a husband or a guardian. They had minimal rights over their own property – it simply made them into suitable marriage alliances.

The lack of freedom of aristocratic women was fundamentally connected to the centrality of private property. It was essential for a lord to defend the property rights of his family against any intrusion. He wanted to be sure that his land would be passed on to his heirs and them alone. A major interest of every feudal landowning family was to extend their property – to make good marriages which would result in this, to buy up whatever they could to consolidate their estates, and to increase them by force if the occasion arose. Because property was naturally inherited through the male line and property meant land, men and power, women were inevitably seen as decorative pawns. In a period when conspicuous consumption was becoming an increasingly important symbol of power within the ruling class, to have a leisured lady as a wife followed round by a company of young men who were dying of love for her was one aspect of that consumption. It increased the status of the husband in the eyes of the world.

We can see from the medieval definition of housewife how close a relationship there is between the position of women at work and at home – in a pre-capitalist society, because there is no split between the two, being a housewife means being engaged in a whole range of productive activities centred both in domestic activity for private consumption and in domestic activity which would be marketable. There are two sets of considerations at work in defining women's proper work – firstly, what it is on the whole thought right and proper for women to do and, secondly, what is – given the circumstances of production at the time – practicable for women to do. These two continuously interact on, and constrain, one another. It is the interaction of the ideological with the economic – both levels within the same social formation but having a relative autonomy of their own – which are the major factors in the definition of housewife.

The extended activities of the fourteenth-century household were beginning to disappear by the seventeenth century. The emergence of capitalism led to extensive changes in the organization and function of the family. The family started to be less important in production but at the same time far more important in the creation of the relations of capitalist production – in the production, we might say, of bourgeois men. Women became considerably less important in the direct creation of surplus value but more important in the reproduction of conditions for labour power – the family had to become the training ground of rational men. With the development of capitalism comes the separation of capital from labour, the separation of the home from the place of work and the separation of domestic labour and commodity production. With the development of a capitalist mode of production the household is no longer the central unit of production. We are already beginning to discern the family as a centre of consumption.

This was, of course, a very long-term change, but the separation of work from home has a vital effect on women since it brings with it a much changed conception of the sexual division of labour and what constitutes women's work.

Two of the major functions of the family within capitalism are to act as a centre of consumption and to act as the unit which is responsible for the maintenance and reproduction of labour power.[9] The change in the family, from being the major unit of production in the society, does have quite specific effects on the position of the housewife. As more consumer goods and services become available on the market so there is less need for the household to be a self-sufficient economic unit – a narrowing down of the conception of domestic activities takes place. Alice Clark in her excellent study *The Working Life of Women in the Seventeenth Century* documents, for example, the way in which services which were performed within the family in a pre-capitalist economy became professionalized in the seventeenth century and were taken over by men.[10] This professionalization – which was particularly marked in the medical and educational spheres – was partly a result of the scientific and intellectual developments of the seventeenth century but it was also due to the new division of labour which was taking place in the capitalist organization of trade and industry. Nursing and doctoring, which had been a part of domestic activity, began to be organized and require training and as women were excluded from this specialized training so domestic handling of it came to seem inadequate.

A similar kind of limitation on domestic activity took place because of the developing capitalist organization of those trades which had previously been part of an extended household. Brewing is a classic example: it was, as we have seen, an entrepreneurial area which had been particularly popular with women but by the end of the seventeenth century brewing had become an organized trade and was no longer open to women. The skills which could be acquired domestically were not enough to establish women's position in trade – women could still, of course, brew for their own families if they wanted to, but that became a privatized activity which could not easily be extended into the social sphere. Gradually a change was taking place in the relative efficiency of domestic and capitalist production – a slow decline had set in for the self-sufficient household or country estate as a unit of production. It became more important for men to organize their trades protectively once the separation of capital and labour and of the home from the place of work took place: the separation of commodity production from domestic labour was an inevitable result. Male workers were gathered together and employees began to form associations in addition to the employers' guilds which existed. For journeymen in their new position as wage labourers to be able to bargain well, they had to maintain their exclusive position by long apprenticeships and many restrictions on entry: the easiest group to exclude were women. Both guilds and workers' associations had power and influence stemming from their collective organization which women did not have at their command. A large number of poor women had managed to make a living by selling domestic produce from door to door – the established shopkeepers disliked this competition and managed to restrict unlicensed selling because of their political influence in the localities.

We defined a second function of the capitalist family as the maintenance and reproduction of labour power. This can be divided into two areas – firstly, the material reproduction of the labour force and, secondly, the ideological reproduction of the relations of production. The seventeenth-century housewife is directly responsible for the first and has a limited responsibility for the second. The material reproduction of the labour force is ensured by giving labour power the material means with which to reproduce itself – that is to say, wages. The notion of the individual 'social' wage – enough to support a man and his family – is only beginning in the seventeenth century and it does not receive full recognition until the era of industrial capitalism. But with the separation of work and home within the capitalist-organized trades there comes the much clearer division of labour between the man who goes out to work and the woman who stays at home and organizes the household – which has in any event, as we have seen, come to mean far less than it did and is being progressively reduced to the physical care of husband and children. The maintenance and reproduction of labour power is, and must be, a necessary condition to the reproduction of capital. But the capitalist, as Marx points out, can safely leave this to the labourers' instincts of self-preservation and propagation.[11] Workers, even when not directly engaged in the labour process, are still, therefore, an appendage of capital while an appearance of independence is kept up by the fiction of a free contract between the employer and the labourer.

The reproduction of labour power requires not only material care but also ideological care. Labour power must both reproduce its skills and its submission to the rules of the established order – in other words, as Althusser puts it, the reproduction of submission to the ruling ideology for the workers and the reproduction of the ability to manipulate the ruling ideology correctly for the agents of exploitation and repression.[12] The family, the Church, the army and the schools are all crucial in the reproduction of the relations of production – they socialize people in ways which ensure subjection to the ruling ideology or mastery of its practice. In the medieval period the Church was the most important institution of this type, in that it provided the ideology of feudalism – it deified hierarchical relations. It was for this reason, of course, that religious struggle and dissent was so crucial to the decline of feudalism and the transition to capitalism. With the crisis in the Catholic Church, the Reformation and the development of Puritanism, the Anglican Church in the seventeenth century no longer combined within itself religious, educational, and cultural functions. Consequently the family had become much more formative in the education and socialization of children. As a prayer in the Primer of 1553 put it: 'To have children and servants is thy blessing, O Lord, but not to order them according to thy world deserveth thy dreadful curse.'[13]

The changes which capitalism began to effect in the organization of the household were not experienced in the same way by all women. Up to the Restoration it had been seen as quite natural that the wives of merchants and large farmers should play an active part in business affairs but from 1660 onwards this seems to become increasingly unusual.[14] The idea develops of the upper-class woman as a lady of leisure – a shift takes place from the image of women as active and energetic to the old aristocratic ideal of women as passive and dependent. As Sheila Rowbotham points out, not to work becomes a mark of superiority for upper-middle-class women, just as men establish work as a crucial criterion of dignity and worth.[15] The spread of capitalism brought with it a great increase in wealth which made possible the idleness of a much larger group of women. The bourgeois revolution brought not only an extension of the ruling class but also a new set of values for the wives of the successful bourgeoisie. This process had in fact been going on for a long time. There is a considerable amount of popular literature in the preceding hundred years which documents the emergence of a new leisured middle class and the resulting ambivalent attitudes to women. Most of the literature revolves around the position and behaviour of middle-class wives. The main attacks were on their love of luxury and their vanity. Rich, in a typical pamphlet on 'The Excellency of Good Women', says: 'and what is it that doth make so many citizens and trades men, so commonly to play bankrupt, but the excessive pride that is used by their wives. By this pride of women Hospitality is eaten up and good Housekeeping is banished out of the Country . . .'[16] Or Gainsford, an early-seventeenth-century spokesman for the commercial classes: 'A citizen is more troubled with his wife than his wares: for they are sorted, locked up, and never brought out, but by constraint for the profit of their master; but his wife is decked, adorned, neatly apparelled, sits for the gaze, goes at her pleasure, and will not be restrained from any sights or delights, or merry-meetings; where they may shew their beauties, or riches, or recreate themselves.'[17] The objections were to middle-class women behaving in ways which were not suitable to their position – overreaching themselves. There are many references to the increasing difficulty of distinguishing between countesses, courtesans and merchants' wives. In the more prosperous commercial families, the role of the wife was increasingly that of a leisured lady – the most that she would do would be to supervise the domestic activities of her servants. This also resulted to some extent in a bourgeoisification of the aristocracy. There is a tendency in the seventeenth century towards a reduction in the size of households which was probably connected with development of bourgeois patterns. Aristocratic ladies might, as in the fourteenth century, be concerned with the supervision of the household but essentially their lives were leisured. We do have records of some exceptional figures who were deeply involved with the organization of their estates but what is striking about the diary of Lady Anne Clifford as seen through her biographer, for example, is the extent to which she regards private or domestic events as scarcely worth recording.[18] Time and again the seventeenth-century private records demonstrate the degree to which the inferiority of women and the unimportance of household activities were a part of the cultural apparatus. Public events were the things which where worth recording.

Lady Anne Clifford filled several volumes with the records of her long and active life, but the major issues dealt with are public ones. She had a long struggle over a disputed inheritance which took up a great deal of time and energy. She was obviously an unusual woman in that she would not give in despite very strong pressure from both her husband, who wanted a settlement, and the king – until finally an agreement was made over her head: an arrangement which was only possible, of course, because she was a woman. Once she eventually got hold of her inheritance because of the death of the surviving male heir, her major concern was with the administration of her estates. The only private issue that she deals with is her religious sentiments, and this seems to be a common pattern in seventeenth-century diaries.

In the less wealthy families and in the gentry and clerical families of middling status the housewife continued to play an active part in the organization of the domestic economy. The general impression from Ralph Josselin's diary is that the bond between husband and wife was very strong.[19] There is evidence that they worked together on the farm and it seems as if all important decisions were taken jointly. At the end of one account of some advice given to his son he says 'their mother gave them the same advice'.[20]

Ralph Josselin was a clergyman, but his wife clearly worked. The idea of the leisured lady was only possible when there were no financial problems. Ralph records in his diary felling a tree with his wife – she was used to hard physical labour.

Housewifery seems to have been a valued skill. Thomas Isham of Lamport, when he was looking for a wife, had one possible candidate described to him as 'very vertuously educated by a careful and vigilant mother, and is of an excellent temper and disposition, naturally brisk and cheerful, a notable Housewife and may prove a very endearing consort if well managed'.[21] It seems to have been a common pattern in these sorts of families for the children – both boys and girls – to leave home when they were adolescent. The boys would be apprenticed out to learn a trade, the girls would be sent as servants into other families – presumably to learn housewifery.

The beginning of the separation of the place of work from the home made it more difficult for lower-class women and children to be engaged in productive activity. The wives of journeymen found themselves no longer on the work premises and seriously disadvantaged because of this. If their husbands made enough money they could become dependent – and in the seventeenth century we find the idea developing of husbands keeping their wives rather than a couple being engaged together in economic activity: or they could attempt to find work themselves. But women were in a weak position in the labour market. Once a woman lost the ability to support herself and her family through domestic activity centred on the household, she found herself very disadvantaged compared with men – her family ties now operated as a severe handicap. Capitalism undermined the position of considerable economic independence enjoyed by married women and widows in the tradesmen and middling farmer groupings.[22] The value of a woman's productive capacity to her family was greatly reduced when through poverty she was obliged to work for wages – spinsters, for example, suffered from extremely low wages because of the combination of disorganization and a lack of bargaining power, both of which resulted mainly from the fact that they worked at home.[23] Consequently a large proportion of the produce of a woman's labour was diverted from her family to the capitalist or consumer, whereas when a woman was fully employed in the household the whole value of what she produced was retained by the family. Capitalist organization tended to deprive women of the opportunities to share in the more profitable forms of production – it confined them as wage-earners to the unprotected trades. Any family which had sufficient resources would employ the woman within the household in some form of domestic industry – women were only driven on to the labour market from necessity.

The development of Puritanism marked a change in the importance given to the family. In using the example of the Puritans I am not claiming that they were a representative group in the society but rather that they reflected the emergence of new attitudes to the family which were centrally related to the development of a capitalist ethic. As the Puritans did not have control of the ruling institutions and, indeed, for much of the seventeenth century were subject to active persecution and repression, it was essential for them to develop counter-institutions, of which the family was one. In the spiritual withdrawal of 'the saints' for the years to come, the family became a focus of organization and discipline. The Puritans were extremely well aware of the centrality of proper socialization and they saw the family or household unit as vital to this. For the Puritans, the lowest unit in the hierarchy of discipline was the household – for 'Who is anywhere,' says a preacher in 1608, 'but is of some man's family, and within some man's gates?'[24] They believed in the spiritualization of the whole life and the household was a starting point for this process. The influence of God must be felt at all levels and in all spheres. One of the key elements in socialization was the taboo on idleness and the imposition of a labour discipline, as Christopher Hill has demonstrated.[25] The father and master of the household was given the main responsibility for this but the mother was seen as his lieutenant. Elizabeth Joceline in *The Mother's Legacie To her Unborne Childe* of 1632 says, 'Be ashamed of idleness as thou art a man, but tremble at it as thou art a Christian . . . What more wretched estate can there be in the world? First to be hated of God an idle drone, not fit for this service; then through extreme poverty to be contemned of all the world.'[26] A Puritan homily against idleness stresses that children must be trained to work so as to be able 'not only to sustain themselves competently, but also to relieve and supply the necessity and want of others'.[27] From the seventeenth century onwards there is much more emphasis on work in the parish provisions for orphaned children. The fact that the father was charged with the responsibility for the moral welfare of his household enhanced his dignity and made everyone else more dependent on him – as the Hallers put it: 'In the society which the preachers were helping to shape, the family household, with its extensions in farmstead and shop, and in its relation to religious life, was assuming an importance it had not had in feudal, monastic, or courtly society. The preachers described it again and again as a little church, a little state – for which the head of the household was responsible.'[28] Calamy, in *England's Looking-Glasse* of 1642, says, 'First reform your own families and then you will be the fitter to reform the family of God. Let the master reform his servant, the father his child, the husband his wife.'[29]

Yet there were contradictory influences within Puritanism; one of these was the emphasis on regarding morality as an affair of the inner spirit rather than depending on the opinion of the world. Paradoxically, this emphasis on the inner spiritual life was, it has been argued, one of the major reasons for the Puritan success in the business world, in that subjecting the spiritual life to godly discipline and setting the whole of a man's life under the eye of God led to the extension of rational calculation and organization in the world of trade as well. Thus, in assisting the husband to discipline the family, women no doubt played a crucial role in the character formation and training of the children who were to grow up to be 'proper bourgeois men'. Within the Puritan family, however, strict hierarchy was maintained – the man remained the head of the household. As Benjamin Wadsworth put it in *The Well Ordered Family*, 'Though the husband is to rule his Family and his Wife, yet his government of his wife should not be with rigour, hautiness, harshness, severity; but with the greatest love, gentleness, kindness, tenderness that may be. Though he governs her he must not treat her as a servant, but as his *own flesh*: he must love her as himself, Eph. 5 33. He should make his government of her, as easie and gentle as possible; and strive more to be loved than feared; though neither is to be excluded.'[30] The Puritan God was undoubtedly masculine and Puritanism, in abolishing the cult of the Virgin Mary, had undoubtedly abolished whatever moderating feminine influence the Virgin had had on rampant Catholic male chauvinism! Some of the radical Puritan sects recognized the spiritual equality of the woman with the man and this produced, at the ideological level at least, some early and quite radical statements on the position of women. Even they, however, as Keith Thomas has suggested, did not carry this beyond the spiritual arena.[31] The dominant tendency Puritanism remained that of seeing women as subordinate helpmeets – the image of the sun and moon is very often used for the husband and wife. As Adam says in *Paradise Lost*:

> For nothing lovelier can be found
> in woman, than to study household good
> and good works in her husband to promote.[32]

Milton makes it clear that Adam should have exercised his proper authority over Eve – he attributes Adam's failure to his dependence on his wife and insufficient control over his instincts. Lucy Hutchinson, the wife of a Puritan commander in the Civil

War, shares Milton's attitudes – she firmly believed in the subjection of women. When describing her husband she says,

> For conjugal affection to his wife it was such in him as whosoever would draw out a rule of honour, kindness and religion to be practised in that estate, need no more but to draw out exactly his example. Never man had a greater passion for a woman, nor a more honourable esteem of a wife; yet he was not uxorious, nor remitted not that just rule which it was her honour to obey, but managed the reins of government with such prudence and affection that she who would not delight in such an honourable and advantageable subjection must have wanted a reasonable soul. He governed by persuasion . . . all that she was, was him, while he was here, and all that she is now at best is but his pale shade.[33]

She describes her own mother's role as 'The care of the worship and service of God, both in her soul and her house, and the education of her children.'[34] But what authority the mother did have over her children was received from the father. Daniel Rogers, in his *Matrimonial Honour* of 1642, illustrates how unimportant it was if a mother objected to a marriage alliance – it was the father that mattered.[35] Women were expected to give some religious instruction – special 'mothers' catechisms' were produced – but again it was as the father's lieutenant. The Puritans assumed that babies were born evil and ignorant but that this could be overcome by education. The task of instruction and discipline must be started very early – they realized how much easier it was to train young children than adolescents. The mother's role as educator and socializer of her children was certainly recognized in the seventeenth century but it was a limited and narrowly defined and ultimately dependent responsibility which she had. Lucy Hutchinson remarks in her few autobiographical notes that her mother did not approve of the amount of intellectually oriented education which her father arranged for her.[36]

We can see from the seventeenth-century definition of housewife the way in which the role is subject to change. The establishment of a more clearly defined sexual division of labour within the developing capitalist mode of production has a crucial effect on the position of women both inside and outside the home. It would be wrong to overemphasize the separation of work from home – even the big London merchants did not begin to live systematically away from their counting-houses until the eighteenth century and for the shopkeeper separation comes very much later. However, the economic status of women was declining – often, no doubt, with their active connivance since there were clearly many advantages in being 'leisured'. Women are now defined both economically and ideologically as secondary – as people who care for, and support, others rather than themselves being active in the world. There is less tension between the economic and the ideological spheres than there was in pre-capitalist society because the woman's two main economic functions have become, firstly, the organization of a household which is no longer the central unit of production; and, secondly, the provision of a cheap supply of labour. There are increasing numbers of ladies at one end of the social scale and exploited women at the other end: somewhere in the middle, the traditional housewife is trying to defend her position.

The third definition of housework that I want to look at is the one which was current in early Victorian society. The dominant ideal definition was one which was established by the Victorian middle class and which was highly unsuited to working-class experience. One of the major functions of the Victorian family was to provide a privatized haven for the man who was subject day in and day out to the pressures of competition in the new industrial world. This feminine role was, one might say, a new aspect of the material reproduction of labour power – to provide men at home with the emotional support to face the world of work outside. As Engels says, the family is not only the sum of its economic functions; it is not just a serving-house for capitalism, standing in a one-to-one relationship with the mode of production – it is also itself a system of relations and emotional needs which shape responses in the world and are created and defined with peculiar strength within the intimate sphere of the family.[37] So, just as we have seen how in the seventeenth century women became much less directly concerned with the creation of surplus value and much more concerned with the production of the proper conditions for capitalist production – with the coming of industrial capitalism, the more total separation of work from home and the public from the private, the proper role of women was increasingly seen to be *at home.* The family was at the centre of Victorian middle-class social life and the fulcrum for the complex set of social values which comprised middle-class respectability. We now know something of the degree of double standards and the mechanism of psychological projection which sustained this ethic. As Marx was the first to point out, the respectable middle-class lady and the prostitute were two sides of the same coin – one might almost say bedfellows! The rich harvest of Victorian pornography would not exist without the Victorian gentleman's ability to travel constantly between virginal ladies upstairs and easy prey below stairs. So it became essential for the preservation of family life that women should be at one and the same time exalted and despised. Thomas Arnold talked of that peculiar sense of solemnity with which the very idea of domestic life was invested: the conception of the home as a source of virtues and emotions which could not be found elsewhere.[38] As Ruskin puts it in *Sesame and Lilies*,

> This is the true nature of home – it is the place of peace – the shelter not only from all injury, but from all terror, doubt and division. In so far as it is not this, it is not home; so far as the anxieties of the outer life penetrate into it, and the inconsistently minded, unknown, unloved, or hostile society of the outer world is allowed by either husband or wife to cross the threshold, it ceases to be home.[39]

William Thompson, in his *Appeal on Behalf of One Half of the Human Race*, was somewhat sceptical of the male-oriented view of the home. 'Home,' he writes, 'was the eternal prison house of the wife; her husband painted it as the abode of calm bliss, but took care to find outside its doors a species of bliss not quite so calm, but of a much more varied and stimulating description.'[40] The Victorians needed to sentimentalize the home in order to give themselves some relief from the anxieties of the public world. Tennyson ironically epitomises the new tradition in *The Princess*:

> Man for the field and woman for the hearth;
> Man for the sword, and for the needle she;
> Man with the head and woman with the heart;
> Man to command, and woman to obey;
> All else confusion.[41]

As endless manuals reminded the Victorian wife and mother, her job was to be 'a companion who will raise the tone of a man's mind from low anxieties and vulgar cares' and preserve an exalted love free from the taint of sexuality or passion. Love should be an uplifting experience and belonged at home – sex was a different matter. Middle-class women, who saw themselves as tending the household and maintaining its moral tone, provided sex on demand for their husbands along with preserves, clean linen and roast meat. The notion of autonomous sexual pleasure for themselves was unthought of: sex was a necessary obligation owed to men and not one which women were permitted to talk or think about as owed to themselves. Mrs Ellis, in her manual *Daughters of England*, gives us a rich Victorian middle-class definition of love:

> 'What, then, I would ask again, is love in its highest, holiest character?' It is woman's all – her health, her power, her very being. Man, let him love as he may, has ever an existence distinct from that of his affections. He has his worldly interests, his public character, his ambition, his competition with other men – but woman centres all in that one feeling, and 'in that *she* lives, or else *she* has no life'. In woman's love is mingled the trusting dependence of a child, for she ever looks up to man as her protector, and her guide; the frankness, the social feeling, and the tenderness of a sister – for is not man her friend? The solicitude, the anxiety, the careful watching of the mother – for would she not suffer to preserve him from harm? Such is love in a noble mind . . .[42]

As the rapidly expanding bourgeoisie extended its range of power and influence – as it established itself not only economically but also politically, so it took on – as the seventeenth-century bourgeoisie had done – the ideas of the ruling class about the proper activities of women: namely, economic idleness. As a result of the increase in wealth and consumer developments which came with the Industrial Revolution, women's activities were restricted in various directions. The employment of servants and the mass production of articles formerly made in the home gradually made such idleness physically possible for the privileged. The industrialization in textiles made redundant one of women's most traditional skills – spinning – and the invention of the sewing-machine, for example, altered conditions even further in the direction of the leisured lady. Increasing wealth brought new standards of luxury and new ideas of refinement which prevented women in the trading and business classes from taking any further share in their husband's concerns. In the eighteenth century many of women's entrepreneurial activities had been based on experience rather than training – but as the division of labour developed, and education and skill became more important, there was no provision for the training and education of women. The process which had begun in the seventeenth century with the emergence of capitalism was carried several stages further and affected much greater numbers of women in the nineteenth century. Margaretta Greg, in her diary in 1853, wrote:

> A lady, to be such, must be a mere lady and nothing else. She must not work for profit, or engage in any profit that money can

> command . . . The conventional barrier that pronounces it ungenteel to be behind a counter, or serving the public in any mercantile capacity, is greatly extended. The same in household economy. Servants must be up to their offices which is very well; but ladies, dismissed from the dairy, the confectionery, the store room, the still room, the poultry yard, the kitchen garden and the orchard, have hardly yet found themselves a sphere equally useful in the pursuits of trade and art to which to apply their too abundant leisure.[43]

The mid-nineteenth-century feminists were extremely concerned with the lack of useful employment available to women. By the 1870s there were complaints that women were no longer involved even in supervising servants. George Eliot says of Mrs Amos Barton, 'You would never have asked, at any period in Mrs A. B's life, if she sketched or played the piano, you would even, perhaps, have been rather scandalized if she had descended from the serene dignity of being to the assiduous unrest of doing.'[44] For women not to work reflected the success of their men – whether father or husband. The education and training of girls was to prepare them for courtship and marriage. Much more attention was paid to the education of boys, for they had to make their own way in the world – a woman could, if she was lucky, rely on somebody else doing it for her. If she did not marry, her life was likely to be a hard one. Fathers tended to be responsible for the education of their sons – for, after all, their mothers could scarcely carry this out, given their own limited experience. The importance of the mother as a primary agent in the socialization of children only emerges in the nuclear family when the mother is more or less solely responsible for the pre-school child. The twentieth-century 'myth of motherhood' associated with Bowlby, Spock and others is one of the end products of this historical process of narrowing the definition of the family. Victorian middle-class mothers usually had limited contact with their children so they were not seen as the key person in the reproduction of the ideological relations of production. The utilitarian educators of the nineteenth century located the crucial years as those at school and laid great emphasis on the importance of establishing, through education, either a proper ruling ideology or a proper work discipline. They saw working-class parental attitudes as both inadequate and decadent and sought to substitute the teacher and the school as the dominant inculcators of values.[45] The Schools Enquiry Commission of 1867 complained that the major problem in the education of girls was their parents' attitude.[46] As Mr Gibson put it in *Wives and Daughters*, 'Don't teach Molly too much: she must sew and read, and write and do her sums . . . After all, I'm not sure that reading or writing is necessary."[47] Music, drawing, painting, French, fancy work, gossip and fashion were the stuff of a Victorian girl's life – all designed to prepare her to catch a man. Mrs Ellis, in her chapter on the training of girls, says:

> It is sometimes spoken of as a defect in women, that they have less power of abstraction than men; and certainly if they were required to take part in all the occupations of the other sex, it would be so; but for my own part, I must confess, I never could see it an advantage to any woman, to be capable of abstraction beyond a certain extent . . . a woman, I would humbly suggest, has no business to be so far absorbed in any purely intellectual pursuit, as not to know when water is boiling over on the fire.[48]

There was no training in the practical duties of a housewife even in many lower-middle-class households for it was seen as an unladylike activity. Once married, housekeeping presented many problems, as Rosamund Vincy in *Middlemarch* experienced so bitterly. Even Lydgate – a thinking man in many ways – wanted for a wife 'an accomplished creature who venerated his high musings and momentous labours, and would never interfere with them'.[49] The Victorian middle-class obsession with cleanliness hardened the division between the housewife as organizer and those who actually did the work. A lady must have white shapely hands free from dirt and must never be seen outside the house without gloves. A. J. Munby gives us considerable insight into the symbolic power of hands as distinguishing between those who worked and those who didn't.[50]

The leisure of the Victorian lady was necessarily bound up with the exploitation of her less fortunate sisters. She relied on lower- middle- and working-class women to nurse and train her children and to do the domestic work associated with her household. Her own involvement would be confined to supervision. Servants were of course found right down the social scale – even in some working-class households. But whereas in upper-class households the mistress would be engaged in a system of labour relations, in small units with only one or two servants the 'housewife' would be more actively engaged herself – in thinking out menus, for example. The image of the housewife as lady, therefore, was the one propagandized by the dominant class in the nineteenth century. Middle-class women who were driven by economic necessity out to work, mainly as governesses, were able despite the poverty and loneliness of their situations to maintain an aura of gentility. Middle-class women did have to work to earn money in considerable numbers – but they were a depressed minority. Feminists argued that it was vital to recognize the existence of this group and allow them to work. As Mary Carpenter put it,

> It is work we ask, room to work, encouragement to work, an open field with a fair day's wages for a fair day's work; it is an injustice, we feel, the injustice of men, who arrogate to themselves all profitable employments . . . and . . . drive women to the lowest depths of penury and suffering . . . Could Providence have created several thousand superfluous women for the purpose of rendering them burdens on society, as inmates of our prisons, workhouses and charitable institutions? Or is it that there is something wrong in our social arrangements, whereby they are unfairly deprived of occupations?[51]

Being themselves Victorians, the feminists could not help arguing within those terms. Their new model woman would 'become, in a better sense than they have ever been before, companions and helpmeets to men'.[52] But the idea of women working was very much disapproved of by the Victorian middle class – it did not go well with the deification of the home and the idea of women and children as helpless dependants who had to be protected.

However, this ideology of domesticity was far in advance of the practice. Not only did considerable numbers of middle-class women have to go out to work but the vast majority of working-class women were engaged in work either inside or outside the home. A working-class woman at home might very well be engaged in something else as well as running the house – taking in laundry, for example, or outwork, or running a trading sideline or a shop. Practice was wildly at variance with the social ideal canvassed by bourgeois and clerical moralists. What changes, as Margaret Hewitt points out, is that the middle class try and impose their new standards on the working class[53] and the power of their dominant ideology is such that it would seem to have been to some extent adopted and internalized by working-class men and women as early as the mid-nineteenth century. There were, of course, many contradictory influences at work and attitudes and expectations would vary very much from region to region according to the work available and other factors. The situation was clearly different in areas like Lancashire, where there was factory work available for women, from areas where the only kind of available employment was as servants. In addition, patterns of housewifery would be different in towns from those in rural areas. It was typical of Victorian hypocrisy that they should combine the exploitation of women as factory workers, domestic servants, needlewomen and agricultural workers with lectures and homilies on the disgraceful way in which these women were neglecting the care of their families. A factory deputation from Yorkshire on the ten-hour day, in the 1840s, pressed for the gradual withdrawal of women from factories on the grounds that 'the home, its cares and employments are the woman's true spheres'.[54]

No doubt fears on the men's part about losing their own jobs combined with a degree of acceptance of the prevailing view that woman's place was in the home. Engels reminds us that the early heavy employment of women in the textile industries particularly brought about something of a reversal of the economic position of men and women.[55] This exacerbates the internal divisions in the working class created by the sexual division of labour. Of course, this was hardly a new view – one of the major changes which industrialization brought was that women who had been employed as outworkers in the home were now employed in factories in some areas, and their hours and conditions were on view in a way that they had never been before. 'The idea of women's work outside the home in industry', as Winifred Holtby puts it, 'became associated with squalor, fatigue, bad cooking and neglected children, just as women's work in the professions became associated with celibacy, aggressiveness or impropriety and with everything contradictory to the ideal of ladyhood.'[56]

The articulate and interfering sections of the Victorian middle class were united in their disapproval of the disastrous effects of factory labour, in particular on the family. By keeping women at work, thought Ashley, 'You are poisoning the very sources of order and happiness and virtue; you are tearing up root and branch all relations of families to one another; you are annulling, as it were, the institution of domestic life decreed by Providence Himself, . . . the mainstay of peace and virtue and therein of national security.'[57] Dr Andrew Ure, usually the most hard-headed of political economists, remarked what a good thing it was that women were paid low wages since it would make the idea of staying at home and doing their natural job more attractive to them.[58] However, economic necessity did send many women out to work and households had to be organized on that basis. Domestic obligation was outridden on the labour market. In the early days of industrialization in Lancashire when father, mother and children would all be working, the home was little but a shelter. When both parents were working it was generally understood that the woman organized the household as well. In Birmingham in the 1840s Monday was still often regarded as a holiday but only for the men – the women then had to do the washing, shopping and other domestic work.[59] Hawkins, a factory inspector in the north, reported in 1861:

> I scarcely need argue that there can be comparatively no comfort in the dwelling of a working man whose wife is away from home from 5.30 in the morning till 6.30 in the evening, except at mealtimes, for she is compelled to leave her children and her household to other hands; and, having so little experience of her own, is quite unable to teach her daughter those attractive qualifications with which women keep their husbands from disreputable associations.[60]

Large numbers of women were employed in service capacities to the mill women – to fulfil the domestic activities which they had not time to do themselves – as tea-makers, washerwomen, needlewomen, cleaners, and to nurse children. The critics of the new factory age attacked this whole system of domestic economy – they were shocked by the handing out of laundry and that women did not know how to sew and mend. The middle-class commentators were particularly shocked by the standards of housewifery of the factory operatives but it seems that they were very little different from those of other working-class women – and how could it be otherwise? It was a piece of double-think, as Ivy Pinchbeck points out, to go on about the dirt and squalor and lack of domestic pride among the working class – given the material circumstances in which they lived.[61] But the combination of the doctrine of *laissez-faire* with the ideal of the sanctity of the home made it impossible for a long time for the Victorian moral entrepreneurs to do more than bemoan the inadequacies of working-class family life. Again the hypocrisy was quite astounding – the conditions of that life were the creation of that same bourgeoisie which imposed quite other standards in ideological terms. By the mid-century the importance of educating working women was beginning to attract considerable attention. *Household Words*, in 1832, describes a new school for wives in Birmingham – the first evening school which taught sewing including mending, reading, writing, arithmetic – so that they could check whether they were being swindled by shopkeepers – and the Bible.[62] From about 1870, domestic economy did begin to be introduced in some schools.

So we can see how, in the nineteenth century, the pattern established in the seventeenth century with the development of the capitalist mode of production has been strengthened and extended with the formation of industrial capitalism. The sexual division of labour rigidifies as the capitalist division of labour becomes more refined and job specialization increases. The bourgeoisie make their wives into ladies in a position of dependence economically and subordination ideologically and then use lower-middle-class and working-class women to service their households and produce their textiles. It is only when the capitalist economy needs women in large numbers that the image of the idealized wife and mother changes somewhat and a new note is introduced. The society can organize crèches and canteens and substantially reduce the need for privatized domestic labour, as can clearly be seen from the experience of the two world wars. To understand the position of women in the home it is necessary to see the way in which women provide an industrial reserve army of labour which can be drawn upon in different ways at different times. The ideology of domesticity which ties women into the home and stresses their role as wife and mother has, since the early nineteenth century, been a key to the sexual division of labour as we know it. The fact that a woman's place is in the home justifies the definition of her work outside the home as secondary – and, therefore, typically low-paid and unskilled. But this is not a natural phenomenon, it is a cultural creation. A crucial missing element in our knowledge of the past is a history of the housewife.

NOTES

1 Anon., *Seneschaucie*, in James Bruce Ross and Mary Martin McLaughlin (eds), *The Portable Medieval Reader* (Viking, New York, 1949), p. 135.
2 Margery Kempe, *The Book of Margery Kempe*. A modern version by W. Butler-Bowden (Cape, London, 1936), p. 82.
3 Chrétien de Troyes, *Arthurian Romances* (Dent, London, 1965).
4 R. H. Hilton, *The English Peasantry in the Later Middle Ages* (Clarendon, Oxford, 1975). See particularly the chapter on 'Women in the Village'. I have greatly benefited in preparing the medieval section of this chapter, and especially this paragraph, from discussions with Professor Hilton and access to his unpublished material.

5 Pattingham, Staffs. Court Rolls, 1369, 1388.
6 Halesowen, Worcs. Court Rolls, 1386.
7 Kempe, *The Book of Margery Kempe*, p. 28.
8 Anon., *The Goodman of Paris*, in Ross and McLaughlin (eds), *The Portable Medieval Reader*, p. 155.
9 For the developing Marxist-feminist analysis of the family under capitalism, see, *inter alia*, Juliet Mitchell, *Women's Estate* (Penguin, Harmondsworth, 1972); Sheila Rowbotham, *Woman's Consciousness, Man's World* (Penguin, Harmondsworth, 1973); Mariarosa Dalla Costa, *The Power of Women and the Subversion of the Community* (Falling Wall Press, Bristol, 1972).
10 Alice Clark, *The Working Life of Women in the Seventeenth Century* (Frank Cass, London, 1968). See particularly ch. 6.
11 Karl Marx, *Capital*, vol. 1 (Foreign Languages Publishing House, Moscow, 1961).
12 Louis Althusser, 'Ideology and Ideological State Apparatuses', in *Lenin and Philosophy, and Other Essays* (New Left Books, London, 1971).
13 J. Ketley (ed.) *The Two Liturgies in the Reign of King Edward VI* (Parker Society, 1844). Quoted in Christopher Hill, *Society and Puritanism in Pre-Revolutionary England* (Secker & Warburg, London, 1964), p. 447.
14 Clark, *Working Life*, See particularly ch. 2.
15 Sheila Rowbotham, *Women, Resistance and Revolution*, Allen Lane, London, 1972. See particularly ch. 1.
16 Rich, 'The Excellency of Good Women', quoted in Louis B. Wright, *Middle-Class Culture in Elizabethan England* (North Carolina Univer-isty Press, Chapel Hill, 1935), p. 473.
17 Gainsford, quoted in Wright, *Middle-Class Culture*, p. 491.
18 George C. Williamson, *Lady Anne Clifford, Countess of Dorset, Pembroke and Montgomery* (T. Wilson & Son, Kendal, 1922).
19 Alan Macfarlane, *The Family Life of Ralph Josselin: a seventeenth-century clergyman* (Cambridge Univeristy Press, London, 1970); (ed.) *The Diary of Ralph Josselin 1616–1683* (Oxford University Press, London, 1976).
20 Macfarlane, *The Family Life*, p. 109.
21 Sir Giles Isham (ed.), *The Journal of Thomas Isham of Lamport* (Miller & Leavins, Norwich, 1875), p. 43.
22 For more detail on this, see Clark, *Working Life*, chs 3, 5.
23 Clark, *Working Life*, ch. 4.
24 Quoted in Keith Thomas, 'Women and the Civil War Sects', *Past and Present*, no. 13, April 1958.
25 Hill, *Society and Puritanism*, ch. 13.
26 Elizabeth Joceline, *The Mother's Legacie to her Unborne Child* (1632), quoted in Hill, *Society and Puritanism,* p. 124.
27 'Homily Against Idleness', quoted in Hill, *Society and Puritanism*, p. 139.

28 W. and M. Haller, 'The Puritan Art of Love', *Huntingdon Library Quarterly*, V, p. 247.
29 E. Calamy, *England's Looking-Glasse* (1642), quoted in Hill, *Society and Puritanism*, p. 445.
30 Benjamin Wadsworth, *The Well Ordered Family*, quoted in E. S. Morgan, *The Puritan Family. Essays on religious and domestic relations in seventeenth-century New England* (Boston, Mass., 1944), p. 11.
31 Thomas, 'Women and the Civil War Sects'.
32 John Milton, *Paradise Lost* (Longman, London, 1968), Bk 9.
33 Lucy Hutchinson, *Memoirs of the Life of Colonel Hutchinson* (Oxford University Press, London, 1973), p. 9.
34 Hutchinson, *Memoirs of the Life of Colonel Hutchinson*, pp. 25–8.
35 Daniel Rogers, *Matrimonial Honour* (1642), quoted in L. L. Schuecking, *The Puritan Family* (Routledge & Kegan Paul, London, 1969).
36 Hutchinson, *Memoirs*, p. 288.
37 Frederick Engels, *The Origin of the Family, Private Property and the State* (Lawrence & Wishart, London, 1940).
38 Thomas Arnold quoted in Walter Houghton, *The Victorian Frame of Mind* (Yale Univeristy Press, New Haven, 1957), p. 343.
39 John Ruskin, quoted in Houghton, *The Victorian Frame of Mind*, p. 343.
40 William Thompson, *Appeal on Behalf of One Half of the Human Race, Women, Against the Pretensions of the Other Half, Men, to Retain Them in Civil and Domestic Slavery* (London, 1825), p. 79.
41 Alfred, Lord Tennyson, *The Princess* (Moxon, London, 1847), p. 116.
42 Mrs Sarah Stickney Ellis, *The Daughters of England. Their Position in Society, Character and Responsibilities.* (London Printing and Publishing Co., London, n.d.), p. 318.
43 Quoted in Ivy Pinchbeck, *Women Workers and the Industrial Revolution 1750–1850* (Frank Cess, London, 1969), pp. 315–16.
44 George Eliot, *Scenes of Clerical Life*, 'Amos Barton' (Penguin, Harmondsworth, 1980), p. 54.
45 Richard Johnson, 'Educational Policy and Social Control in early Victorian England', *Past and Present*, no. 49, November 1970.
46 See Wanda Neff, *Victorian Working Women 1838–50* (Allen & Unwin, London, 1929), especially the chapter on 'The Idle Woman'.
47 Mrs Elizabeth Gaskell, *Wives and Daughters* (Penguin, Harmondsworth, 1980), pp. 104–5.
48 Mrs Sarah Stickney Ellis, *Mothers of England* (Peter Jackson & Co., London, 1843), p. 321.
49 George Eliot, *Middlemarch* (Penguin, Harmondsworth, 1987), p. 121.
50 Derek Hudson, *Munby: Man of Two Worlds* (Abacus, London, 1974).
51 Quoted in Lee Holcombe, *Victorian Ladies at Work 1850–1940* (David & Charles, Newton Abbot, 1973), especially ch. 1.
52 Holcombe, *Victorian Ladies.*

53 Margaret Hewitt, *Wives and Mothers in Victorian Industry* (Rockliff, London, 1958).
54 Hewitt, *Wives and Mothers*, p. 23.
55 Frederick Engels, *The Condition of the Working Class in England in 1844* (Blackwell, Oxford, 1958).
56 Winifred Holtby, *Women, a Changing Civilisation* (London, 1934), p. 37.
57 Quoted in Hewitt, *Wives and Mothers*, p. 49.
58 Andrew Ure, quoted in Neff, *Victorian Working Women*, p. 29.
59 There are complaints in the diaries and accounts of small masters in particular of the problems posed by 'Saint Monday'.
60 Quoted in Hewitt, *Wives and Mothers*, p. 63.
61 Pinchbeck, *Women Workers*, p. 107.
62 Quoted in Neff, *Victorian Working Women*, p. 78.

PART II

Gender and Class

3 The Early Formation of Victorian Domestic Ideology

The Victorian middle-class ideal of womanhood is one that is well documented – the 'angel in the house', the 'relative creature' who maintained the home as a haven, is familiar from novels, manuals and even government reports. There is plenty of evidence to suggest that by the 1830s and 1840s the definition of women as primarily relating to home and family was well established. But what were the origins of this ideal? 1780–1830 has been called the period of the making of the industrial bourgeoisie. That class defined itself not only in opposition to the new proletariat, but also to the classes of landed capitalism – the gentry and the aristocracy. Their class definition was built not only at the level of the political and the economic – the historic confrontations of 1832 and 1846 – but also at the level of culture and ideology. The new bourgeois way of life involved a recodification of ideas about women. Central to those new ideas was an emphasis on women as domestic beings, as primarily wives and mothers. Evangelicalism provided one crucial influence on this definition of home and family. Between 1780 and 1820, in the Evangelical struggle over anti-slavery and over the reform of manners and morals, a new view of the nation, of political power and of family life was forged. This view was to become a dominant one in the 1830s and 1840s. The Evangelical emphasis on the creation of a new life-style, a new ethic, provided the framework for the emergence of the Victorian bourgeoisie.

It has been argued that Evangelical morality was probably the single most widespread influence in Victorian England.[1] Evangelicals were staunch members of the Church of England who believed in reform from within rather than in following the example of John Wesley, who in the 1780s had in effect seceded from the established Church to form the Methodist sect. The crucially important position of the Clapham Sect, as leaders of the Evangelicals, and their influence on nineteenth-century England has long been recognized. They occupy a position of distinction in Whig history, but have been less revered by radicals.[2] The Whig interpretation sees the Sect as having played a vital role, not only in establishing the great nineteenth-century tradition of extra-Parliamentary agitation, but also as a group marked by moral superiority and freedom from self-interest. The origins of the group lay in Henry Thornton's house at Clapham and the focus which that provided for a number of prominent Evangelicals at the end of the eighteenth century. The Thornton family were prosperous bankers and John Thornton, Henry's father, was an influential Evangelical. Clapham became a centre for a number of families who were united in their interests and interconnected by marriage. The major figures were Henry Thornton, William Wilberforce, Zachary Macaulay (who was Editor of the Evangelical *Christian Observer* and did much of the research and writing on the slavery issue), James Stephen (a barrister) and Lord Teignmouth (who was Governor General of India for five years). All of them lived in Clapham for long periods, where an Evangelical, John Venn, held the living. In addition, there were other people who were very closely associated and paid frequent visits – Thomas Gisborne, for example, a country gentleman, cleric and author; Hannah More, the celebrated author; and Charles Simeon, who was the Evangelical leader in Cambridge. The Sect's work was primarily devoted to the furtherance of Evangelical principles in various political and social fields. They are best known for their contributory effort to the abolition of the slave trade and of slavery, their missionary activities both within and beyond England, and their influence on the foundation of Sunday schools and many other philanthropic and reforming institutions. In a much quoted entry in his diary in 1787, Wilberforce wrote that his mission was to abolish the slave trade and reform the manners and morals of the nation; virtually all the activities of the Clapham Sect sprang from these two commitments.

The Sect's second campaign – the attempt to transform national morality – had less clear legislative goals than the anti-slavery movement. Its concern was to redefine the available cultural norms and to encourage a new seriousness and respectability in life. The Clapham Sect aimed to provide a new model that would displace the licentiousness and immorality which they saw around them. This *modus vivendi* would be widely propagated by means of pamphlets, manuals, sermons, and as many other media as could be utilized. At the same time it would be reinforced institutionally by getting legislation passed on such issues as public amusements, sabbatarianism and obscene publications. The onslaught on morality was a highly organized campaign, and although it did not fire the national imagination in the same way that the anti-slavery issue had, it nevertheless had an important impact on manners at the beginning of the nineteenth century.[3]

The Evangelical concern with national morality had, as its premiss, the belief of the Sect that religion should be a daily rule of life rather than a question of doctrinal purity. Like the Methodists, they emphasized the importance of a well-ordered daily routine. Their overwhelming sense of sin necessitated the formulation of rules for daily life, in an attempt to reduce the possibilities of collapse into the natural condition. Hannah More and Wilberforce wrote journals which give us considerable insight into the practices of Evangelical living. Both of them see self-examination as absolutely central in their attempt to live according to God. Passivity and obedience were demanded in relation to God's word. A vital distinction was made between nominal and real Christianity: the nominal Christian accepts only the forms. The eighteenth-century religious revival was concerned with an attempt to get beneath the forms, to transform the meaning of religion *from within*. The Evangelical decision to stay inside the established Church meant that pressure for internal reconstruction was perhaps even stronger on them than on the Methodists – since the latter were creating new external forms of religious organization as well.

Wilberforce's immensely influential *Practical Christianity* gives us one of the clearest statements of Evangelical views. He insisted on the distinction between real and nominal belief. Christianity, he argued, 'is a state into which we are not born, but into which we must be translated; a nature which we do not inherit, but into which we are to be created anew . . . This is a matter of labour and difficulty, requiring continual watchfulness, and unceasing effort, and unwearied patience'.[4] Life is a journey towards salvation and the image of the pilgrim is constantly there. Wilberforce and

Hannah More both experienced conversion in adulthood and, as a result, reconstructed their lives. Wilberforce aimed to live by rule and to subject his life to constant scrutiny in an attempt to be of the greatest productive use to others. He believed that an individual's only strength sprang from a deep and abiding sense of his own weakness and inadequacy – hence the constant need for self-criticism and self-examination. Criticism, moreover, should be not just an individual practice but a mutual practice amongst the believers. Self-discipline was therefore a *sine qua non* in the Evangelicals' philosophy. Their letters and diaries bear constant witness to the difficulties of achieving it. It is important not to read back into this early phase of Evangelicalism the critique of its aspects in Victorian England with which we are familiar from Dickens, Thackeray or Butler. Between 1790 and 1820 the movement was in struggle, constantly on the attack against the evils it saw surrounding it, and attempting to transform English life. After 1820 Evangelicalism increasingly established itself as a part of the dominant culture. It lost its early purity and could justly be accused of priggishness, conventionality, hypocrisy and conservatism. But the first generation of the Clapham Sect were unceasingly diligent in their efforts to behave properly, to live as *real* Christians should, and to change their way of life.

In the 1780s the Evangelicals were convinced of the necessity for a national reform of manners. They wanted to attack the aristocracy's laxness and impose a new rule of life. In current political weakness they saw a reflection of moral depravity. It seemed clear that moral reform was impossible without the support of the ruling class and the established Church – and those were their initial constituencies. If – as they believed – Wesley's attempt at it had been doomed from the start by his reliance on preaching the Word, then they instead would exploit any political channels open to them. Society was seen to be in need of effective leadership and guidance. The growth of the middle class made this particularly urgent because it was in danger of adopting the lax principles of those of higher rank; furthermore, the commercial spirit did not appear naturally favourable to the maintenance of religious principles.

The attack on manners and morals was initially organized mainly around producing propaganda aimed at the upper classes.[5] It took the French Revolution to transform a modest campaign into a major national force. In the dangerous years of the 1790s a simple, repressive policy was not enough; an active regeneration was also necessary in support of England. As Lady Shelley wrote in her diary: 'The awakening of the labouring classes after the first shocks of the French Revolution, made the upper classes tremble. Every man felt the necessity for putting his house in order.' E. P. Thompson had added to this: 'To be more accurate, most men and women of property felt the necessity for putting the houses of the poor in order.'[6] But to put the houses of the poor in order was only one part of the Evangelical campaign. They believed in self-regeneration as well as the proper instruction of the poor, and it was this duality which gave their movement such power. Their position cannot be equated with Toryism – they were subject to vitriolic attacks from sections of the ruling class as well as from radicals. The Evangelicals only ever had a limited amount of support from aristocratic and landed circles. Their major support, despite the intentions of the Clapham Sect, came from the middle ranks.

Between 1780 and 1832 England was in a period of transition – from an aristocratic and mercantile capitalist society, where land was still the major source of power, to an industrial capitalist society with a large and influential bourgeoisie. The Evangelicals were able to play a mediating role in this transition. They neither unquestioningly supported the old society nor uncritically welcomed the new. Their religious position drew on some of the same criticisms of established religious forms as had the Methodists, yet they remained staunch Anglicans; and unlike the Methodists, they never developed a popular base amongst the labouring classes. They insisted on the possibility of reform from within, rather than by creating new structures. Similarly, in political terms, they advocated transformation from within, rather than a direct change in the distribution of political power. They believed in the traditional power of the aristocracy and appealed to the old ruling groups, yet their desire for particular kinds of change drove them to seek support from the expanding middle class. In order to achieve the abolition of the slave trade and of slavery, for example, they needed pressure group organization on a massive scale – yet they still believed in the absolute power of an unreformed House of Commons to make legislative decisions. The success of the anti-slavery campaign marked an important transitional moment on the way to a full demand for recognition of middle-class power.[7]

The religious base of the Evangelicals allowed them to insist that the issues they took up were moral, not political. Anti-slavery came to be seen as 'above politics'. Their solution to the political problems facing England in the wake of the French Revolution was declared to be a religious solution – not a political one. It was the religious consciousness of England, they argued, which determined her political condition.

> To the decline of Religion and morality our national difficulties must both indirectly and directly be chiefly ascribed . . . My only solid hopes for the well-being of my country depend not so much on her fleets and armies, not so much on the wisdom of her rulers, or the spirit of her people, as on the persuasion that she still contains many, who in a degenerate age, love and obey the Gospel of Christ; on the humble trust that the intercession of these may still be prevalent, that for the sake of these Heaven may still look upon us with an eye of favour.[8]

Real Christianity must be cultivated to arrest the progress of political decay.

The Clapham Sect members were neither old-style aristocrats nor new-style manufacturers. Yet they came to be seen as representing the interests of England and of sections of the middle classes. The major interests of the Sect were in financial and mercantile capital. The Wilberforce family money came from the Baltic trade and by the 1770s had been partly invested in land. The Thorntons were well-established bankers. Macaulay's money derived from African trade. There were remarkably few manufacturers involved. The Evangelicals always looked for wealthy and aristocratic support; they believed in the importance of influencing the great, and rejoiced in titled and royal backing. Wilberforce was one of Pitt's closest friends and mixed regularly with the governing elite. Nevertheless, this group was associated from its early days with the new middle-class culture of industrial England. The Clapham Sect came to articulate and represent the needs and changing consciousness of a new society. Their own links with the old mercantile bourgeoisie and the landed aristocracy enabled them to form a bridge between the old ruling groups and the aspirant middle classes. Organizations like the anti-slavery movement created a forum where these different class fractions could meet and cooperate. The Evangelicals were able to bridge class divisions because they had a strikingly new view of desirable life-styles and political responsibilities. Their great influence lay not only in their own power, but also in having the ear of others in authority. An important geographical factor was also involved in their potential to form a link between classes: London was the capital and the centre of political life, and the Sect was effectively based there. London was also a major centre of middle-class life. It was, however, not an expanding area for the factory system – and it remained the heartland of financial and commercial capitalism where the Evangelicals were so well represented. When manufacturers and industrialists came to London, they did so partly to enjoy metropolitan life and to engage in London politics. Consequently it was possible for the Sect to bridge the gap in London more easily than in Manchester or Rochdale, where the balance of class forces was different.

It is important to take account of the hostility of sections of the ruling class to Evangelicalism and the attempted reforms. Once the first fury of the French Revolution was over, with its initial effect of binding all property owners together, the High Church began to attack the Evangelicals. In the Evangelical campaign, 1797 had been a crucial year – a year of moral panic in England.[9] There were mutinies in the fleet, fears of a French invasion and of rebellion in Ireland, and a widespread belief in a conspiracy to undermine religion and morality. The fears about internal conditions had been manageable until there was also a serious threat from outside. Then the combination of the threat both from without and within England provoked a grave crisis of confidence; it was in this context that Wilberforce published *Practical Christianity*, with such immediate success. Moral and sexual subversion seemed to many to be the greatest dangers facing the country. But a High Church/Evangelical alliance over the moral dangers confronting the nation was not to last. High Churchmen associated immorality with French influence and mismanagement. The Evangelicals saw it as the result of the lack of true religion and the sinful heart of man. This marked a fundamental disagreement and the High Church inaugurated a campaign against the attempted Evangelical infiltration of the seats of power.[10] This was a struggle within sections of the ruling class and the Evangelicals were increasingly forced to look for support to the middle ranks.

In the wake of the French Revolution England was split politically. Evangelicalism provided a rallying point against Jacobinism. The beliefs and values of the truly religious were totally opposed to those of Godwin and the Jacobin circles. Because they regarded themselves as a campaigning movement engaged in struggle, the Evangelicals built a network and an organization across the country which permeated English life. By means of the anti-slavery associations, the Cheap Repository Tracts, the Sunday schools and many other societies, they penetrated aspects of daily life and provided a politics and morality that recognized the power of the French and industrial revolutions and responded to that challenge. That response was in open conflict with both new working-class organization and consciousness, and with Old Corruption. It is not that the Clapham Sect simply represented and reflected the interests of the new capitalist class: at a particular historical moment a particular class fraction or group can represent the interests of other factions or classes and can embody ideas and practices which have repercussions far beyond them. It is in this sense that the Clapham Sect spoke for others and, therefore, came to be seen as something other than what it was. It was understood selectively and taken up in part.

Central to the Evangelicals' attempt to reconstruct daily life and create a new morality with liberal and humanist parameters on the one hand (the attack on slavery), yet buttressed by social conservatism on the other (the reform of manners and morals), was the redefinition of the position of the woman in the family. The Evangelical attempt to transform daily life was based on the belief in the universality of sin and the need for constant struggle against it. A primary arena of this struggle must be the home and family. The Evangelical ideal of the family and the woman at home was developed well before the French Revolution. Cowper, for example, 'the poet of domesticity', was writing in the 1780s. But it was the debate about the nature and the role of women, produced by the Revolution, which opened the floodgates of manuals from Evangelical pens. Mary Wollstonecraft's *Vindication of the Rights of Women* was first published in 1792 – before the tide had really been turned in England by the Terror. Hannah More was appalled by the book and she became the major protagonist of an alternative stance.

The *Vindication* is basically a plea for equality with bourgeois men – educational, legal and political equality. It is also an attack on the idea of femininity. Wollstonecraft was fired by the example of the Revolution to demand an extension of the rights of men to women. She saw women's inferior status as resulting from their environment – not from a lack of natural abilities. She argued for better education for women, to equip them for the world.[11] The Evangelicals started from a fundamentally different position: men and women are not equal; the sexes are naturally distinct; women should be better educated, but only to make them better wives and mothers. The 1790s saw a flood of writing defining, arguing and extending this position. The feminist belief in the equality of the sexes was absolutely rejected. Thomas Paine was dangerous in that he proposed equality between men, but if that argument were to be extended to women the whole social fabric would be under attack. At least it could be demonstrated that there was a *natural* division between the sexes. Arguments about social hierarchies also began with assumptions about nature, but less easily gained acceptance: the ideological underpinning of the 'natural constitution' was more apparent than beliefs in the inevitable concomitants of the sexual division. The debate on women, the family and the sexual division of labour was thus an integral part of the 1790s discussions about the organization of society. The Evangelical beliefs in the special and important duties of women in the home again played a mediating role between Radicals and Old Corruption. It is dependence which binds people together, argues More, both in the family and in the social hierarchy.

> Now it is pretty clear, in spite of modern theories, that the very frame and being of societies, whether great or small, public or private, is jointed and glued together by dependence. Those attachments which arise from, and are compacted by, a sense of mutual wants, mutual affection, mutual benefit, and mutual obligation, are the cement which secures the union of the family as well as of the State.[12]

The Evangelicals pilloried aristocractic ideals of women – they attacked as inadequate the way in which women were educated and the refusal to take them seriously. They denounced the double standard and championed the value of a good marriage. They drew on the eighteenth-century debate about women – they admired Richardson and agreed with the early Cobbett about, for example, the unfortunate aping of their betters by aspirant farmers' wives. They were responding again to the major social transformation which was taking place in England as a result of the development of capitalism. They were concerned with the problem of defining for the middle ranks a way of life best suited to their affluence and leisure. By the 1780s, existing material conditions enabled many more women to forgo employment – and a 'lady of leisure' enjoyed the hallmark of gentility. As Pinchbeck has demonstrated, the number of well-to-do women in mercantile and commercial ventures was dropping.[13] How were these women, with their new-found wealth and time, to behave? And who was to provide the model? Hannah More, Gisborne, Wilberforce, Mrs West, Mrs Sherwood and many others were adept and successful in assuming the role of mentors.

Evangelicalism has been described as 'the religion of the household' and it is clear that the notion of home and family was central to their religious views. Cowper refers to

> Domestic happiness, thou only bliss
> Of paradise that has survived the Fall.[14]

Home was one place where attempts could be made to curb sin – in the world outside it was obviously far more difficult. The household was seen as the basis for a proper religious life – morality began at home. The Clapham Sect were champions of family life themselves and in many ways lived like a large extended family. They lived with each other (often for long periods), they intermarried, they went on holiday together, and the men worked together. The values of domestic life were highly prized. Stephen, in his essay on the Sect, takes the unusual step of including domestic portraits of the key members as well as a discussion of their public contributions. He sees Wilberforce as at his best in the home and argues that the example of his household was a wonderful incentive to the practice of religion. 'There is something peculiar in Wilberforce's character and situation,' he writes, 'that seems to point it out as the design of Providence, that he should serve his Master in this high and special walk, and should have, so to speak, a kind of *domestic publicity* – that he should be at home a candle set on a candlestick as well as abroad a city built upon a hill.'[15]

Hannah More, in her novel *Coelebs*, offers the ideal example of the religious home. Set in their country house, the Stanley family are presented as the epitome of a religious household, living out their Evangelical and Utilitarian practice on a daily basis.[16] The country ambience is important. More, like Gisborne and other Evangelicals, believed that the ideal of a new-style benevolent paternalism was more viable in a rural than in an urban environment. Religious and domestic virtues were linked in the concept of a religious household. Sunday abstinence, for example, acquired significance when Sunday was defined as a family day. This linking of the religious with the domestic was extended to the division between the public and the private sphere, and was crucial to

Evangelical thinking about the home. The basic split was between the world as hostile and the home as loving – a split that became commonplace in Victorian England.

The Evangelical movement was both intensely public and intensely private. The emphasis on the individual religious life came from a view of the world as immoral and distracting. But once people had been converted, they were needed in that world as moral missionaries. They were fired by the most private of passions – for sincerity and terrible truthfulness, with great emotional warmth on moral issues – and they had to carry all this with them into a public sphere which might be indifferent, cynical or hostile. 'They' were all men (except in philanthropy, where women were allowed a supporting role); consequently, the split between the private and the public spheres became a split between the sexes of a peculiarly exaggerated kind. Home became the sphere of women and the family; the world outside became the sphere of men. Wilberforce's letters abound with the imagery of conflict and trouble in the world, peace and calm at home. When away from his family on business, he wrote to his wife very regularly. 'Pray for me,' he wrote just before Parliament reassembled, 'that I may be enlightened and strengthened for the duties of this important and critical session. Hitherto God has wonderfully supported and blessed me; oh how much beyond my deserts! It will be a comfort to me to know that you all who are, as it were, on the top of the mountain, withdrawn from and above the storm, are thus interceding for me who am scuffling in the vale below.'[17] This idealized view of the home was common to the Clapham Sect. Family prayers became a symbol of the togetherness. Cowper evokes the warmth and cosiness of an Evangelical family evening:

> Now stir the fire and close the shutters fast,
> Let fall the curtains, wheel the sofa round,
> And, while the bubbling and loud hissing urn
> Throws up a steaming column, and the cups
> That cheer but not inebriate, wait on each
> So let us welcome peaceful evenings in.[18]

Within the household it was quite clearly established that men and women had their separate spheres. Hannah More defined certain qualities and dispositions as 'peculiarly feminine'. Cultural differences were seen as natural. Women were naturally more delicate, more fragile, morally weaker, and all this demanded a greater degree of caution, retirement and reserve. 'Men, on the contrary, are formed for the more public exhibition on the great theatre of human life';[19] men had grandeur, dignity and force; women had ease, simplicity and purity. This absolute distinction between men and women is repeated time and again in Evangelical writing.

Evangelicals expected women to sustain and even to improve the moral qualities of the opposite sex. It is at this level that the Evangelicals offered women an area of importance which, therefore, holds within itself considerable contradictions. Women, it was believed, could act as the moral regenerators of the nation. They occupied a key position in the struggle to reform and revive the nation. Women in the home could provide, as it were, a revolutionary base from which their influence could shine forth: 'If our women lose their domestic virtues, all the charities will be dissolved, for which our country is a name so dear. The men will be profligate, the public will be betrayed, and whatever has blessed or distinguished the English nation on the Continent will disappear,' wrote a friend to More, congratulating her on her book on female education.[20] That book, published in 1799 in the wake of the moral panic, exhorted women to play their part in the struggle for national survival. They were being offered a field where they could be allowed to wield some power and influence within the moral sphere. They could play an important part in the reform of manners and morals. Wilberforce made a similar plea for women's support in *Practical Christianity*. He argued that women were especially disposed to religion; this was partly because their education was limited and they were not exposed to the moral dangers of the classics. The woman, therefore, had the particular duty of encouraging her husband's religious sensibilities: 'when the husband should return to his family, worn and harassed by worldly cares or professional labours, the wife, habitually preserving a warmer and more unimpaired spirit of devotion, than is perhaps consistent with being immersed in the bustle of life, might revive his languid piety.' Women had open to them a most noble office: 'we would make them as it were the medium of our intercourse with the heavenly world, the faithful repositories of the religious principle, for the benefit both of the present and the rising generation.'[21] Because the major problem in England was seen by the Evangelicals as being the prevalent state of religious and moral decadence, this emphasis on the religious power of the woman considerably modified their emphasis elsewhere on subordination. In a later period, Victorian feminists like Mrs Jameson were to build on this contradiction.

The good Evangelical woman had recognizable characteristics: she was modest, unassuming, unaffected and rational. ('Rational' was used as the opposite to 'sentimental' or 'subject to violent feeling'.) Babington, a prominent figure in the Clapham Sect, wrote to Macaulay on the eve of his marriage in 1799, detailing the distinction between the male and female spheres:

> You have been a grave and active African governor, surrounded by business and difficulties and dangers, and enjoying little affectionate and no female society. Selina has been entirely with females, and her companions have been her near relations and friends. Under these circumstances you meet as man and wife, with habits of domestic life more different than those of men and women, who act on the same principle, generally are. She must endeavour to assimilate herself to you, and you to her, without either of you departing from your proper sphere ... Hours of relaxation are among the most useful, as well as most pleasant seasons of matrimonial life, if they do not recur too frequently, and if the source of enjoyment be pure and hallowed ... In general you should lead her through cheerful cornfields, and pastures, and when opportunity offers go out of your way a little to show a flowery meadow or a winding stream.[22]

The implication is clear that the man is wiser and will guide the woman into the area appropriate to her, occasionally introducing her to new ideas.

The right choice in marriage was seen as vital to a good Evangelical life. Since the religious household was the basis of Christian practice, it was essential to find the right partner. *Coelebs* is structured around the hero's search for a wife:

> In such a companion I do not want a Helen, a Saint Cecilia, or a Madame Dacier; yet she must be elegant or I should not love her; sensible, or I should not respect her; prudent, or I should not confide in her; well-informed, or she could not educate my children; well-bred, or she could not entertain my friends; consistent, or I should offend the shade of my mother; pious, or I should not be happy with her.[23]

The striking feature of this passage is that the woman is seen only in relation to the man. She is, in Mrs Ellis's later phrase, a 'relative creature'. Hannah More, although herself an independent and unmarried woman, consistently relegated women to a dependent role. There can be no higher praise for a woman than that she is worthy of her husband, whose happiness she creates. As Coelebs puts it, 'It appears to me that three of the great inducements in the choice of a wife are, that a man may have a directress for his family, a preceptress for his children, and a companion for himself.'[24] There is no suggestion of what the woman might want for *herself.* The letters and diaries of the Clapham Sect demonstrate the degree to which these views were lived through – they were not simply presented in manuals for others. Women were both central to, and absent from, the Clapham Sect. They were central in that the definition of their position constituted a major area of Evangelical thought and writing. They were absent in that the absolute assumption of their subordination meant that their activities were hidden. Apart from Hannah More, the majority of writing about the Sect was by men. This was no doubt partly because the women's letters were not seen as worth keeping. Halévy describes More as 'one of the great men of the party'[25] – since she does not fit the stereotypes of what an Evangelical woman, or indeed any woman, should be, she is presented as exceptional. When Stephen described the domestic lives of the Sect, the wives were there as supportive backcloth, helpmeets to their husbands. Wilberforce frequently gave an account of family parties and documented all those present, except his wife. It is tempting to assume that this was because she was so taken for granted that she did not have to be mentioned. The woman, after all, was private property. Gisborne saw the duties of the woman as three-fold: first, to look after husbands, parents, children, relatives and friends; second, to set a good example to men and improve manners by that example; third, to care for children.[26] The whole notion of duty was, of course, central to Evangelicalism.

The unmarried woman had to do what she could; basically, Evangelical writing on women assumed marriage and the family. Within marriage it was quite clear that the wife was subordinate to her husband – it was not a question open to 'speculative arguments'. Faithful and willing obedience on the part of the wife was essential, even in cases of domestic management. The first set of duties – looking after the home and family – was, in St Paul's terms, 'guiding the house'. The superintendence of domestic management is clearly demarcated from doing the work itself; there was an absolute assumption that servants would be available. Domestic management required regularity of accounts and the proper care of money. Home should be seen as the wife's centre. There she could influence to the good her children, her servants, and her neighbours. It is in the home that 'the general character, the acknowledged property, and the established connections of her husband, will contribute with more force than they can possess elsewhere, to give weight and impressiveness to all her proceedings'.[27] Women were consequently advised not to leave home too much – it was only there that they could achieve moral excellence.

A great deal of emphasis was placed by the Evangelicals on the power of women to demonstrate by example. Daily practice in the home must be an attempt to live out principles. The letters and journals of the Clapham Sect would suggest that their daughters and wives did try to do this. But there was also one public arena open to them and that was philanthropy. The activities of women in charitable organizations between 1790 and 1830 give us the most concrete evidence so far available of the power of the Evangelical example on women's lives.[28] Charity was seen as the proper activity of a lady. 'I have often heard it regretted,' says Mrs Stanley in *Coelebs*, 'that ladies have no stated employment, no profession. It is a mistake. Charity is the calling of a lady; the care of the poor is her profession.'[29] More argued that women were peculiarly suited to philanthropic activities – they had leisure, an acquaintance with domestic wants and more sympathy with female complaints. Charity should become a part of daily life. Being philanthropic was, of course, both a reflection of virtue and a relief from a life bounded by the home.

If women were to be able to exercise a proper moral influence, they must be well educated. A clear distinction was made between the education of the daughters of the poor and those of the upper and middle classes. The daughters of the poor should be trained as servants or as good wives; the emphasis in their schooling should be on industry, frugality, diligence and good management. The daughters of the well-to-do, on the other hand, should be educated for moral excellence, and that meant that the traditional girls' training which they had been receiving was quite inadequate. To be able to dress well, to dance and play the piano, was not enough. 'The profession of ladies,' wrote More, 'is that of daughters, wives, mothers and mistresses of families.'[30] They should, therefore, be trained for that. Given these considerations, there was much to be said for educating girls at home. A mother was the best person to train her daughter. The purpose of that training was not to enable women to compete with men, but to prepare them in the best possible way for their relative sphere. Mothers were responsible for the children of both sexes in infancy, for their daughters until they left home. The Evangelicals stressed the importance of parental responsibility and the religious implications of good motherhood. The fathers took especial responsibility for their sons, but often had very close domestic ties with their daughters as well.

The Evangelical ideology of domesticity, it has been argued here, was not an ideal constructed for others, but an attempt to reconstruct family life and the relations between the sexes on the basis of 'real' Christianity. The Puritans had developed many similar views on marriage in an earlier period. The two groups shared the experience of living through a period of very rapid social, political and economic change; the articulation of their response was in religious terms, but it cannot be understood outside the particular historical conjuncture. Changing ideas about women and the family must be seen in relation to changes in the mode of production and in the social relations of production and reproduction. The Puritans and the Evangelicals shared a need to build a protected space in a hostile world, from which the great campaign of evangelization could be securely launched. The home was an area which could be controlled and which was relatively independent of what went on outside. The home did provide a haven. The expansion of capitalist relations of production in the late eighteenth century meant that homes were increasingly separated from workplaces, although this was a lengthy process and, in some trades, family workshops survived for a very long time. It has also been suggested that domestic demand for such items of household utility as china provided one of the main factors in the industrial 'take-off' at the end of the eighteenth century.[31] In other words, the emergence of a particular kind of home was directly related to the expansion of productive forces. But the way that home was realized, lived in and experienced within the middle ranks was crucially mediated by Evangelicalism.

The Clapham Sect, as we have seen, set some of the boundaries for public and domestic life in Victorian England. Their ideas were not, however, always understood in the way that they would have wished. They were benevolent paternalists but they were understood as the precursors of Utilitarianism and the power of the bourgeoisie. They were mercantile princes and clerics but they ushered in the machine age. They were a group with aristocratic connections, some of them belonging to the governing elite of

England, yet they paved the way for the alliance between that old ruling class and the manufacturers. Their importance lies in the mediating role which they were able to play, by virtue of their class position, in the transitional period between the era of mercantile capitalism and the recognized dominance of industrial capitalism. They belonged to neither side and so were able to speak to both.

The campaign on slavery gave the Sect national status; it established the claim to represent the middle classes and articulate their demands. The campaign in itself was massively influential in shaping those demands – steering the 'middling ranks' towards liberalism and a national consensus rather than towards a more radical perspective and an alliance with the new industrial proletariat. The campaign on manners and morals would undoubtedly have been far less effective if the anti-slavery movement had not been such a success. The religious principles of the Evangelicals drove them from within. They became moral entrepreneurs committed to struggling for widescale conversion to their views. Their evangelizing campaign gained massive support, but only up to a certain point. Anti-slavery became identified as the British way. England claimed moral superiority in her style of colonization. Respectability and decorum ruled, but the double standard reigned supreme in Victorian England. The split between the public and the private sphere, the subordination of the woman in the family, and the protection of private property were key features of nineteenth-century England; but the truly religious households remained a minority phenomenon. The forms, shaped by the Evangelicals for one purpose, were moulded to another. Just as the Puritan notion of the family was partly a response to the development of productive forces and partly an ideological form that must be understood in terms of its own logic, so was the Evangelical. But the Evangelical capacity to respond to the changing social relations of industrial capitalism and redefine the family form ensured that notions of home and domesticity in the nineteenth century would be heavily influenced by the Mores, Gisbornes, and Thorntons of this world.

Inside that dynamic, the bourgeois ideal of the family became a part of the dominant culture and, by the 1830s and 1840s, was being promoted through propaganda as the only proper way to live.[32] In the government reports of that period, working wives and mothers are presented as something unnatural and immoral. Working-class women were castigated for being poor housewives and inadequate mothers. If married women were to enter paid employment, they should not be seen; they should work at home. The should not flaunt their independence as the mill girls did. It is worth noting that the early campaigns to improve the working conditions of women focused on the factory system and the mines and did not come to grips with more hidden areas, such as the sweated trades. The bourgeois family was seen as the proper family, and that meant that married women should not work. The ideology of the family thus obscured class relations, for it came to appear above class. That ideology also obscured the cultural definition of the sexual division of labour, since the split between men and women came to be seen as naturally ordained. Nature decreed that all women were first and foremost wives and mothers.

NOTES

1 E.g. Noel Annan, *Leslie Stephen* (Macgibbon & Kee, London, 1951).
2 Cf. George O. Trevelyan, *The Life and Letters of Lord Macaulay* (Longmans, Green & Co., London, 1876). A more recent version is E. M. Howse, *Saints in Politics* (Allen & Unwin, London, 1953). For a contemporary radical critique, see William Cobbett, *Political Register*, 3 October 1818.
3 The most helpful secondary source on this is Maurice Quinlan, *Victorian Prelude: A History of English Manners 1700–1830* (Columbia University Press, London, 1941).
4 William Wilberforce, *A Practical View of the Prevailing Religious System of Professed Christians in the Higher and Middle Classes in this Country Contrasted with Real Christianity* (T. Cadell Jun. and W. Davies, London, 1797), p. 298.
5 The first major statement was Hannah More, *Thoughts on the Importance of the Manners of the Great to General Society* (T. Cadell Jun. and W. Davies, London, 1788).
6 E. P. Thompson, *The Making of the English Working Class* (Penguin, Harmondsworth, 1968), p. 60.
7 For an interesting discussion of the importance of the anti-slavery agitation in terms of a political transition, see David Brion Davis, *The Problem of Slavery in the Age of Revolution* (Cornell University Press, London, 1975).
8 R. I. and S. Wilberforce, *The Life of William Wilberforce*, vol. 3 (John Murray, London, 1838), p. 487.
9 For a good account of 1797, see Eric Trudgill, *Madonnas and Magdalens* (Heinemann, London, 1976).
10 One of the best examples of this division is the Blagdon Controversy over Hannah More's running of Sunday schools. Cf. W. Roberts (ed.), *The Life and Correspondence of Mrs Hannah More* (R. B. Seeley and

W. Burnside, London, 1834), and Ford K. Brown, *Fathers of the Victorians* (Cambridge University Press, Cambridge, 1961).

11 For an interesting discussion of Wollstonecraft from a feminist perspective, see Margaret Walters, 'The Rights and Wrongs of Women: Mary Wollstonecraft, Harriet Martineau, Simone de Beauvoir', in Juliet Mitchell and Ann Oakley (eds), *The Rights and Wrongs of Women* (Penguin, Harmondsworth, 1976).

12 Hannah More, *Strictures on the Modern System of Female Education*, vol. 2 (T. Cadell Jun. and W. Davies, London, 1799), pp. 186–7.

13 Ivy Pinchbeck, *Women Workers and the Industrial Revolution 1750–1850* (Frank Cass, London, 1969).

14 William Cowper, *The Task*, in W. Benham (ed.), *Selected Works of William Cowper* (Macmillan & Co., London, 1889).

15 James Stephen, *Essays in Ecclesiastical Biography* (Longman, Brown, Green & Longman, London, 1845), p. 510.

16 E. Halévy was one of the first to discuss the connections between Evangelicalism and Utilitarianism in *England in 1815* (Ernest Benn, London, 1913). That discussion is developed in Davis, *The Problem of Slavery*.

17 Wilberforce, *The Life of William Wilberforce*, vol. 5, p. 77.

18 Cowper, *The Task*, Bk 4.

19 Hannah More, *Essays Principally Designed for Young Ladies* (R. B. Seeley and W. Burnside, London, 1777), p. 5.

20 In a letter to Hannah More, in Roberts (ed.), *Life and Correspondence*, vol. 3, p. 453.

21 Wilberforce, *A Practical View*, p. 453.

22 Viscountess Knutsford, *Life and Letters of Zachary Macaulay* (Edward Arnold, London, 1900), p. 234.

23 Hannah More, *Coelebs in Search of a Wife*, vol. 1 (R. B. Seeley and W. Burnside, London, 1809), p. 23.

24 More, *Coelebs*, p. 78.

25 Halévy, *England in 1815*.

26 Thomas Gisborne, *Duties of the Female Sex* (T. Cadell Jun. and W. Davies, London, 1801).

27 Gisborne, *Duties*.

28 Cf. F. R. Prochaska, 'Women in English Philanthropy 1790–1830', *International Review of Social History*, vol. 19, pt 3, 1974; Brown, *Fathers of the Victorians*.

29 More, *Coelebs*, vol. 2, p. 20.

30 More, *Coelebs*, vol. 2, p. 20.

31 Neil McKendrick, 'A New Look at the Contribution of the Employment of Women and Children to the Industrial Revolution', in Neil McKendrick (ed.), *Historical Perspectives: Studies in English Thought and Society in Honour of J. H. Plumb* (Europa, London, 1974).

32 Cf. Sally Alexander, 'Women's Work in Nineteenth-Century London' in Mitchell and Oakley (eds), *The Rights and Wrongs of Women*.

4 Gender Divisions and Class Formation in the Birmingham Middle Class, 1780–1850

The flowering of socialist historiography in the last fifteen years, of which the History Workshop is of course one very important instance, has seen an enormous development in working-class and people's history. This development has not been complemented by an equivalent amount of research into the dominant classes; the emphasis for socialist historians has been on cultures of opposition and resistance and on the mechanisms of control and subordination, rather than on the culture of the ruling class. The same point can be made about feminist history, which in England has been profoundly influenced by the particular way in which social history has developed. The vast majority of the work done so far has been on working-class women and the working-class family. This is entirely understandable, particularly in a period when the importance of our struggle has been stressed politically, as it has been, for example, in the women's movement. For most socialists it is clearly more attractive to work on material which offers some assertion and celebration of resistance rather than on material which documents the continuing power, albeit often challenged, of the bourgeoisie. This does leave us, however, which a somewhat unbalanced historiography. Any discussion on the 'making of the English middle class' for example, is infinitely less well documented and theorized than it is on the working class. John Foster's work on the bourgeoisie in his *Class Struggle and the Industrial Revolution*[1] provides us with a starting point, but there is little else that is easily available.

The work that is available on the 'making of the middle class' in the late eighteenth and early nineteenth centuries is not, for the most part, placed within a socialist framework (for example, Briggs[2] or McCord[3]) but it also faces us with a second problem – the absence of gender. The middle class is treated as male and the account of the formation of middle-class consciousness is structured around a series of public events in which women played no part: the imposition of income tax, the reaction to the Orders in Council, the Queen Caroline affair, the 1832 reform agitation and the Anti-Corn Law League are usually seen as the seminal moments in the emergence of the middle class as a powerful and self-confident class. Yet when we come to descriptions of the Victorian family, much emphasis is placed on the part which domesticity played in middle-class culture and on the social importance of the home. That is to say, the class once formed is seen as sexually divided but that process of division is taken as given. Since eighteenth-century middle-class women did not, as far as we can tell, lead the sheltered and domestically defined lives of their Victorian counterparts it seems important to explore the relation between the process of class formation and gender division. Was 'the separation of spheres' and the division between the public and the private a given, or was it constructed as an integral part of middle-class culture and self-identity? The development of the middle class between 1780 and 1850 must be thought of as gendered; the ideals of masculinity and femininity are important to the middle-class sense of self and the ideology of separate spheres played a crucial part in the construction of a specifically middle-class culture – separating them off from both the aristocracy and gentry above them and from the working class below them.

Gender divisions appear also to have played an important part in unifying the middle class. The class is significantly divided, as Marx pointed out, between the bourgeoisie and the petite bourgeoisie. Foster uses this division and helps to extend its meaning, as does R. J. Morris in his work.[4] The two groups are divided economically, socially and politically, and much of the political history of the period is concerned with the shifting alliances between these two factions and other classes – as, for example, in Birmingham over the reform agitation and the movement into Chartism. But one of the ways in which the middle class was held together, despite the many divisive factors, was by their ideas about masculinity and femininity. Men came to share a sense of what constituted masculinity and women a sense of what constituted femininity. One central opposition was that masculinity meant having dependants, femininity meant being dependent. Inevitably, the available ideals were not always ones which could be acted upon – petit-bourgeois men would often need their wives to work in the business, but they would often also aspire for that not to be so. Clearly, looking at gender divisions as having a unifying theme within the middle class is only one way of approaching the subject; it would be equally possible to examine the way in which it unites men across classes, or the way in which it creates contradictions within the middle class which led to the emergence of bourgeois feminism in the second half of the nineteenth century. For the moment it seems important to stress the class-specific nature of masculinity and femininity in this period; the idea of a universal womanhood is weak in comparison with the idea of certain types of sexual differentiation being a necessary part of class identity. This may help to explain the relative absence and weakness of feminism in the first half of the nineteenth century – *Jane Eyre*, for example, provides us with a very sensitive account of the limitations of middle-class femininity which leaves little space for the possibility of a cross-class alliance.

This general theme of the importance of a sharpened division between men and women, between the public and the private, and its relation to class formation can be illustrated by looking at the development of the Birmingham middle class between 1780 and 1850. The account that is being offered here is extremely sketchy, but can perhaps provide a framework for further discussion. Birmingham was a fast-growing industrial town by the late eighteenth century – its population of only 35,000 in 1780 had grown to 250,000 by 1850. Its wealth was built on the metal industries and had been made possible by its strategic position in relation to coal and iron. The town has usually been taken, following Asa Briggs, as one dominated by small masters with workshops but recent work, particularly that of Clive Behagg, has somewhat modified this view and suggested that factory production was better established by the 1830s and 1840s than has usually been thought. Although Birmingham had been gradually expanding since the seventeenth century, the impression by the end of the eighteenth century is that the middle class within the town are only gradually coming to realize their potential strength and power. Consequently, Birmingham offers us a relatively uncomplicated account of the emergence of the middle class – uncomplicated by factors such as the struggle between the well-established merchant class of the eighteenth century and the new manufacturers, which took place in Leeds.

We can briefly examine the separation between the sexes as it took place in Birmingham in this period at three levels – those of the economic, the political and social, and the ideological. If we look first at the economic level it is important to stress from the beginning that the ideology of separate spheres has an economic effectivity. Clearly, the crucial problem which faces us is the question of what the relation is between the emergence of separate spheres and the development of industrial capitalism. Is there any relation at all? At this point it is only possible to say that women seem to be increasingly defined as economically dependent in our period, and that this economic dependence has important consequences for the ways in which industrial capitalism developed. That is to say, we cannot argue that industrial capitalism would not have developed without sexual divisions, but that the increasingly polarized form which sexual divisions took affected the forms of capitalist social relations and of capitalist accumulation.

The legal framework for this is provided by the centrality of the notion of dependence in marriage – Blackstone's famous dictum that the husband and wife are one person and that person is the husband. Married women's property passed automatically to their husbands unless a settlement had been made in the courts of equity. Married women had no right to sue or be sued or to make contracts. For working-class families, the idea of the family wage came to encapsulate the idea of economic dependence – though we know that in reality few working-class families were in a position to afford to do without the earnings which a wife could bring in. For middle-class families there is no equivalent concept, since the men do not earn *wages*, but still the economic dependence of the wife and children was assumed. Amongst the aristocracy and gentry, patrilineal rights to property had been established for a very long time, but although the middle class broke with their 'betters' at many other points the connection between masculinity and property rights was not broken. Two interrelated points need to be made here; first, the importance of marriage settlements in capital accumulation and, second, the sexual specificity of inheritance practices. Neither of these are new developments – making an advantageous marriage had long been a crucial way of getting on in the world – but whereas in the past the gentry and aristocracy had for the most part used money so acquired to enlarge their houses or consolidate their estates, small producers were now using it to build up their businesses. Archibald Kenrick, for example, a Birmingham buckle-maker in the late 1780s who was caught up in the decline of the buckle trade, got married in 1790 and used his wife's marriage settlement to set up in business as an iron founder in 1791.[5] Sometimes the capital would come from a mother rather than a wife, for amongst the wealthier bourgeoisie it was common practice to have a marriage settlement which protected the wife's property whereas amongst the petite bourgeoisie this would have been very unusual. Richard and George Cadbury both inherited a substantial amount from their mother, Candia Barrow, at a time when the family business was doing rather badly and used the capital to reorganize and revitalize the business.[6]

Marx noted that the bourgeoisie practised partible inheritance rather than primogeniture and widows and daughters were not disinherited, but the forms of female inheritance tended increasingly to be linked to dependence. In general, boys would receive an education and training to enter a business or profession and then would be given either a share in the existing family business or capital to invest in another business. Thomas Southall, for example, who came to Birmingham in 1820 to set up in business as a chemist, had been educated and apprenticed by his father who had a mixed retailing business himself and set up each of his sons in one aspect – one as a draper, one as a vintner and one as a chemist.[7] Daughters, on the other hand, would either be given a lump sum as a marriage settlement (though it should be noted that they were sometimes not allowed to marry because of the impossibility of removing capital from the business) or they would be left money in trust, usually under the aegis of a male relative, to provide an income for them together with their widowed mothers. The money in trust would then often be available for the male relatives to invest as they pleased. It should be pointed out, however, that widows amongst the petite bourgeoisie often were left the business to manage – it might be a shop, for example – and this different pattern of inheritance marks an important division between the two groups in the middle class. Rights of dower were finally abolished in 1833 but long before that it was accepted that men had a right to leave their property as they liked. Life insurance developed in the late eighteenth century as a way of providing for dependants, and this is another example of the way in which sexual divisions structure the forms of capitalist development – insurance companies became important sources of capital accumulation which could not have existed without the notion of dependants.

Meanwhile, the kinds of businesses which women were running seem to have altered. An examination of the Birmingham Directories reveals women working in surprising trades throughout our period; only in very small numbers it is true, but still they survived. To take a few examples, there were women brass founders at the end of the eighteenth century, a bedscrew-maker and a coach-maker in 1803, several women engaged in aspects of the gun trade in 1812, an engine cutter and an iron and steel merchant in 1821, plumbers and painters in the 1830s and 1840s, burnishers and brush-makers in the 1850s. There are certain trades in which women never seem to appear as the owners – awl-blade making, for example, or iron founders. But although the percentage of women to men engaged in business goes up rather than down in the early nineteenth century, at least according to the evidence provided by the Directories, there seems to be a significant shift towards the concentration of women in certain trades. In the late eighteenth century women were well represented among the button-makers, and button making was one of the staple trades of Birmingham. Sketchley's Directory of 1767 described the button trade as:

> very extensive and distinguished under the following heads viz. Gilt, Plated, Silvered, Lacquered, and Pinchback, the beautiful new Manufactures Platina, Inlaid, Glass, Horn, Ivory, and Pearl: Metal Buttons such as Bath, Hard and Soft White etc. there is likewise made Link Buttons in most of the above Metals, as well as of Paste, Stones, etc. in short the vast variety of sorts in both Branches is really amazing, and we may with Truth aver that this is the cheapest Market in the world for these Articles.

But by the 1830s and 1840s women were concentrated in what became traditional women's trades – in dressmaking, millinery, school-teaching and the retail trade. Women were no longer engaged as employers in the central productive trades of the town in any number, they were marginalized into the servicing sector, though, of course, it should be clear that many working-class women continued as employers in, for example, the metal trades. G. J. Holyoake described in his autobiography his own mother's disappearance from business:

> In those days horn buttons were made in Birmingham, and my mother had a workshop attached to the house, in which she conducted a business herself, employing several hands. She had the business before her marriage. She received the orders; made the purchases of materials; superintended the making of the goods; made out the accounts; and received the money; besides taking care of her growing family. There were no 'Rights of Women' thought of

> in her day, but she was an entirely self-acting, managing mistress . . . The button business died out while I was young, and from the remarks which came from merchants, I learned that my mother was the last maker of that kind of button in the town.[8]

It is worth remarking that Holyoake's mother became a keen attender at Carr's Lane Chapel where, as we shall see, John Angell James taught the domestic subordination of women from the pulpit for fifty years. Women increasingly did not have the necessary forms of knowledge and expertise to enter many businesses – jobs were being redefined as managerial or skilled and, therefore, masculine. For instance, as Michael Ignatieff points out, women goalers were actually excluded by statute as not fitted to the job.[9] Women could manage the family and the household but not the workshop or the factory. Furthermore, a whole series of new financial institutions was being developed in this period which also specifically excluded women – trusts, for example, and forms of partnership. Ivy Pinchbeck has argued that women were gradually being excluded from a sphere which they had previously occupied; it appears that in addition they were never allowed into a whole new economic sphere.

The separation of work from home obviously played an important part in this process of demarcation between men's work and women's work. That separation has often been thought of as the material basis of separate spheres. But once the enormous variety of types of middle-class housing has been established, that argument can no longer be maintained. Separating work from home was one way of concretizing the division between the sexes, but since it was often not possible it cannot be seen as the crucial factor in establishing domesticity. The many other ways in which the division was established have to be remembered. For doctors there could often be no separation, whereas for iron founders the separation was almost automatic. In some trades the question of scale was vital – in the Birmingham metal trades some workshops had houses attached but in many cases they were separated. Sometimes there is a house attached and yet the chief employee lived there rather than the family. James Luckcock, for example, the Birmingham jeweller, when he was just starting up in business on his own not only lived next to his workshop but also used the labour of his wife and children. As soon as he could afford it he moved out and moved his manager into the house and his wife stopped working in the business.[10] Shopkeepers moving out of their premises and establishing separate homes for their families obviously lost the assistance of wives and daughters in the shop – Mrs Cadbury and her daughters all helped in the shop until the family moved out to Edgbaston.

So far I have tried to suggest that the economic basis for the expansion of the middle class is underpinned by assumptions of male superiority and female dependence. When we turn to the level of the political and social we can see the construction in our period of a whole new public world in which women have no part. That world is built on the basis of those who are defined as individuals – men with property. The Birmingham middle class had developed very little in the way of institutions or organizations by the mid-eighteenth century, but by the end of the century a whole new range had appeared. In the voluntary societies which sprang up in the town the male middle class learned the skills of local government and established their rights to political leadership. These societies placed women on the periphery, if they placed them at all. Dorothy Thompson has argued in her essay on working-class women in Radical politics that as organizations became more formal so women were increasingly marginalized.[11] This process took place earlier for the middle class since their formal organizations were being established from the mid-eighteenth century.

As in all other towns and cities Birmingham societies covered an extraordinarily wide range of activities through religion, philanthropy, trade, finance and politics. The personnel of these societies were often the same people who were finding their way on to the boards of local banks, insurance companies and municipal trusts. In Birmingham there was a series of political struggles between the governing classes and the middle class in our period which resulted in the formation of political organizations; to take one example, the Chamber of Commerce, founded in 1785, was the first attempt to bring manufacturers together to protect their interests and had no place for women. The Birmingham Political Union, the Complete Suffrage Union, the dissenting organizations to fight the established Church, the organizations which worked for municipal incorporation and the Anti-Corn Law League were all male bodies. It is interesting to note that the BPU made provision for the wives of artisans in the Female Political Union, but there was no equivalent provision for middle-class ladies. Women were not defined by the middle class as political – they could play a supportive role, for example fund-raising for the Anti-Corn Law League, but that marked the limit. The only political organization in which they did play an important part was the anti-slavery movement where separate ladies' auxiliary committees were set up after considerable argument within the movement, but even here their real contribution was viewed as a moral one. Women were appealed to as mothers to save their 'dusky sisters' from having their children torn from them, but the activities which women could engage in to achieve this end were strictly limited. It was often the very weakness of women which was called upon – as God's poorest creatures perhaps their prayers would be heard.

Similarly the relationship of women to new social organizations and institutions was strictly limited. They could not be full members of the libraries and reading rooms, or of the literary and philosophical societies; even the concerts and assemblies were organized by male committees. When we look at the huge range of philanthropic societies, again the pattern is that men hold all the positions of power – more specifically the bourgeoisie provide the governors and managing committees while the petite bourgeoisie sit on the committees of the less prestigious institutions and do much of the work of day-to-day maintenance. Women are used by some societies as visitors, or tract distributors, or collectors of money, but they are never, formally at least, the decision-makers. Even in an institution like the Protestant Dissenting Charity School, which was a girls' school in Birmingham, there was a ladies' committee involved with the daily maintenance of the school but any decision of importance had to be taken by the men's managing committee and membership of the ladies' committee was achieved by recommendation from the men. Ladies could be subscribers to the charity but their subscription did not carry the same rights as it did for the men – for example, ladies could only sponsor girls to be taken into the school by proxy. The ladies' committee had no formal status and relied on informal contact with the men – often taking the form of a wife promising that she would pass some point on to her husband who would then raise it with them. The constitution of most kinds of society, whether political or cultural, usually either formally excluded women from full membership by detailing the partial forms of membership they could enjoy, or never even thought the question worth discussing. Women never became officers, they never spoke in large meetings, indeed they could not attend most meetings either because they were formally excluded or because the informal exclusion mechanisms were so powerful – for example, having meetings which were centred around a dinner in an hotel, a place where ladies were clearly not expected to be. Nor did women sign the letters and petitions which frequently appeared in the press.

So far, I hope that I have succeeded in establishing that at both the economic and political level middle-class women were increasingly being defined as subordinate and marginal; anything to do with the public world was not their sphere. At the same time a whole range of new activities was opening up for men, and men had the freedom to move between the public and the private. It is at the level of the ideological that we find the articulation of separate spheres which informed many of the developments we have looked at. The period 1780–1850 saw a constant stream of pamphlets and books – the best-known authors of which are probably Hannah More and Sarah Stickney Ellis – telling middle-class women how to behave. But domesticity was a local issue as well as a national one, and the activities of the Birmingham clergy in our period give us plenty of evidence of the way in which congregations were left in no uncertain state as to the relative positions of men and women. John Angell James has already been referred to. He was the minister of the most important Independent church in the town from 1805–57 and was recognized as a great preacher and prolific writer. Carr's Lane had a large membership drawn from both the bourgeoisie and the petite bourgeoisie whilst several hundred working-class children attended the Sunday schools. James's books sold extremely well and his series on the family – *Female Piety, The Young Man's Friend and Guide Through Life to Immortality* and *The Family Monitor, or a Help to Domestic Happiness* – were long-term best-sellers.[12] James believed that women were naturally subordinate to men – it was decreed in the Scriptures.

> Every family, when directed as it should be, has a sacred character, inasmuch as the head of it acts the part of both the prophet and the priest of his household, in instructing them in the knowledge, and leading them in the worship, of God; and, at the same time, he discharges the duty of a king, by supporting a system of order, subordination and discipline.

Furthermore, home was the woman's proper sphere:

> In general, it is for the benefit of a family that a married woman should devote her time and attention almost exclusively to the ways of her household: her place is in the centre of domestic cares. What is gained by her in the shop is oftentimes lost in the house, for want

> of the judicious superintendence of a mother and a mistress. Comforts and order, as well as money, are domestic wealth; and can these be rationally expected in the absence of female management? The children always want a mother's eye and hand, and should always have them. Let the husband, then, have the care of providing for the necessities of the family, and the wife that of personally superintending it: for this is the rule both of reason and of revelation.[13]

James's ideas were not simply spoken from the pulpit; the domination of such ideas was reflected in the organization of his church and in the way in which church societies were established. Nor were such ideas limited to the Independents. The Quakers and the Unitarians were both important groups in Birmingham – many of the most influential families in the town were in one of these two groups. Both Quakers and Unitarians inherited a fairly radical view of the relations between the sexes but the Quakers in the late eighteenth century were moving towards a more formal subordination of women, introducing, for example, separate seating for men and women. However, the Quakers still offered women the opportunity to preach and thus guaranteed the maintenance of a spiritual significance for women. The Unitarians, though believing in some education for women, maintained strict lines of demarcation, as has already been mentioned in connection with the Protestant Dissenting Charity School which was a Unitarian foundation. But it should not be thought that it was left to Nonconformists to lead the way on questions relating to the divisions between the sexes. Birmingham saw a considerable Evangelical revival from the late 1820s, associated with the influence of the Evangelical Bishop Ryder in Coventry and Lichfield. There is substantial evidence of the emphasis which Evangelicals placed on the importance of a proper home and family life, and the belief they had in the centrality of the religious household in the struggle to reconstruct a properly Christian community. Christ Church, a large Anglican church in the town centre, was occupied by an enthusiastic Evangelical minister in the 1830s who inaugurated separate benches for men and women; this led to a popular rhyme:

> The churches in general we everywhere find,
> Are places where men to the women are joined;
> But at *Christ Church*, it seems, they are more cruel hearted,
> For men and their wives are brought here to be parted.[14]

The Revd John Casebow Barrett, the Rector of St Mary's from the late 1830s and a much liked and admired preacher in the town, maintained a similar stance from his pulpit, as in his sermon in memory of Adelaide Queen Dowager in 1849 where he extolled her virtues as an ordinary wife and mother:

> As a *wife*, her conduct was unexceptionable; and her devotedness, her untiring watchfulness to her royal consort during his last illness, stands forth as a bright model, which the wives of England will do well to imitate. Here, in her husband's sick chamber, by day and by night, she – then the Queen of this mighty Empire – proved herself the fond and loving wife, the meek and feeling woman, the careful and uncomplaining nurse. *Her* eye watched the royal sufferer: *her* hand administered the medicine and smoothed the pillow: *her* feet hastened to give relief by changing the position: *her* voice was heard in prayer, or in the reading of the words of eternal life. And the character she then exhibited won for her – which we believe in her estimation was more precious than the crown she wore – the deep respect, the high approval, the honest, truthful love of an entire nation, which, whatever its other faults may be, is not insensible to those charities and affections, which give a bright and transcendent charm to the circle of every home.[15]

Domesticitiy often seems to have an important religious component, but it was not always expressed in religious terms. The local papers often carried poems with a heavily idealized domestic content and the ideology of separate spheres seems to have gained very wide usage. James Luckcock, the Birmingham jeweller who has already been mentioned, was deeply attached to the domestic ideal. He was a political Radical, a great friend of George Edmonds, and was very active in the Birmingham Political Union. There seems to be no evidence that an attachment to domesticity had anything to do with political allegiances – it appears to have cut cleanly across party lines. Luckcock loved the idea of both his home and garden – particularly the home which he built for his wife and himself for his retirement in leafy Edgbaston. His relationship with his two sons seems in reality to have been fraught with tension but he continued to celebrate poetically the joys of domestic bliss. At one point when he was seriously ill and thought he might die he composed a poem for his wife about himself; it was entitled 'My Husband' and catalogued his thoughtfulness and caring qualities as a husband and father:

> Who first inspir'd my virgin breast,
> With tumults not to be express'd,

And gave to life unwonted zest?
My husband.

Who told me that his gains were small,
But that whatever might befal,
To me he'd gladly yield them all?
My husband.

Who shun'd the giddy town's turmoil,
To share with me the garden's toil,
And joy with labour reconcile?
My husband.

Whose arduous struggles long maintain'd
Adversity's cold hand restrain'd
And competence at length attain'd?
My husband's.[16]

Unfortunately we do not even know the name of James Luckcock's wife, much less her reaction to this poem!

In this brief and introductory essay I have tried to suggest how central gender divisions were to the middle class in the period 1780–1850. Definitions of masculinity and femininity played an important part in marking out the middle class, separating it off from other classes and creating strong links between disparate groups within that class – Nonconformists and Anglicans, Radicals and conservatives, the richer bourgeoisie and the petite bourgeoisie. The separation between the sexes was marked out at every level within the society – in manufacturing, the retail trades and the professions, in public life of all kinds, in the churches, in the press and in the home. The separation of spheres was one of the fundamental organizing characteristics of middle-class society in late-eighteenth and early-nineteenth-century England.

NOTES

1 John Foster, *Class Struggle and the Industrial Revolution. Early industrial capitalism in three English towns* (Weidenfeld and Nicholson, London, 1974).
2 Asa Briggs, *The Age of Improvement 1783–1867* (Longmans, Green and Co. Ltd., London, 1959), *Victorian Cities* (Odhams, London, 1963).
3 Norman McCord, *The Anti-Corn Law League 1838–46* (Allen & Unwin, London, 1958).

4 Robert J. Morris, 'The Making of the British Middle Class' (unpublished paper, University of Birmingham Social History Seminar, 1979).
5 Roy A. Church, *Kenricks in Hardware. A Family Business 1791–1966* (David & Charles, Newton Abbot, 1969).
6 A. G. Gardiner, *Life of George Cadbury* (Cassell, London, 1923).
7 C. Southall, *Records of the Southall Family* (private publication, London, 1932).
8 George S. Holyoake, *Sixty Years of an Agitator's Life* (T. Fisher Unwin, London, 1900).
9 Michael Ignatieff, *A Just Measure of Pain: The Penitentiary in the Industrial Revolution 1750–1850* (Macmillan, London, 1978).
10 James Luckcock, *Sequel to Memoirs in Humble Life* (J. Belcher, Birmingham, 1825).
11 Dorothy Thompson, 'Women and Nineteenth-Century Radical Politics: A Lost Dimension', in Juliet Mitchell and Ann Oakley (eds), *The Rights and Wrongs of Women* (Penguin, Harmondsworth, 1976).
12 John Angell James, *Female Piety or the Young Woman's Friend and Guide Through Life to Immortality*, 5th edn (Hamilton Adams & Co., London, 1856); *The Young Man's Friend and Guide Through Life to Immortality* (Hamilton Adams & Co., London, 1851); *The Family Monitor, or a Help to Domestic Happiness*, first published 1828, reprinted in T. S. James (ed.) *The Works of John Angell James*, 17 vols (Hudson & Co., Birmingham, 1860–64).
13 James, *The Family Monitor*, pp. 17, 56.
14 W. Bates, *A Pictorial Guide to Birmingham* (Josiah Allen & Son, Birmingham, 1849), p. 46.
15 Revd John Casebow Barrett, *Sermon in Memory of Adelaide Queen Dowager* (T. Ragg, Birmingham, 1849), p. 11.
16 Luckcock, *Sequel to Memoirs in Humble Life*, p. 49.

5 The Butcher, the Baker, the Candlestick-maker: the shop and the family in the Industrial Revolution

In Mrs Gaskell's famous novel *Cranford*, Miss Matty, the kind-hearted and genteel friend of the narrator, loses all her money in the collapse of a country bank. Faced with surviving on a tiny income, it is proposed to her that she could add to it by selling tea. She is assured that she could maintain her gentility and that only small alterations would need to be made to her home:

> The small dining-parlour was to be converted into a shop, without any of its degrading characteristics; a table was to be the counter; one window was to be retained unaltered, and the other changed into a glass door.[1]

Mrs Gaskell published *Cranford* in 1853, but she was describing the culture of a small country town in her childhood – looking back to those days before the face of England had been significantly altered by the growth of industrial towns and cities, of factory production and of new transport systems. A less obvious feature of that transformation, and one which Mrs Gaskell may have had in mind when she described the simple alterations needed to turn Miss Matty's dining parlour into a shop, were the changes which had taken place in the organization of shopping. Between 1780 and 1850, developments in the pattern of production, of distribution and of consumption combined to alter some of the physical characteristics of shops and the ways in which people acquired their food and clothing. These changes provided the necessary preconditions for the 'retailing revolution' of the second half of the nineteenth century – when consumer goods started to be mass-produced and shops both increased in size and amalgamated into chains.[2]

It is the shopkeepers themselves that we are primarily concerned with in this chapter – the butchers, bakers and candlestick-makers of the late eighteenth and early nineteenth century – and the changes which took place in the organization of the shop and the family. Furthermore, it is a substantial middle-class sector – those with their specialized shops on the high streets of the rapidly growing towns – whose custom came mainly from the local middle class. Their counterparts were the small shopkeepers running general stores who serviced the working-class population. Such small shops for the working classes were rapidly on the increase in the early nineteenth century. Rural immigrants, who had been able to grow a good deal of their own produce in the country, mainly had to rely on buying food in the towns and came to rely on local general shops. Markets and itinerant traders also continued to play an important part in retailing: they were the hawkers and sellers so powerfully portrayed by the journalist and commentator Mayhew in his series on London life in the 1850s.[3] Small shopkeepers and traders were certainly not a part of the middle class. Their links were far more with both the 'respectable' and the 'rough' working class who provided their clientele and their neighbours.

High-street traders, however, were a different matter. Their customers might range from the local gentry coming into town for business and services, to the best paid of the skilled artisans. They would primarily have relied, however, on the urban middle class – those merchants, manufacturers and professionals whose numbers were growing in an economy which was rapidly being industrialized – and on farmers. Such traders were running good-sized businesses, with none of the 'degrading characteristics' referred to by Miss Matty, and were themselves living the life of the middle class. The men were becoming the backbone of their churches and philanthropic and voluntary societies, they were mixing with professionals and small manufacturers, and they were regarded as respected members of the community. Such small traders with their established tradition of retailing respectability are nicely evoked in a memoir of a distinguished Birmingham Unitarian minister whose father was a draper. Though such men stood behind counters, they had a 'quiet, gentlemanly dignity of bearing' which challenged the old adage that a tradesman could not be a gentleman.[4] Arnold Bennett placed a draper's establishment at the heart of his most popular novel, *The Old Wives' Tale*. The shop was in St Luke's Square, the centre of Bursley's retail trade. The Square,

> . . . contained five public-houses, a bank, a barber's, a confectioner's, three grocers', two chemists', an ironmonger's, a clothier's, and five drapers'. These were all the catalogue, St Luke's Square had no room for minor establishments. The aristocracy of the Square undoubtedly consisted of the drapers (for the bank was impersonal); and among the five the shop of Baines stood supreme. No business establishment could possibly be more respected than that of Mr Baines was respected. And though John Baines had been bedridden for a dozen years, he still lived on the lips of admiring, ceremonious burgesses as 'our honoured fellow-townsman'.[5]

Businesses such as Baines the drapers were family affairs. Mrs Baines helped in the shop at busy times, but reserved Friday for pastry-making and early Saturday morning for her own shopping. After her husband's illness, the shop was basically managed by one of the young men who had been apprenticed there and she continued to help when necessary.

But this sexual division of labour within the shopkeeping family, associated with a physical environment which combined work and home, was gradually changing in our period. From the late seventeenth century the wives of wealthy London tradesmen had been castigated by commentators such as Defoe for their attempts to be genteel.[6] The most prosperous were furnishing their living apartments elegantly, putting their servants into livery, and refusing to be seen in the shop themselves, as it was not considered ladylike. As the businesses of provincial tradesmen expanded in the late eighteenth and early nineteenth century, so their aspirations also grew. They increasingly wanted their homes to be separated from their workplace and their wives and daughters to be dependent on them; these had become powerful symbols of belonging to the middle class. By 1851 the numbers of lock-up shops in town centres, with their proprietors living elsewhere, were on the increase.[7] This separation between work and home had important effects on the organization of work within the family and the marking out of male and female spheres.[8] Men were increasingly associated with business and public activities which were physically and socially separated from the home; women with the home and with children.

For working-class families the separation between work and home was rooted in the changes in the organization of production.

A family producing woollen cloth at home in the late eighteenth century, for example, with the wife spinning and the husband weaving, would by the mid-nineteenth century have been forced into factory production because they would not have been able to compete with the cheaper cloth produced by mechanized processes in the factory.[9] This separation between work and home, between the production of things and the reproduction of people, which has had such far-reaching effects on industrial capitalist societies, did of course take place at significantly different times in different trades. Some trades were mechanical much later than others, and at mid-century many working-class men and women were still working inside the home. Industrial capitalism did not only mean factory production – it also brought with it a vast expansion of the sweated trades and of outwork.[10]

Within the middle class, too, the separation between production and reproduction was also a long-drawn-out and uneven process, depending in part on the particular kinds of work which people were doing. Clergymen, for example, have never quite lived in their workplaces though they have often lived next door to them. Doctors and dentists, on the other hand, until the recent advent of health centres were still likely in the twentieth century to combine home and workplace. Large-scale manufacturers often lived next door to their factories so that they could easily oversee them – as did Mr Thornton in Mrs Gaskell's novel *North and South*, or indeed the first generation of the Greg family in Styal on whom it is thought Mrs Gaskell may have based her picture of the hard-nosed industrial capitalist.[11] For those small manufacturers who relied on workshop production, it was most convenient to combine home and workplace and many merchants had their warehouse at the back of their living quarters. Technological advances which revolutionized the labour process rarely forced those in middle-class occupations to establish a home away from work, yet by the mid-nineteenth century this separation was becoming increasingly popular.

Take a town like Birmingham. Birmingham had grown from a population of around 35,000 in 1780 to a quarter of a million in 1850, its expansion being based on the metal trades for which it was famous. It had always been the pattern for the most prosperous members of the middle class to move to the small versions of the gentleman's country house which ringed the town when they could afford it. Joseph Priestley for example, the well-known scientist, theologian and minister of one of the Unitarian congregations in

Birmingham, was living at Fair Hill about two miles from the town centre in the 1780s, and Dr William Withering, another member of the famous Birmingham Lunar Society and an eminent physician in the town, was living at Edgbaston Hall – a charming rural retreat away from the hustle and bustle of the town centre. By the 1820s and 1830s they were being followed by families who were considerably less wealthy, but were looking for a modest version of country living in houses which were close enough to the town for the men to walk daily to their places of work. By the mid-1840s Edgbaston, the leafy suburb of Birmingham, carefully planned with restrictive leases that prevented the building of workshops in gardens or the opening of shops on the premises, was growing apace and the most popular domestic retreat of the growing Birmingham middle class.[12]

The domestic ideal which underpinned such a development was premissed on the notion of a male head of household who supported his dependent wife and children. The women and children were able to be sheltered from the anxieties of the competitive public world by living in their 'haven' or home – away from the political dangers associated with such movements as Chartism, and the business worries of the town. This ideal was popularized from the late eighteenth century particularly by Evangelical Christians who believed that a proper religious household must form the basis of a reformed society.[13] The pulpit, the tract and the manual of behaviour provided some of the main vehicles for the promulgation of such ideas. The ideas were institutionalized in the new organizations formed by the middle classes – the self-improvement societies and the philanthropic societies, for example – in their business practices and in the new schools which they established for their sons, and eventually for their daughters.[14] Well-to-do shopkeepers were not slow to attach themselves to such ideas – ideas which called for significant changes in their established way of life 'above the shop'.

What was this established way of life? The records of the Cadbury family in Birmingham provide a valuable insight into the changing patterns of moderately successful shopkeepers over three generations.[15] Richard Tapper Cadbury, the originator of the Birmingham dynasty, arrived in the town in 1794, and having done his apprenticeship in Gloucester and served as a journeyman in London, he set up in business in Bull Street – a major Birmingham shopping street – as a silk mercer and draper. In 1800 he moved in with his wife and rapidly growing family above the shop. Elizabeth Cadbury was clearly actively engaged in the business, though she had not of course had access to the kind of training her husband had acquired. She helped in the shop when it was necessary, she looked after affairs when her husband was away and she organized the large household which included apprentices and female shop assistants as well as her own immediate family. That immediate family consisted of ten children – eight of whom survived, and her own mother who lived with them in her old age. In addition there were at least two women servants who helped with the organization of the household.

The provision of meals and linen for such a household, at a time when there were no mechanical aids and not even piped water, must have been an enormously time-consuming activity. It also has to be remembered that Elizabeth Cadbury had a baby every one to two years for the first fifteen years of her married life. Yet at the same time she was taking an active part in the business and living above the shop at a time when virtually no limitations existed on shop hours. This meant that household affairs had to be organized to fit in with those hours. In 1815, for example, when Richard was away in London buying fabrics for the shop, one of his letters to his wife included not only family news and inquiries about the children but also information about his commercial activities. He had already sent 'some coloured and scarlet whittles and scarves', some with the car men and others to go in the coach the next day. 'Bombazines I have been after', he told her, 'but I find it difficult to get all my colours. Such as I have met with are very nice and tomorrow I am to look out my black ones.' He was anxious to know whether she had had any news from Ireland about the linens; meanwhile he had ordered a bonnet for his daughter Sarah and assured his wife that the fresh eggs from Birmingham which she had sent had arrived safely.

In 1812 business was going sufficiently well for Richard Tapper Cadbury to take a modest second house in Islington Row, on the outskirts of the town and virtually in the country. The younger children went there to live with their nurse whilst their parents got away from the business as often as they could to visit them. The family kept pigeons, rabbits, a dog and a cat at the country house and since the garden was small, a second plot of land was rented nearby where strawberries and other fruit and vegetables were grown. Mrs Cadbury was now supervising two households and, with her own older daughters, she moved constantly between them. In 1827 she was unwell and soon after, Richard was glad to be able to report to his youngest daughter Emma that he had been gratified to find her well enough 'to see her walk to town, and to bustle about all day without apparent fatigue'. The sons followed in their father's footsteps and were apprenticed – the eldest, Benjamin, to a draper in London in training to take over the family business. The second son, John, was apprenticed to a tea and coffee dealer in Leeds and in 1824, after a spell in London to gain more experience, he came back to Birmingham and set up in business next door to his father and brother.

The daughters, again like their mother, had no formal apprenticeship. Indeed there were very few trades where it was possible for girls to be apprenticed, since craft rules had always been concerned with the guarding of skills for men. But the Cadbury girls had informal domestic apprenticeships. They learned to help their mother from a very early age and Maria and Ann would often assist their father in the shop. They were clearly brought up to see this as in no way reflecting on their femininity or gentility. Like their mother, they were no doubt just as much at home cooking, preserving, or preparing the house for winter by putting old extra carpets down. The business was a part of the life of every member of the family; as Elizabeth Cadbury wrote when, in 1828, the Bull Street premises were being altered and they were worried as to the effect this would have on the light in the parlour, '. . . I suppose we must not complain as it is for the business'.

Richard Tapper Cadbury's business was clearly doing quite well in the 1820s and he was publicly regarded as one of the substantial Birmingham tradesmen. But he could not afford to let matters drift, for around him the patterns of retailing were changing and this offered considerable opportunities. Despite the absence of a technological revolution in the retail trade, its organization was soon marked by the changes associated with the early development of industrial capitalism. Population growth and urbanization meant that there were large concentrations of people needing to buy. Factory production meant that some consumer items became much more easily and cheaply available – the Staffordshire pots for which the region was famous are examples of such items. In time the transport revolution meant that distribution networks could be established and transport speeded up. The traditional fairs and markets which had been central to eighteenth-century consumer patterns were not specialized enough to supply the new demands. Sometimes consumers themselves tried to organize adequate supplies of what they saw as important items. A public subscription was established in Birmingham in 1791 to try to get a good fish shop set up in the town. This effort, together with other consumer-oriented activities, was lauded by James Bisset in his *Poetic Survey around Birmingham* of 1800:

> And Epicureans, then, may have their wish,
> And tho' an inland place, find good fresh fish,
> For many schemes suggested have been tried,
> To have our markets constantly supplied
> With ev'ry thing that's good, and cheap in reason
> Fruit, fish or fowl, and rarities in season . . .[16]

Weekly markets remained very important for the sale of foodstuffs; in fact there was no national marketing system for food until after 1850, but gradually the markets became more organized. In the late eighteenth century a cattle market would often occupy the main street of a town one day a week, and this interfered considerably with other kinds of business and trading. Mrs Lucy Benton recalled New Street, which became one of Birmingham's main shopping streets, in the year 1817; there was an inn, the Old Crown, where the pig market was held:

> . . . all respectable females who traversed the street on market days had to turn into the middle of it to preserve their cleanliness, the footpaths being reserved for the special accommodation of the superior animal to whom the spot was devoted . . .[17]

Such an arrangement would hardly do for a town which depended economically on attracting buyers and selling its products to the rest of the country. The Birmingham markets were first centralized into the Bull Ring, and then construction of a market hall began in 1833, authorized by one of the town improvement acts and with a market committee responsible for its good order.[18]

Meanwhile shopkeepers were beginning to think about changing their practices. Larger towns meant the decline of custom based on kinship and on friendship – customers now had to be attracted from the streets and into the shops. This meant that the display of wares assumed a new importance and changes had to be made in the appearance of shops. John Cadbury was the first retailer in Birmingham to introduce plate glass windows which allowed for a much more attractive display. His friend Thomas Southall, who had a chemist's shop opposite, also had the new windows installed and the two of them would chat whilst they carefully polished them up in the mornings. A guidebook to Birmingham in 1825 referred to the town as in 'the high tide of retail trade'. 'The shops', it continued, 'of the higher degrees are very handsomely fitted up; the form and sweep of the windows, and the style of the decorations, emulating those of the Metropolis.'[19] Superior shopkeepers began to advertise in the local press as another way of attracting trade, though some of the old-established families were shocked at this 'puffing', as it was called. Richard Tapper Cadbury made a regular practice of advertising in *Aris's Birmingham Gazette* and, like many other drapers, he would make a particular point of advertising when he had just brought in his new stock from London.

Contemporaries who commented on improvements in the organization of shopping tended to refer to the drapery business for it was the first branch of the trade to exhibit the characteristics of modern retailing systematically. Many traders in the eighteenth and early nineteenth century combined production and distribution: the butcher killed and cut his meat, the baker baked and sold his bread, the candlestick-maker produced his metal goods as well as retailing them. This combination of production and distribution, based on a large household which utilized the labour of all family members, was in decline – at least in the large towns – by the mid-nineteenth century. Town butchers were increasingly specializing in killing and cutting on the one hand and retailing on the other. Candlestick-makers no longer existed as such; the production of hardware in workshops and small factories had become the staple trade of the Black Country and ironmongers would then sell these products. Baking, however, was still dominated by the independent master who baked and sold – the big change there had been from home-baking. The draper had the advantage of being relatively free from production functions; the only item which required preparing for sale was thread. Developments in textile production, particularly cotton, meant that there was an expanding mass market for cloth and by the 1820s the drapery shops in towns and cities were bigger than any other shops. Drapers were able to concentrate their capital on shop improvements. They were frequently the first to introduce plate glass windows, window displays and gas lighting, and they also led the field in price ticketing and cash trading which were two of the next developments.[20]

Despite the advantages of his trade, however, Benjamin Head Cadbury, who took over the drapery business from his father, does not seem to have been such a good businessman as his brother, John. John not only introduced the latest retailing improvements in his tea and coffee shop; he also decided to branch out into the manufacture of cocoa, made possible by the introduction of cocoa powder around 1830, as soon as he had the capital available. In 1831 he set up a small factory for this purpose around the corner from the shop and ran the two sides of the business simultaneously for as long as he could. His first wife, Priscilla, whom he had married in 1826, died two years later and in 1832 John married Candia Barrow, the daughter of a Quaker shipping merchant. Initially the couple lived over the shop, but after the birth of their first son John, they moved to Edgbaston and soon found the house which became the family home for nearly forty years. It was not a large house but they gradually altered and extended it. Their daughter Maria, in her recollections of her childhood, commented on the fact that her mother lived on the business premises initially; by the time that Maria was writing it was obviously something that had to be explained, and her account was that Candia liked to be beside her husband all the day in the early part of their marriage. There was no mention of the importance of her contribution to the work which had to be done. The profits from the shop and the factory had been sufficient to warrant setting up a suburban home, but there was no money to spare. Candia could cook and she supervised the home wash once a fortnight in the back kitchen. But she was used to country living and it was these standards which they sought in their Edgbaston home, as Maria described it:

> . . . it was almost cottage like in appearance and too small without many alterations, but its countrylike surroundings decided our parents to take it, make more rooms, and lay out the gardens to their own taste . . . our Mother was exceedingly fond of gardening, but our Father was greatly occupied with business and town affairs and other interests and he had very little time during the week for his garden.

The house soon had a playroom, which was later turned into a schoolroom, and a nursery upstairs for the little ones. Such a differentiation between rooms had not been possible in the combined home/workplace in Bull Street. Suburban housing allowed for a different notion of childhood as well as a different role for women, and this differentiation of role was mirrored in the new definitions of physical space. Candia and her children's lives were focused on home and school, whilst her husband used the Edgbaston home as a happy family base for his business and public activities. 'Our dear Father was a very steady industrious man, noted for punctuality, and took great pride in his business, everything being arranged in beautiful order,' wrote Maria. In 1847 John Cadbury opened larger premises for his cocoa production, some way from the shop but nearer to home, where his time was increasingly spent. Cocoa production provided a popular drink for temperance advocates in this period, and John and Candia were amongst the earliest supporters of the temperance movement. Indeed family habits clearly involved some small-scale advertising in themselves; when Maria was sent away to school her father sent some cocoa to the Misses Dymond who ran the school. Maria reported in one of her regular letters home that 'Miriam Dymond told me that they liked Father's cocoas so much that they have persuaded their grocer to supply them regularly with it, and we have it regularly every 5th day morning for breakfast.'

Meanwhile Richard Tapper Cadbury had decided to retire. At the age of sixty-four he left the business in the hands of his eldest son, Benjamin, and also bought a house in Edgbaston, where he lived with his wife and two remaining unmarried daughters on a 'modest competency'. He still went into town a great deal, however, in connection either with his public activities or his business interests. For his wife and daughters, it was a very different matter. Once they had physically moved from the workplace it became marginal to their lives – the business was simply where the money came from, rather than something which occupied many of their working hours. It was Elizabeth's daughter-in-law, another Candia – Candia Wadkin – who now took over the responsibilities in the shop. The Bull Street house had been smartened up before Benjamin and Candia moved in and an effort was made to make it more comfortable as a home. Candia was impressed to find it so

> ... completely metamorphosed that it was almost difficult to recognize it as the old family mansion, the difference of furniture and the addition of window curtains have given the parlour quite another character, it now appears a much squarer room and more comfortable and had been dressed out with flowers ... some hyacinths on the chimney piece are in full bloom, in addition to this there are several plants in full blossom so that we have quite a country appearance ...

Obviously every effort was being made to downplay the urban features of Bull Street life. The yard had been whitewashed and the upstairs sitting room and bedrooms comfortably fitted up. Candia was kept extremely busy with a growing family: she soon had six daughters and a son, and the same kind of business responsibilities that her mother-in-law had assumed. In the 1830s, for example, she gave Benjamin news of the shop when he was away: 'Customers have been flowing in very satisfactorily today and all has, I believe, gone on comfortably, all appear attentive, equally so or more anxious to be so than if thou wast at home . . .'

Candia was closely involved in the education of her children, as were her sisters-in-law. The girl's education was started at home and then they went to a Birmingham day school before going to the same Quaker boarding school as their cousin Maria. They were given an early training in domesticity; dolls, prams, pin-cushions and workboxes figure prominently as presents, and they were taught to knit and to sew, to make their own clothes and to repair them. The family stayed in the Bull Street house until 1844 and then they too moved into the outskirts of Edgbaston; the last clear links were cut between the women and the family businesses. In 1846 Benjamin gave up the drapery business and went into partnership with John, presumably having decided that with the new, larger factory there would be plenty of work and enough profits for the two of them.

The separation between home and work made substantial differences to the daily lives of both men and women in middle-class families. The Cadbury men still went to work every day and then came home to their families. This meant that there was a much clearer distinction between work-time and leisure-time and there was also a much clearer distinction between public and private life. As long as home and workplace were combined it must often have been difficult to categorize whether activities which went on there were 'public' or 'private' and indeed it would probably have been a pretty irrelevant question. Was feeding an apprentice, for example, who would usually have been the son of a friend and who would have generally been treated as one of the family, a business or domestic matter? The point is, of course, that they were one and the same thing, and one clear demonstration of this is that shopkeepers such as the Cadburys started to keep separate household accounts only when the separation had taken place between work and home. The physical separation of the two was the culmination of a long process during which time middle-class men's activities had become increasingly differentiated from those of middle-class women. Women's participation in family businesses had always tended to be an informal affair; the fact that married women had no property rights meant that the business was always legally owned by the husband as long as he lived. Only widows and spinsters could run their own businesses in their own names. Furthermore the training and skills had always been tied to masculinity – women were not apprenticed to drapers or to tea and coffee dealers. But the increasing complexity of the commercial world and its increasing formalization in this period meant that it was becoming more difficult for women to participate even informally, especially since the training which encouraged the new retailing skills was not available to them. The informal 'picking up' of the business, which was what women relied on, was no longer necessarily enough.

But in addition to the increasing difficulty of women learning how to do business, there were the aspirations for a separate domestic sphere and the positive desire to move away from the shop if this were financially possible. Initially efforts were often made to make the shop more like a 'home' – as, for example, when the Bull Street parlour was made more comfortable with curtains for Benjamin and Candia, and an attempt was made to make it look more countrylike by putting in flowers and plants. But in the end the only way to have a fully private home, where family time would not be interrupted by the apprentices, late customers or visiting business contacts, was by geographically dividing the home from the workplace. The most crucial effect of this in terms of sexual divisions was that it meant wives and daughters were no longer there to be called upon for help. Daughters were educated to be wives and mothers and to expect to be financially dependent on their husbands. This did not mean that women no longer had any financial relation to the business. Their money, acquired through marriage settlements, remained a vital source of capital. In fact John Cadbury's sons saved the family cocoa business, which went through a bad patch in the 1850s, by investing some money left to them by their mother. But the *direct* working relation of women to the business had gone and 'work' was now what their husbands did when they left the house in the morning.

Women were furthermore increasingly cut off from the variety of other *public* activities which their menfolk engaged in. The period 1780–1850 was the age of societies, which were formed in aid of every possible cause. These societies ranged from ones with a primarily political orientation to those concerned with commercial activities, self-education in its broadest sense and philanthropic works. It was exceedingly difficult for women to be involved in any of these except the philanthropic societies, and even there they were encouraged to participate privately and informally rather than being engaged in the public activities – the meetings and the dinners.[21] A typical day for John Cadbury might have involved an early rise, a walk with some of the children and the dogs, back home for breakfast, a walk into town to work, a morning in the shop or factory, a twelve o'clock meeting at the Public Office of the Street Commissioners (the oligarchic elite which was responsible for some aspects of town government up to 1851 and of which he was a member for many years), followed by something to eat in the respectable hostelry next door where street commissioners often gathered, an afternoon back at the business with a five o'clock philanthropic meeting of one of the many committees of which he was an active member, after which he would have returned home for what was left of the day. Candia, by contrast, would have spent her day in Edgbaston caring for the children both physically and educationally and supervising the household. In 1851, when they had six children, she had two female servants in the house and this was certainly not a generous number for a middle-class household, given the amount of domestic labour required in a pre-mechanical age.

If she had a little spare time she might have visited one or two poor families in whom she took a special interest, but as her daughter Maria recalled, she rarely left home:

> Our precious Mother had a very busy home life with her five boys and one girl, living amongst them as much as possible; she was a lovingly watchful and affectionate wife and mother seldom visiting from home . . .

Candia's social life centred on her extended family and the Quaker network of Friends. Candia was indeed an essentially 'private person' whilst her husband was well known as a 'public man'. Such a social demarcation of male as 'public' and female as 'private' was both reinforced and encouraged by the physical separation between work and home.

NOTES

1 Mrs Elizabeth Gaskell, *Cranford* (Dent, London, 1964).
2 Alison Adburgham, *Shops and Shopping 1800–1914* (Allen & Unwin, London, 1964); Dorothy Davis, *A History of Shopping* (Routledge &

Kegan Paul, London, 1966); D. Alexander, *Retailing in England during the Industrial Revolution* (Athlone, London, 1970).
3 E. P. Thompson and Eileen Yeo, *The Unknown Mayhew. Selections from the Morning Chronicle 1849–50* (Penguin, Harmondsworth, 1973).
4 J. Kenrick, *Memoir of the Rev. John Kentish* (William Grew & Son, Birmingham, 1854), p. 9.
5 Arnold Bennett, *The Old Wives' Tale* (Pan, London, 1964), p. 30.
6 Davis, *A History of Shopping.*
7 Alexander, *Retailing in England.*
8 This separation between the shop and the home was confined to the most prosperous tradesmen, while many shops still combined workplace and home in the late nineteenth century. See Thea Vigne and Alan Howkins, 'The small shopkeeper in industrial and market towns', in Geoffrey Crossick (ed.), *The Lower Middle Class in Britain 1870–1914* (Croom Helm, London, 1977).
9 Catherine Hall, 'The home turned upside down? The working-class family in cotton textiles in the early nineteenth century', in Elizabeth Whitelegge et al. (eds), *The Changing Experience of Women* (Martin Robertson, Oxford, 1982).
10 See Raphael Samuel, 'The workshop of the world; steampower and hand technology in mid-Victorian Britain', *History Workshop Journal*, no. 3, Spring 1977.
11 Mrs Elizabeth Gaskell, *North and South* (Penguin, Harmondsworth, 1970); M. B. Rose, *The Gregs of Styal* (Quarry Bank Mill Development Trust, London, 1978).
12 Leonore Davidoff and Catherine Hall, 'The architecture of public and private life: English middle-class society in a provincial town 1780–1850', in Derek Fraser and Anthony Sutcliffe (eds), *The Pursuit of Urban History* (Edward Arnold, London, 1983).
13 Catherine Hall, 'The Early Formation of Victorian Domestic Ideology', in this volume.
14 Robert J. Morris, 'Voluntary Societies and British Urban Elites, 1780–1850: an analysis', *The Historical Journal*, vol. 26, no. 1, 1983.
15 The material on the Cadburys which forms most of the rest of the paper is drawn from the Cadbury Collection. The Collection, which is housed in Birmingham Reference Library, comprises a rich series of manuscripts plus drawings and illustrations.
16 James Bisset, *A Poetic Survey around Birmingham* (Birmingham, 1800).
17 Mrs Lucy Benton, *Recollections of New Street in the Year 1817* (J. J. Davis, Birmingham, 1877).
18 On the municipal history of Birmingham, see Conrad Gill, *History of Birmingham*, vol. 1 (Oxford University Press, London, 1952).
19 James Drake, *The Picture of Birmingham* (J. Drake, Birmingham, 1825), p. 69.

20 Alexander, *Retailing in England.*
21 F. K. Prochaska, *Women and Philanthropy in Nineteenth-Century England* (Oxford University Press, London, 1980).

6 The Tale of Samuel and Jemima: gender and working-class culture in early-nineteenth-century England

Samuel Bamford, the Radical weaver, described in his famous autobiography *Passages in the Life of a Radical* his experience of the Peterloo massacre of 1819.[1] The account has rightly become a classic. Bamford first recounted how the restoration of habeus corpus in 1818 made it possible to campaign again openly for reform. The decision was taken in the North to hold a reform meeting in St Peter's Field, Manchester. Committees were set up to organize the event and issued their first injunctions, *Cleanliness, Sobriety* and *Order*, to which was added *Peace* on the suggestion of Orator Henry Hunt. Then came the weeks of drilling by 'the lads' on the moors, after work and on Sunday mornings, learning 'to march with a steadiness and regularity which would not have disgraced a regiment on parade'. As a reward maidens with milkcans, 'nymphs blushing and laughing' would sometimes refresh the men with 'delicious draughts, new from the churn'.[2] Then came the day of the gathering of the procession in Bamford's native town of Middleton. At the front were

> twelve of the most comely and decent-looking youths, who were placed in two rows of six each, with each a branch of laurel held presented in his hand, as a token of amity and peace, – then followed the men of several districts in fives, – then the band of music, an excellent one, – then the colours; a blue one of silk with inscriptions in golden letters, 'UNITY AND STRENGTH'. 'LIBERTY AND FRATERNITY'. A green one of silk, with golden letters, 'PARLIAMENTS ANNUAL'. 'SUFFRAGE UNIVERSAL'; and betwixt them on a staff, a handsome cap of crimson velvet, with a tuft of laurel, and the cap tastefully braided with the word, LIBERTAS in front.

Next came the men from Middleton and its surroundings, every hundred with its leader who had a sprig of laurel in his hat, the 3,000 men all ready to obey the commands of a 'principal conductor', 'who took his place at the head of the column with a bugleman to sound his orders'. Bamford addressed the men before they set off, reminding them that it was essential that they should behave with dignity and with discipline and so confound their enemies who represented them as a 'mob-like rabble'. Bamford recalled the procession as 'a most respectable assemblage of labouring men', all decently if humbly attired and wearing their Sunday white shirts and neck-cloths.[3]

The Middleton column soon met with the Rochdale column and between them, Bamford estimates, there were probably 6,000 men. At their head were now about 200 of their most handsome young women supporters, including Bamford's wife, some of whom were singing and dancing to the music. The reformers arrived in Manchester, having changed their route following the personal request of Hunt that they would lead his group in. This did not particularly please Bamford, who had elevated views of his own dignity as leader and was not especially sympathetic to Hunt, but he agreed and then, while the speeches were going on, he and a friend, not expecting to hear anything new, went to look for some refreshment. It was at this point that the cavalry attacked and that the great demonstration was broken up with terrible brutality. Hundreds were wounded, eleven killed. Bamford managed to get away and after much anxiety met up with his wife, from whom he had been separated for some hours.

The human horror of Peterloo was differently experienced by Jemima Bamford, for from the moment of realizing that something had gone badly wrong her anxieties and fears were focused on her husband's safety. As a leader of the reformers he would be particularly subject to persecution and, indeed, was arrested and charged with high treason soon afterwards. Reform demonstrations were predominantly male occasions, as we can see from the description of the Middleton procession. There was usually a good sprinkling of women present and 'a neatly dressed female, supporting a small flag' was sitting on the driving seat of Hunt's carriage.[4] Mary Fildes, President of the Female Reform Society of Manchester, was on the platform, dressed all in white. Over a hundred women were wounded in St Peter's Field and two were killed, but nevertheless the majority of participants, of speakers and of recognized leaders, were men.[5]

When Bamford first began to worry as to where his wife was he blamed himself that he had allowed her to come at all. In her account she says that she was determined to go to the meeting and would have followed it even if her husband had not consented to her going with the procession. She was worried before the event that something would go wrong and preferred to be near Samuel. He finally agreed and she arranged to leave their little girl, Ann, with a 'careful neighbour' and joined some other 'married females' at the head of the procession. She was dressed simply, as a countrywoman, in her 'second best attire'. Separated from her husband and the majority of the Middleton men by the crowd, she was terrified when the soldiers started the attack and managed to escape into a cellar. There she hid until the carnage was over when she crept out, helped by the kindly people in the house, and went in search of Samuel, who was first reported as dead, next said to be in the infirmary, then in the prison, but with whom she was eventually reunited. At the end of the tragic day, Bamford tells us,

> Her anxiety being now removed by the assurance of my safety, she hastened forward to console our child. I rejoined my comrades, and forming about a thousand of them into file, we set off to the sound of fife and drum, with our only banner waving, and in that form we re-entered the town of Middleton.[6]

Peterloo was a formative experience in the development of popular consciousness in the early nineteenth century and Bamford's account takes us into the question of the meanings of sexual difference within working-class culture. In E. P. Thompson's classic account of the making of the English working class, that process whereby groups of stockingers and weavers, factory workers and agricultural labourers, those in the old centres of commerce and the new industrial towns came to see themselves as having interests in common as against those of other classes, Peterloo is seen as one of the decisive moments, significantly shifting disparate individuals and groups towards a defined political consciousness.[7] By 1832, Thompson claims, working people had built up a sense of collective identity and shared struggle, had come to see themselves as belonging to a class. Placing the emphasis on class as process and as relationship rather than 'thing' or fixed structure, Thompson argued that 'class happens when some men, as a result of common experiences (inherited or shared), feel and articulate the identity of their interests as between themselves, and as against other men whose interests are different from (and usually opposed to) theirs'.[8] Shifting away from the classical Marxist emphasis on relationships of production, he focused on the experience of new forms of exploitation and the meanings given to that experience through the construction of a class-consciousness. *The Making of the English Working Class* documented and celebrated the emergence of that working-class consciousness between the 1790s, when a distinctively English artisanal Radicalism came to threaten the established social and political order, and the early 1830s, which saw the beginnings of Chartism, a national political movement dominated by working-class people. Working people's consciousness, Thompson argued, was embedded in their cultural institutions, their traditions and their ideas. *The Making* thus departed radically from the established routes of Marxists and of labour historians in its stress on the cultural and ideological aspects of class politics.

The book constituted a major political and intellectual intervention and has remained at the centre of debates on history, class and culture ever since. As a history undergraduate in 1963 when it was published, I devoured it and tried slowly to come to terms with its theoretical implications. More than twenty years later and now teaching it myself to students I still feel excited by its story, its rich material, the power of its political vision. In 1963 the re-emergence of feminism was still to come but from the beginning of that new dawn, the first national event of which took place under the aegis of the History Workshop (itself deeply indebted to Thompson's work), feminist history has been powerfully influenced by Thompsonian social history. His insistence on the rescue of 'the poor stockinger, the Luddite cropper, the "obsolete" hand-loom weaver, the "utopian" artisan, and even the deluded follower of Joanna Southcott, from the enormous condescension of posterity' and his triumphant demonstration of the possibility of such a rescue was echoed in the feminist commitment to recover the forgotten sex, captured in Sheila Rowbotham's *Hidden From History*.[9]

The Making of the English Working Class featured women political activists – members of reform societies and trade unionists – as well as the occasional female prophet or seer. In the context of the early 1960s, Thompson was certainly attentive to those women who appeared in the historical records which he examined. But feminism was to recast ways of thinking about women's political and cultural space. In 1983, Barbara Taylor published *Eve and the New Jerusalem* which both built upon Thompson's achievement and extended his analysis. In her account of the place of skilled workers in the Owenite movement, for example, she used the framework established by Thompson in his seminal chapters on artisans and weavers but looked beyond the threat posed to those workers by the forces of new methods and relations of production to the tensions and antagonisms which this fostered between male and female workers. The fragile unity of the English working class in the 1830s, she argued, was constructed within a sexually divided world, when on occasion, as one Owenite woman put it, 'the men are as bad as their masters'.[10]

This recognition that class identity, once theorized as essentially male or gender-neutral, is always articulated with a masculine or feminine subject, has been a central feminist insight and the story of Samuel and Jemima helps us to pursue the implications of this insight for the radical working-class culture of the early nineteenth century. The culture to which Bamford belonged was a culture that originated with artisans but extended to factory operatives, a culture that stressed moral sobriety and the search for useful knowledge, that valued intellectual inquiry, that saw mutual study and disputation as methods of learning and self-improvement. Such a culture placed men and women differently and the highlighting of these forms of sexual division can give us some access to the gendered nature of popular culture in the early nineteenth century.

Men and women experienced that culture in very different ways, as we can see from Bamford's story. He had been involved with the organization of the day, with the training of the men so that they would march in disciplined procession, with the arrangements as to the route, with the ceremonial and ritual which would help to give the reformers a sense of strength and power. He belonged unambiguously to the struggle; as a leader he was concerned to articulate the demands of honest weavers, to help to develop strategies which would make possible the winning of reform. For his wife it was a very different matter. She too had a commitment to the cause but it was her husband who wrote down her tale, hoping that it would not be 'devoid of interest to the reader'.[11] Her arrangements were to do with their child; her first concern, once she knew that Samuel was safe, was to get back to her. Like the majority of female reformers at the time she positioned herself, and was positioned by others, as a wife and mother supporting the cause of working men. The men, on the other hand, like her husband, entered the political fray as independent subjects, fighting for their own right to vote, their own capacity to play a part in determining forms of government. It is this distinction, between men as independent political beings and women as dependants, that the tale of Samuel and Jemima vividly illustrates.

The emergence of the working man as a political subject in his own right was part of the process of the development of male working-class consciousness. As E. P. Thompson has demonstrated, eighteenth-century society had not primarily been dominated by class issues and class struggles. It was King Property who ruled and the hegemony established by the landowning classes and the gentry rested on an acceptance of a patriarchal and hierarchical society. Consent had been won to the exercise of power by the propertied in part through the shared acceptance of a set of beliefs and customs, the 'moral economy' of the society, which unlike the new political economy of the nineteenth century, recognized communal norms and obligations and judged that the rich would respect the rights of the poor, particularly when it came to the issue of a 'just price' for bread. When that moral economy was transgressed, eighteenth-century crowds believed they had the right to defend their traditional customs. Bread riots, focused on soaring prices, malpractices among dealers, or just plain hunger, were one of the most popular forms of protest. Women were often the initiators of riots for they were the most involved in buying and inevitably the more sensitive to evidence of short weight or adulteration. Their concern was the subsistence of their families.[12]

But traditional ideas of family and household were shifting at the end of the eighteenth and beginning of the nineteenth centuries. In some regions the traditional family economy was breaking up as new productive processes required different forms of labour and proletarianzation gathered pace.[13] Such changes played a part in structuring and organizing the family and shaping ideas about marriage and parenthood. Among the rural poor of the South and East, for example, as John Gillis has argued, typical labouring families, which no longer owned their means of production, were driven to push their children into the labour market in order to survive. Couples could scarcely support their little ones, never mind their kin. At the same time, the decline of living-in servants meant more sexual and marital freedom than had previously been hoped for from servants in husbandry. From the late eighteenth century, employers and overseers in this area were likely to favour marriage as a source of cheap and docile labour whereas previously they had favoured celibacy among living-in servants. Labouring couples developed what might be described as a 'narrow conjugality' in these circumstances. In the North and West, however, particularly in the areas of proto-industrialization, the family remained the economic unit and kinship continued to be a powerful bond while master artisans in the old urban centres clung to their tradition of late marriage. But this richness or variety in familial and marital patterns, which even extended to sexual radicalism among some pockets of Owenites, freethinkers and radical Christians, gave way by the 1850s to what Gillis sees as an era of 'mandatory marriage'.[14] There was no longer a viable alternative to the nuclear family and heterosexual monogamy for working people and the undermining of the independence of the family economy went together with the recognition of the man as the breadwinner, the woman as dependant. As yet, historians have not charted in any detail the interconnections and dissonances between the narratives of family and sexuality and the narrative of politics, more narrowly defined. The separation between market-place and home, between production and consumption, so powerfully inscribed in our culture, has been difficult enough to begin to repair.[15] Next must come the insistence that the politics of gender does not rest with issues around state regulation of the family and sexuality but affects such apparently gender-neutral arenas as foreign affairs and diplomatic relations, commercial and financial policy, as well as ideas of nation and nationality.

English politics took a sharp turn in the turbulent decade of the 1790s when the established hierarchy was challenged and the movement began towards a new sense of distinctive interests, of class interests, not only for working people but for aristocrats and entrepreneurs as well.[16] The degree of sympathy which food rioters had been able to expect from some magistrates disappeared and more punitive strategies began to be adopted by the authorities after the start of Jacobin activities in England. The repudiation of customary rights by those in power meant that such expectations had to be rethought and reinterpreted. It was the writings of Thomas Paine and the revolutionary ideals of liberty, equality and fraternity that inspired the 1790s version of the 'freeborn Englishman' and the creation of new traditions of Radicalism and protest. In the clubs and the meeting places of the 1790s, serious reformers gathered to discuss the vital subject of the day – Parliamentary Reform. As Thomas Hardy, the first secretary of the London Corresponding Society, wrote in his autobiography, describing their first meeting,

> After having had their bread and cheese and porter for supper, as usual, and their pipes afterwards, with some conversation on the hardness of the times and the dearness of all the necessaries of life . . . the business for which they had met was brought forward – *Parliamentary Reform* – an important subject to be deliberated upon and dealt with by such a class of men.[17]

The artisans and small tradesmen of the reforming societies had come to the conclusion that their demand must be for political representation. It was Parliament that carried the key to a better future. With the moral consensus eroded and the refusal of the rich to take their responsibilities seriously, whether in the field of wages, the customary control of labour, or poverty and hunger, the only solution could be to change the government for the better. It was men who were in the forefront of formulating such demands. Drawing on and reworking the established traditions of English liberalism and dissent, they defined themselves as political agents while their wives, mothers and daughters were primarily defined as supporters and dependants. As bread riots gave way to new forms of political protest, whether constitutional societies, demonstrations for reform or machine-smashing, it was men who led the way organizationally, who dominated the meetings and defined the agendas for reform. This is not to say women were not represented. Indeed Samuel Bamford regarded himself as the initiator of female voting and even of female philanthropic societies, an idea that would have astonished the many women who had been active in such organizations since the 1790s. When speaking at Saddleworth he recounts,

> I, in the course of an address, insisted on the right, and the propriety also, of females who were present at such assemblages, voting by show of hand, for, or against the resolutions. This was a new idea; and the women who attended numerously on that bleak ridge, were mightily pleased with it, – and the men being nothing dissentient, – when the resolution was put, the women held up their hands, amid much laughter; and ever from that time, females voted with the men at the radical meetings.[18]

Females may have voted with the men at many of the Radical meetings but females certainly did not carry the same weight in the overall political process. The later decision by the Chartists to abandon universal suffrage in favour of universal male suffrage depended on the notion of men representing women.

Jemima 'never deemed any trouble too great' if bestowed for the cause, according to Samuel, but the troubles that visited her were different from those of her husband.[19] Samuel was arrested and tried for high treason, found guilty and imprisoned. In the course of all this he had to get himself to London twice, mostly by walking, be interviewed by Lord Sidmouth, have a defence committee set up in his name, meet many of the prominent reformers of the period and have his trial reported in the national press. Jemima, on the other hand, stayed at home working on the loom to support herself and her child while Samuel was away, sending him clean linen when she could, venturing out for two visits to Lincoln Gaol to stay with him while their daughter was cared for by an aunt and uncle. Home was for Samuel, as he tells us, his 'dove-nest' to which he could return after the storm. His first description of it comes when he had risked a trip home while lying low in fear of arrest, coming in from the 'frozen rain' and the night wind. He emphasizes the good fire, the clean, swept hearth and his wife darning, while their child read to her from the Bible, 'Blessed are the meek for they shall inherit the earth.' 'Such were the treasures,' he tells us, 'I had hoarded in that lowly cell.'[20]

As working men defined themselves as political subjects of a new kind, 'craving for something for "the nation"' beyond the contentment of domestic blessings, as they learned organizational skills, made contacts across the country, opened up new avenues for themselves as Radical journalists or political activists, so they increasingly saw themselves as representatives of their families in the new public world.[21] Radical working-class culture came to rest on a set of common-sense assumptions about the relative places of men and women which were not subjected to the same critical scrutiny as were the monarchy, the aristocracy, representative forms of government and the other institutions of Old Corruption.

What were the beliefs, practices and institutions of this working-class culture that emerged in the early nineteenth century, and in what ways did they legitimate men and women differently? It was the reform movement that lay at the heart of that culture. This does not, of course, mean that there were not other extremely significant elements within popular culture. Methodism, for example, provided one such alternative discourse, intersecting at some points with the beliefs of serious and improving artisans, as in their shared concern to challenge the evils of alcohol, but at other points having sharply different concerns. Meanwhile heavy drinking and gambling remained very popular pastimes for sections of the working class, however much the sober and respectable disapproved of them. But in Thompson's powerful narrative it was the characteristic beliefs and institutions of the Radicals that emerged as the leading element within working-class culture in the early nineteenth century, carrying more resonance, and with a stronger institutional base, than any other.[22] The main thrust behind the reform movement came from the 'industrious classes – stockingers, handloom weavers, cotton-spinners, artisans and, in association with these, a widespread scattering of small masters, tradesmen, publicans, booksellers and professional men.[23] These different groups were able to come together and on the basis of their shared political and industrial organization, through the Hampden Clubs, the constitutional societies, the trade unions, the friendly societies, the educational groups and the self-improvement societies they were able to come to feel an identity of interest. Such clubs and societies were, therefore, central to the task of building a common culture but such locations offered a much easier space for men to operate in than for women.

Bamford tells us of the Hampden Clubs and their importance:

> Instead of riots and destruction of property, Hampden clubs were now established in many of our large towns, and the villages and districts around them; Cobbett's books were printed in a cheap form; the labourers read them and thenceforward became deliberate and systematic in their proceedings. Nor were there wanting men of their own class, to encourage and direct the new converts; the Sunday Schools of the preceding thirty years, had produced many working men of sufficient talent to become readers, writers, and speakers in the village meetings for parliamentary reform; some also were found to possess a rude poetic talent, which rendered their effusions popular, and bestowed an additional charm on their assemblages, and by such various means, anxious listeners at first, and then zealous proselytes, were drawn from the cottages of quiet nooks and dingles, to the weekly readings and discussions of the Hampden clubs.[24]

Bamford is describing male gatherings; the men who had learned to read and write in the Sunday schools of the late eighteenth century made use of their new talents, spoke to others, sometimes even in popular poetic form, and built up weekly reading and discussion meetings. Work on literacy rates suggests that working-class women lagged significantly behind men.[25] Teachers were less likely to give them time and energy. They were less likely to have time or space or freedom to pursue study and discussion. As David Vincent has shown, the difficulties associated with women writing are reflected in the autobiographical material which has survived. Of the 142 autobiographies which he has analysed, only six were by women. He attributes this silence in part to the lack of self-confidence among women, for who could possibly be interested in their lives? We remember Jemima Bamford, writing her few notes to be included in her husband's story. Vincent also points to women's subordinate position within the family. Men could demand that their wives and children would recognize their need for quiet and privacy in circumstances where such conditions were almost impossible to obtain. The wife would hush the children and quell the storms while her husband struggled with his exercises in reading and writing. Such efforts were rarely forthcoming for women. Furthermore, self-improvement societies were normally for men only. It was hard for women in these circumstances to have the same kind of commitment to intellectual inquiry and the search for useful knowledge, values which were central to Radical culture.[26]

But the characteristics of the subordinate position of women within the family were not fixed and unchanging. Customary assumptions about 'a woman's place' were rethought and reworked in this period. There was nothing new in the assumption that men and women were different and that women were inferior in some respects. There was a great deal that was new in the political, economic and cultural relations within which traditional notions of sexual difference were being articulated. Take the new political culture of the reform movement. As Dorothy Thompson has argued, the replacements of the more informal and communal protests of the eighteenth century with the more organized movements of the nineteenth century resulted in the increasing marginalization of women.[27] As formal societies with constitutions and officers replaced customary patterns of crowd mobilization, women withdrew. Many meetings were seen as occasions for male conviviality and women were excluded informally if not formally. Meetings might be held at times when they could not go, for once they were removed from the street the automatic participation of men, women and children was broken. They were often held in places to which it was difficult for them to go, for pubs were coming to be seen as unsuitable places for respectable women. If they did manage to get there, they might well feel alienated by the official jargon and constitutional procedures so beloved by some Radical men.[28]

Radical men were certainly sometimes happy to welcome women as supporters of their demands. In the Birmingham Political Union, for example, resuscitated in 1837 after its triumphs in the lead-up to the Reform Act 1832, a Female Political Union was established through the efforts of Titus Salt, a leading Radical, who argued that the support that women could provide would be invaluable. At a giant tea-party held by the Female Political Union in the grand, new Town Hall in the city, the male leaders of the BPU demonstrated the ambiguous and contradictory nature of their feelings about women's engagement in politics. Tea and plum cake were served to the assembled thousand and then the men on the platform delivered their addresses. Thomas Attwood, the hero of 1832, spoke first. 'My kind and fair and most dear countrywomen', he began, 'I most solemnly declare my affection for the women of England has been mainly instrumental in causing all my exertions in the public cause, not that I do not feel for the men, but I have a stronger desire to promote the comforts of the women.'

The women, according to the report of the *Birmingham Journal*, the mouthpiece of the Radicals, were suitably grateful for his efforts on their behalf. After Attwood came Scholefield, the first MP for the city, elected after the triumph of Reform. Scholefield proceeded to enunciate his contradictory impulses to his audience. 'It was gratifying to him to meet so many excellent and intelligent women', he began, 'who, by their presence, showed very plainly that they took a lively interest in all that concerned the welfare of their husbands, fathers, brothers and sons, and which also', he added, 'deeply affected their own interests'. Scholefield went on to argue for women's politics, citing the importance of the women's storming of the Bastille. He concluded, however, that he was 'far from wishing that politics should ever supersede the important duties of social and domestic life, which constituted the chief business of the female'; but he also hoped 'the women of Birmingham would never become indifferent to politics'.

Titus Salt followed Scholefield, arguing that by their good conduct the women had won over everybody to the cause of female unions and that, 'by a continuance of the same conduct, and the force of moral power, they would gain all they required'. All these Radical men wanted support from women. Their capacity for fund-raising was particularly welcomed. But in seeking this support they were breaking in part with traditional assumptions about politics being a male sphere, traditional assumptions which had been rudely challenged by the female revolutionaries in France who were constantly involved in the debate over women's political activity. Not surprisingly, many men had mixed feelings about this potential field of action for 'the fair sex'. So, indeed, did many women. Attwood's patronage of his female audience, Scholefield's insistence that they were involved primarily for their menfolk, Salt's emphasis on good conduct and moral force as the ways in which women could be politically effective, all point to the difficulties arising from the mobilization of women, the tensions generated by the spectacle of 1,000 women in the Birmingham Town Hall and what they might do. Would they properly recognize that Attwood had achieved reform for them? Would they be content with acting for their fathers, husbands and sons? Would they continue to behave well and conduct themselves according to female proprieties? Could the men control them? Would Mrs Bamford have gone to Manchester without her husband's permission? What was a woman's place? The women were certainly not willing to be rendered silent. At a subsequent Female Political Union meeting with a Mrs Spinks in the chair, Mr Collins, a prominent BPU member, spoke. Birmingham had at last achieved incorporation and the right to representative local government. Mr Collins said, 'He could not but congratulate them on the glorious victory that had been that day achieved in the Town Hall by the men of Birmingham.' A woman in the meeting, resenting this slur on her sex, piped up, 'And by the women, Mr Collins; for we were there.' Mr Collins had to admit 'the assistance the women had rendered'.[29]

Given the institutional framework of Radical working-class culture, it was difficult for women to engage straightforwardly in it as political agents in their own right. Nevertheless, they were there in considerable numbers and with considerable strength, in Female Reform Associations, in the Owenite communities and among the Chartists.[30] For the most part it seems that they sought primarily to advance the cause of their menfolk, and, in the case of Chartism, to ensure that the male voice could be properly represented in Parliament. But there were sounds of discord. Discussion as to the nature of womanhood was an ever-present feature of both working-class and middle-class society in this period. Debates over the character of woman's moral influence, over her potential for moral inspiration, over the tension between spiritual equality and social subordination, over the proper nature of woman's work, permeated political, religious and scientific discourses as well as the fields of literary and visual representation.

Radical circles provided no exception to this. Attempts by feminists such as Mary Wollstonecraft to open up questions of sexual difference and sexual equality in the 1790s had met with a barrage of hostility. But those women who wanted to question the primacy of women's status as wives and mothers, who wanted to argue for women to have rights for themselves, not only the right to improve men through their spiritual inspiration, but to be independent workers in the vineyards of Radical and socialist culture, were able to use and subvert the language of moral influence to make new claims for themselves as women. As Barbara Taylor has shown, the most sustained attempts to interpret political Radicalism as centrally to do with not only class politics but also gender politics, came from the Owenite feminists.[31] Owenism provided less stony ground than other varieties of Radicalism and socialism for the development of new forms of socialist feminism. Its commitment to love and cooperation as against competition and its critique of the relations of domination and subordination, whether between masters and men or men and women, meant that Owenite analysis potentially focused on all the social relations of capitalism, including the institutions of marriage and the family.

But the Owenite moment was a transitional political moment. Owenite men were not immune to the sexual antagonism fostered by new methods of production which aimed to marginalize skilled men and make use of the cheap labour of women and children. Even within the movement, Owenite feminists had to struggle to be heard and as Owenism declined in strength and Chartism increasingly occupied centre-stage within Radical culture, feminist voices were quietened. The institutions of Radical working-class culture, as we have seen, tended to centre on men and legitimate male belonging. The self-improvement clubs, the debating societies, the Hampden Clubs and the mutual education evenings were more accessible to men than to women. If the institutional framework positioned men as agents and women as supporters, what of the belief system?

Paineite Radicalism was central to the political discourses of working people at this time. With its stress on Radical egalitarianism, its rejection of the traditions of the past, its conviction that the future could be different, its belief in natural rights and the power of reason, its questioning of established institutions and its firm commitment to the view that government must represent the people, it gave a cutting thrust to Radical demands.[32] Mary Wollstonecraft was to build on that Radical egalitarianism and extend the demand for individual rights to women. In her new moral world women would be full subjects, able to participate as rational beings, no longer tied into the constraining bonds of a frivolous femininity. But her cause won few adherents, the countervailing forces were too strong and her ideal of woman's citizenship, while it survived in feminist thinking and debate, was lost in the more public discourses of Radicalism in the next fifty years.[33]

Paine's stress on individual rights and on the centrality of consent to representative forms of government drew on the classical tradition of Locke, which was itself built on the inalienable Puritan right to individual spiritual life. This tradition had attained considerable power in eighteenth-century England. But Locke's concept of the individual agent never extended beyond men. For him the origins of government lay in the consent of the propertied. The only people who were qualified to give consent were those propertied men who would take responsibility for their dependants, whether wives, children or servants. Political authority for Locke rested with men. Locke then further reinforced the differences between men and women by arguing that within the family men would inevitably carry greater authority than women. In line with the political break he represented with Filmer and conservative ideas of the divine and patriarchal nature of kingly authority, he insisted that marriage was a contractual relation to which both partners had to consent. To this extent Locke was arguing *for* individual rights for women. The husband was not seen as having any absolute sovereignty within the family. But Locke saw it as only to be expected that in every household someone would take command. Both parents had obligations to their children but the superior ability of the husband would give him the right to act as head and arbiter. This was a *natural* outcome. Locke thus distinguished between the 'natural' world of the family in which men would emerge as more powerful than women, and the political world of civil society in which men consented to forms of government.[34] This distinction between the two spheres, the family and civil society, with their different forms and rules, was played upon and developed by Enlightenment thinkers in the eighteenth century. As Jane Rendall has argued, writers across England, France and Scotland elaborated theories of sexual difference which built upon this primary distinction. They stressed that woman's nature was governed more by feeling than by reason, it was imaginative rather than analytic, and that women possessed distinctive moral characteristics which, in the right setting, could be fulfilled. Thus Rousseau combined his critique of the moral and sexual weakness of women with a belief that women could act as sources of moral inspiration and guidance, if they were allowed to blossom in their domestic worlds. The domestic sphere, Enlightenment thinkers argued, could provide a positive role for women but a role that was premissed on an assertion of difference from, rather than similarity to, men.[35]

Radical thinking was embedded in these assumptions about sexual difference. Mary Wollstonecraft herself argued for the rights of women as wives and mothers and thought that most women in the new world would put those duties first. For her, such a view was balanced with her belief that women should have the right to fulfilment for themselves. For others it was only too possible to combine a clear commitment to political Radicalism with a deep and entrenched social conservatism. William Cobbett, the writer and journalist whom E. P. Thompson sees as the most important intellectual influence on post-war Radicalism, was in the forefront of such tendencies. It was Cobbett who created the Radical culture of the 1820s, Thompson argues,

> not because he offered its most original ideas, but in the sense that he found the tone, the style, and the arguments which could bring the weaver, the schoolmaster, and the shipwright, into a common discourse. Out of the diversity of grievances and interests he brought a Radical consensus.[36]

But Cobbett's Radical consensus was one which placed women firmly in the domestic sphere. He came to be categorically in favour of home life and what he saw as established and well-tried household patterns. Wives should be chaste, sober, industrious, frugal, clean, good-tempered and beautiful, with a knowledge of domestic affairs and able to cook. The nation was made up of families, argued Cobbett, and it was essential that families should be happy and well managed, with enough food and decent wages. This was the proper basis of a good society. In writing *Cottage Economy*, Cobbett hoped to contribute to the revival of homely and domestic skills, which he saw as seriously threatened by the development of a wage economy. He offered precise instructions on the brewing of beer, not only because it could be made more cheaply at home, but also because a good home brew would encourage men to spend their evenings with their families rather than at the tavern. A woman who could not bake, Cobbett thought, was 'unworthy of trust and confidence . . . a mere burden upon the community'. He assured fathers that the way to construct a happy marriage for their daughters was to 'make them skilful, able and active in the most necessary concerns of a family'. Dimples and cherry cheeks were not enough; it was knowing how to brew, to bake, to make milk and butter that made a woman into 'a person worthy of respect'. What could please God more, asked Cobbett, than a picture of 'the labourer, after his return from the toils of a cold winter day, sitting with his wife and children round a cheerful fire, while the wind whistles in the chimney and the rain pelts the roof?'[37] Given that so much depended on it, men should take care to exercise their reason as well as their passion in their choice of a wife. Wives should run the household and forget the new-fangled 'accomplishments' of femininity, with which he had no patience. Men should honour and respect their wives and spend their time at home when not occupied away. Cobbett shared the commonly held view that women were more feeling than men and he saw that women had more to lose in marriage, for they gave up their property and their person to their husband. Husbands should consequently be kind to their wives, but there was no question that wives were subject to the authority of their husbands, that they must obey and must not presume to make decisions. Reason and God, thundered Cobbett, both decreed that wives should obey their husbands, there must be a head of every house, he said, echoing Locke, and he must have undivided authority. As the head of the household, men must represent their dependants and themselves enjoy the most salient right of all. There could be no rights, Cobbett believed, without that most central right – 'the right of taking a part in the making of the laws by which we are governed'. Without that, the right to enjoy life and property or to exert physical or mental powers meant nothing. Following directly in the tradition of Locke, Cobbett argued that the right to take part in the making of laws was founded in the state of nature. 'It springs', he argued,

> out of the very principle of civil society; for what compact, what agreement, what common assent, can possibly be imagined by which men would give up all the rights of nature, all the free enjoyment of their bodies and their minds, in order to subject themselves to rules and laws, in the making of which they should have nothing to say,

> and which should be enforced upon them without assent? The great right, therefore, of every man, the right of rights, is the right of having a share in the making of the laws, to which the good of the whole makes it his duty to submit.

Cobbett argued strongly, breaking entirely with Locke at this point, that *no* man should be excluded from this 'right of rights' unless he was insane or had committed an 'indelible crime'. He would have no truck with the view that it was property in the sense of landownership that conferred the right.

For Cobbett, it was those properties associated with 'honourable' labour and property in skill which gave men the right to vote. Minors he saw as automatically excluded from such privileges since the law classified them as infants. But the rights of women to share in the making of the laws, to give their assent to the abandonment of the right of nature and the free enjoyment of their bodies and their minds, he disposed of in one sentence. 'Women are excluded', he wrote, from the right of rights because, 'husbands are answerable in law for their wives, as to their civil damages, and because the very nature of their sex makes the exercise of this right incompatible with the harmony and happiness of society'. There was no escape from this. Single women who wanted to argue that they were legal individuals with civil rights were caught, when it came to political rights, by their *nature*. Women could only become persons 'worthy of respect' through their household skills. Society could only be harmonious and happy if they behaved as wives and daughters, subject to the better judgements of their fathers. By nature the female sex were unsuited to the public sphere.[38]

The positioning of women as wives, mothers and daughters within Radical culture at the same time that men were positioned as active and independent agents was in part connected to similar processes within middle-class culture. The period from the 1790s to the 1830s also saw the emergence of the English middle class, with its own beliefs and practices, its own sense of itself as a class, with interests different from those of other classes. The middle class defined itself in part through certain critical public moments: the affair of Queen Caroline, the events of 1832 and the repeal of the Corn Laws in 1846, but it also defined itself through the establishment of new cultural patterns and new institutional forms. Central to its culture was a marked emphasis on the separation between male and female spheres. Men were to be active in the public world of business and politics. Women were to be gentle and dependent in the private world of the home and family. The two most powerful cultural and intellectual influences on middle-class formation were serious Christianity and political economy. Both, in their own ways, emphasized the different interests of men and women and articulated the discourses of separate spheres.[39]

Middle-class men from the late eighteenth century were striving to establish their power and influence in the provinces, long before they achieved full national recognition. They sought to make their voices heard in both town and countryside, to influence Parliament on matters that concerned them, to intervene in different forms of local government, to establish and maintain religious and cultural institutions, to exercise their charity and to build new mercantile, financial and commercial associations. In every field of interest they were active and energetic, fulfilling the precept that 'a man must act'. Their initiatives were multiple, their fields of enterprise boundless. Assumptions about sexual difference permeated all their schemes. Their political committees excluded women, their churches demarcated male and female spheres, their Botanical Gardens assumed that men would join on behalf of their families, their philanthropic societies treated men and women differently, their business associations were for men only. In defining their own cultural patterns and practices, the men and women of the middle class had a significant impact on working-class culture. The middle class was fighting for political and cultural pre-eminence. In rejecting aristocratic values and the old forms of patronage and influence they sought to define new values, to establish new modes of power. In the process they were both defining themselves as a class and asserting dominance. In many areas, particularly in new industrial towns where aristocratic interest was not well entrenched, they were able to occupy the field, to be the providers of education and philanthropy, to establish whole new ranges of institutions which bore their imprint.

In Birmingham, for example, large numbers of schools, Sunday schools and charitable ventures were established in the late eighteenth and early nineteenth centuries, which all operated with middle-class notions of what were properly male and female. In recommending domestic values to Sunday school pupils, charity school girls or aged and infirm women, middle-class women at one and the same time defined their own 'relative sphere' and their sense of the proper place of working-class women. That proper place was either as servants in the homes of their betters, or as respectable and modest wives and mothers in their own homes. The Birmingham Society for Aged and Infirm Women sought money on behalf of 'those who have discharged the relative duties of a wife and mother' and were left, perhaps deserted, in their old age.

The organizers paid the strictest attention to establishing whether the women really deserved such assistance, whether their lives had been humble and respectable.[40] Schools taught boys and girls separately, often in different buildings and with emphasis on different achievements.[41] Self-improvement societies and debating societies, such as the Birmingham Brotherly Society, were for men only.[42] The new Mechanics' Institute was exclusively male and aimed to train men to become better husbands, servants and fathers. As the first report of the Birmingham Institute stressed, a man's whole family would benefit from his involvement with such an establishment. He himself would become more 'sober, intelligent and tranquil', they claimed,

> his presence at home will diffuse pleasure and tranquillity throughout his household. His own improvement will be reflected in the improved condition of his family. Perceiving the benefit of a judicious economy, he will still be able to command a larger expenditure in the education of his children, and in the accessories of rational enjoyment. Cheerfulness, cleanliness, and the smile of welcome will constantly await his approach to his domestic fireside. Beloved at home and respected abroad, it will not be too much to assert, that he will become a better servant, husband and father; a higher moral character; and consequently a happier man, from his connection with the MECHANICS INSTITUTE.[43]

These were grandiose claims indeed! Not surprisingly, working-class men and women were not miraculously transformed into respectable and sober men, domestic and home-loving women, by the action of institutions inspired by the middle class. But as many historians have demonstrated, nor did they simply refuse the values of this dominant culture. As R. Q. Gray has shown in his perceptive study of the aristocracy of labour in Edinburgh, a process of negotiating took place between dominant and subordinate, negotiation that resulted in the emergence of distinctive concepts of dignity and respectability, influenced by middle-class values yet holding to a belief in trade union action, for example, and a strong sense of class pride.[44] Similarly David Vincent, in his study of the meaning of 'useful knowledge' to working-class autobiographers, has demonstrated the independence from middle-class meanings of the term and the creation of a separate and class-specific concept.[45] The same story could be told in relation to male and female spheres. Working-class men and women did not adopt wholesale the middle-class view of a proper way of life. But aspects of both religious and secular discourses on masculinity, femininity and domestic life did have resonance in some sections of the working class, did make sense of some experience and appeal to some needs.

Take the case of temperance. Temperance, it has been argued, provides a prime example of the successful assertion of middle-class hegemony.[46] Working men became volunteers in the cause of middle-class respectability. They aimed to improve themselves, to educate themselves, to raise themselves to their betters. The initiative for the total abstinence movement had come from class-conscious working men and there were many connections between them and the Chartist movement but the Radical belief in individual improvement was extremely vulnerable to assimilation into the cultural patterns of the middle class. Arguments against drink made heavy use of an appeal to home and family, for one of the major evils associated with alcohol was its propensity to ruin working-class families and reduce them to depravity. In the famous series of Cruikshank plates entitled *The Bottle*, for example, the first image was of a respectable and modest working-class family enjoying a meal in their simple but clean and comfortable home. They represented the model happy family with clothes carefully mended, a family portrait, the young children playing, a fire burning cosily in the grate and a lock on the door ensuring that the home would remain a place of refuge and security. Then the man offered his wife a drink and in scene after scene Cruikshank documented the horrifying destruction of the home and family, ending up with the husband insane, having murdered his wife with a bottle, the youngest child dead and the other two a pimp and a prostitute.[47] It was a cliché of temperance lecturers to rely on the comparison between the unhappy home of the drunkard and the contented domestic idyll of the temperate worker. As a reformed drinker poetically declared:

> I protest that no more I'll get drunk –
> For I find it the bane of my life!
> Henceforth I'll be watchful that nought shall destroy
> That comfort and peace that I ought to enjoy
> In my children, my home and my wife.[48]

Such protestations did not simply imply the acceptance of middle-class ideals of domesticity for working men, and women developed their own notions of manliness and femininity which, while affected by dominant conceptions, nevertheless had inflections of their own. As John Smith, a Birmingham temperance enthusiast argued,

> The happiness of the fireside is involved in the question of temperance, and we know that the chief ornament of that abode of happiness is woman. Most of the comforts of life depend upon our female relatives and friends, whether in infancy, in mature years, or old age . . .[49]

Here he touched on a vital nerve, for the comforts of life for the working man did indeed depend on female relatives. But those female relatives needed different skills from their middle-class sisters. While middle-class ideologues stressed the moral and managerial aspects of womanhood, for wives were to provide moral inspiration and manage the running of their households, working-class blueprints for the good wife and mother emphasized the practical skills associated with household management, cooking, cleaning and bringing up children. For the wife to manage the family finances seems to have been a very widespread pattern in both town and countryside, a distinctive difference from their middle-class counterparts with their exclusion from money matters. The working man was to earn, the working woman to spend, using her hard-won knowledge of domestic needs and the relative merits of available goods, to eke out what money was coming in.[50]

This evaluation of woman's domestic role coincided with the emergence of working women as a publicly defined 'social problem'. As Sally Alexander has argued, the period of the 1830s and 1840s saw the confirmation of men as responsible political subjects while women were largely condemned to public silence.[51] An important aspect of this was the emergence of the idea of the 'family wage', a wage which a male breadwinner would earn, sufficient to support his wife and children.[52] Such an ideal of male support and female dependence was already firmly established within middle-class culture but was to become embedded in working-class practice as well through, for example, the bargaining procedures of skilled trade unions.[53] Again, this did not involve the straightforward acceptance of middle-class standards but rather an adaptation and reshaping of class-specific notions.

In the early 1840s, to take one case, middle-class fears and anxieties about the employment of women in unsuitable work reached a pitch over the issue of women's work in the mines. The commissioners appointed to inquire into the incidence of child labour underground were shocked and horrified at the evidence that emerged of female conditions of work. Bourgeois views of femininity were violently assaulted by the spectacle of women in various stages of undress working alongside men. The affront to public morality and the fears generated as to the imminent collapse of the working-class family and consequently working-class morality, led to the campaign, spearheaded by the Evangelicals, for the exclusion of women from underground work. The Mines and Collieries Act 1842, which excluded women from underground work, marked one attempt by the state, together with other interventions such as the bastardy clause of the New Poor Law, to regulate the form of the working-class family and to legislate a moral code. Many working miners supported the ban on women's work but their reasons were different from those of the middle-class campaigners. As Angela John has shown, they did not accept the judgement of commissioners such as Tremenheere that female exclusion was 'the first step towards raising the standard of domestic habits and the securing of a respectable home'. They resented middle-class interlopers who told them how to live their lives and organize their families. They emphasized working-class control over their own culture. They argued for better lives for their wives and daughters and insisted that if the wives of the owners could stay at home, then so should theirs. They stressed that their wives were entitled to a decent life above ground and attacked those coal-owners, such as the Duke of Hamilton, who continued to employ women illegally.

But the miners had another powerful motive for supporting exclusion. The Miners' Association of Great Britain and Ireland was formed in 1842, three days before the date designated for the exclusion of females under eighteen. As clearly stated in the *Miners Advocate*, the union was firmly against female employment from the start. They sought to control the hours of labour and obtain the highest possible wages. For women to work was seen as a direct threat to this enterprise, for women's work kept down wages. For their own reasons men in the mines preferred, as an ideal, to be able to support their women at home.[54] The women, unable to speak publicly for themselves, were lost. They hated the conditions of work but they needed the money; however, their voices were not heard and in one of the major public debates of the 1840s, blazoned across the press, men were legitimated as workers, women as wives and mothers, by the state, by middle-class philanthropists, and by working men.

Samuel and Jemima went together to Peterloo. They shared the excitement, they shared the horror and the fear. But they experienced it differently on account of their sex. Men and women did not occupy the culture of their class in the same way. Ideologically their differences were emphasized, institutionally they were often segregated. The complexities of the relation between class and culture have received much attention. It is time for gender and culture to be subjected to more critical scrutiny.

NOTES

1 Samuel Bamford, *Passages in the Life of a Radical* (Oxford University Press, London, 1984). The account of Peterloo is on pp. 141–56. Subsequently only direct quotes are footnoted.
2 Bamford, *Passages*, pp. 132–3.
3 Bamford, *Passages*, pp. 146–7.
4 Bamford, *Passages*, pp. 151.
5 Bamford, *Passages*, pp. 161, 150.
6 Bamford, *Passages*, p. 156.
7 E. P. Thompson, *The Making of the English Working Class* (Gollancz, London, 1963).
8 Thompson, *The Making*, p. 9.
9 Thompson, *The Making*, p. 12. Sheila Rowbotham, *Hidden from History. 300 years of Women's Oppression and the Fight Against It* (Pluto, London, 1973). For Sheila Rowbotham's own account of the development of her fascination with history, see 'Search and Subject, Threading Circumstance', in Rowbotham, *Dreams and Dilemmas* (Virago, London, 1983).
10 Barbara Taylor, *Eve and the New Jerusalem. Socialism and Feminism in the Nineteenth Century* (Virago, London, 1983), ch. 4.
11 Bamford, *Passages*, p. 161.
12 On the eighteenth-century crowd, see Edward P. Thompson, 'The Moral Economy of the English Crowd in the Eighteenth Century', *Past and Present*, no. 50, February 1971. See also E. P. Thompson, 'Patrician Society, Plebeian Culture', *Journal of Social History*, vol. 7, no. 4, 1974.
13 For discussions of the family economy, see, for example, Maxine Berg, *The Age of Manufactures 1700–1820* (Blackwell, Oxford, 1985); Louise Tilly and Joan Scott, *Women, Work and Family* (Holt, Rinehart & Winston, New York, 1978).
14 John Gillis, *For Better For Worse. British Marriages 1600 to the present* (Oxford University Press, London, 1985), p. 229.

15 For an attempt to do this in relation to the middle class in the early nineteenth century, see Leonore Davidoff and Catherine Hall, *Family Fortunes: Men and Women of the English Middle Class 1780–1850* (Hutchinson and Chicago University Press, London and Chicago, 1987).

16 The literature on class in the early nineteenth century is extensive. See, for example, Harold Perkin, *The Origins of Modern English Society 1780–1880* (Routledge, London, 1969); Robert J. Morris, *Class and Class Consciousness in the Industrial Revolution* (Macmillan, London, 1979); Asa Briggs, 'The language of "class" in early nineteenth century England', in Asa Briggs and John Saville (eds), *Essays in Labour History* (Macmillan, London, 1960); John Foster, *Class Struggle and the Industrial Revolution: Early Capitalism in Three English Towns* (Methuen, London, 1974); Gareth Stedman Jones, *Languages of Class. Studies in English Working Class History 1832–1982* (Cambridge University Press, Cambridge, 1983).

17 Thomas Hardy, *Memoir of Thomas Hardy . . . Written by Himself* (London, 1832), p. 16.

18 Bamford, *Passages*, p. 123.

19 Bamford, *Passages*, p. 121.

20 Bamford, *Passages*, pp. 110, 61.

21 Bamford, *Passages*, p. 115.

22 Thompson, *The Making*, particularly ch. 16.

23 Thompson, *The Making*, p. 610.

24 Bamford, *Passages*, p. 14.

25 Thomas W. Laqueur, 'Literacy and Social Mobility in the Industrial Revolution in England', *Past and Present*, no. 64, August 1974.

26 David Vincent, *Bread, Knowledge and Freedom: A Study of Nineteenth Century Working-Class Autobiography* (Methuen, London, 1981).

27 Dorothy Thompson, 'Women and Nineteenth-Century Radical Politics: A Lost Dimension', in Juliet Mitchell and Ann Oakley (eds), *The Rights and Wrongs of Women* (Penguin, Harmondsworth, 1976).

28 For a delightful example of such constitutional practice, see Thompson, *The Making*, pp. 738–9.

29 *Birmingham Journal*, 5 January 1839, 12 January 1839, 2 February 1839.

30 On women's militancy and engagement with radical politics, see Ida Beatrice O'Malley, *Women in Subjection: a study of the lives of English-women before 1832* (Duckworth, London, 1933); Taylor, *Eve and the New Jerusalem*; Malcolm I. Thomis and Jennifer Grimmett, *Women in Protest: 1800–1850* (Macmillan, London, 1982); D. Jones, 'Women and Chartism', *History*, no. 68, February 1983. There is an excellent introduction to the literature in Jane Rendall, *The Origins of Modern Feminism: Women in Britain, France and the United States 1780–1860* (Macmillan, London, 1985).

31 Taylor, *Eve and the New Jerusalem.*
32 Thomas Paine, *The Rights of Man* (Penguin, Harmondsworth, 1963). The best discussion of Paine in the context of English Radicalism is in Thompson, *The Making.*
33 Mary Wollstonecraft, *Vindication of the Rights of Woman* (Penguin, Harmondsworth, 1982). There is a voluminous literature on Wollstonecraft. For a particularly interesting analysis, see Mary Poovey, *The Proper Lady and the Woman Writer. Ideology as style in the works of Mary Wollstonecraft, Mary Shelley and Jane Austen* (Chicago University Press, Chicago, 1984).
34 John Locke, *Two Treatises of Government,* (ed.) Peter Laslett (Cambridge University Press, Cambridge, 1960); Gordon Schochet, *Patriarchalism in Political Thought. The Authoritarian Family and Political Speculation and Attitudes, especially in Seventeenth-Century England* (Oxford University Press, London, 1975); Susan Moller Okin, *Women in Western Political Thought* (Blackwell, Oxford, 1975); R. W. Krouse, 'Patriarchal Liberalism and Beyond: from John Stuart Mill to Harriet Taylor', in Jean Bethke Elshtain (ed.), *The Family in Political Thought* (Harvester, Brighton, 1982); Elizabeth Fox-Genovese, 'Property and Patriarchy in Classical Bourgeois Political Theory', *Radical History Review,* vol. 4, nos. 2–3, 1977.
35 Rendall, *The Origins,* ch. 2.
36 Thompson, *The Making,* p. 746.
37 William Cobbett, *Cottage Economy* (C. Clement, London, 1822), pp. 60, 62, 63, 199.
38 William Cobbett, *Advice to Young Men, and Incidentally to Young Women in the Middle and Higher Ranks of Life* (Oxford University Press, London, 1980). See particularly chs 4 and 6. For a discussion of the importance of 'honourable' labour and 'property in skill' to working men's claims for manhood, see Sally Alexander, 'Women, Class and Sexual Differences in the 1830s and 1840s; Some reflections on the writing of a feminist history', *History Workshop Journal,* no. 17, Spring 1984. On independence and self-respect, see Tyrgve Tholfsen, *Working-class Radicalism in Mid-Victorian England* (Columbia University Press, New York, 1976).
39 Davidoff and Hall, *Family Fortunes.*
40 *Aris's Birmingham Gazette,* 17 January 1831, 21 January 1831.
41 For example, the Sunday schools of the Anglican Christ Church in Birmingham. John George Breay, *The Faithful Pastor Delineated* (Beilby, Birmingham, 1839).
42 Birmingham Brotherly Society, Minutes of the Meetings, Birmingham Reference Library, Mss. no. 391175.
43 Birmingham Mechanics' Institute, *Address of the Provisional Committee* (W. Hawkes Smith, Birmingham, 1825).
44 Robert Q. Gray, *The Labour Aristocracy in Victorian Edinburgh* (Oxford University Press, London, 1976). Gray's study deals with the

later nineteenth century. See, also, Tholfsen's discussion of middle-class hegemony in *Working Class Radicalism*; Thomas W. Lacqueur's argument in *Religion and Respectability: Sunday Schools and Working Class Culture 1780–1850* (Yale University Press, New Haven, 1976) that working-class people subverted middle-class intentions and made Sunday schools into institutions of their own culture. For two sensitive accounts of the class-specific mediations which occur in cultural practice, see Robert Colls, *The Collier's Rant. Song and Culture in the Industrial Village* (Croom Helm, London, 1977); and Marina Vitale, 'The Domesticated Heroine in Byron's Corsair and William Hone's Prose Adaptation', *Literature and History*, vol. 10, no. 1, 1984.

45 Vincent, *Bread, Knowledge and Freedom*, especially ch. 7.

46 Tholfsen, *Working Class Radicalism*, especially ch. 7.

47 There is a fascinating discussion of Cruikshank in Louis James, 'Cruikshank and Early Victorian Caricature', *History Workshop Journal*, no. 6, Autumn 1978.

48 A selection of tracts and handbills published in aid of the Temperance Reformation, Birmingham, 1839.

49 John Smith, *Speech at the Birmingham Temperance Meeting* (Birmingham, 1835).

50 Keith D. M. Snell, *Annals of the Labouring Poor. Social Change and Agrarian England* (Cambridge University Press, Cambridge, 1985), especially ch. 7; David Vincent, 'Love and Death and the Nineteenth-Century Working Class', *Social History*, vol. 5, no. 2, May 1980.

51 Alexander, 'Women, Class and Sexual Differences'.

52 For the best introduction to the literature on the family wage, see Hilary Land, 'The Family Wage', *Feminist Review*, no. 6, 1980.

53 For a discussion of sex and its relation to skill, see Anne Phillips and Barbara Taylor, 'Sex and Skill: Notes towards a Feminist Economcis', *Feminist Review*, no. 6, 1980. For the development of a particular union and its restrictive practices, see Jill Liddington and Jill Norris, *'One Hand Tied Behind Us'. The Rise of the Women's Suffrage Movement* (Virago, London, 1978).

54 Angela John, *By the Sweat of Their Brow: Women Workers at Victorian Coal Mines* (Croom Helm, London, 1980); and 'Colliery Legislation and its Consequences: 1842 and the Women Miners of Lancashire', *Bulletin of the John Rylands University Library of Manchester*, vol. 61, no. 1, 1978. Tremenheere, quoted p. 90.

7 Private Persons versus Public Someones: class, gender and politics in England, 1780–1850

In 1810, Martha Syms, the daughter of an Evangelical clergyman, was writing to her father from India, where she was living with her husband who was in the Indian army. 'Syms desires me to present to you his best regards,' she wrote, continuing, 'and to add that he perfectly coincides with you in the political opinion contained in your last letter, I do not understand and therefore do not enter into these subjects myself . . . '[1] Martha's assumption, that she did not understand political matters and would not risk expressing a political opinion, was one that was shared by many middle-class women in the early nineteenth century. But the process whereby that assumption came to be shared is one that is worth examining. Dorothy Thompson has explored the ways in which working-class women became marginalized in Radical politics in the 1830s and 1840s and has demonstrated the extent to which that marginalization was associated with the increasing formalization of working-class politics.[2] Barbara Taylor has analysed the problems involved with developing a socialist feminist politics in the 1820s and 1830s and the decline of that politics as industrial capitalism established a more stable base and ideologies about masculinity and femininity became more rigidly defined.[3] But both these case studies deal with the experience of working-class women in relation to politics and as yet the experience of middle-class women has been relatively neglected. The entry of middle-class women into politics has tended to be constructed in terms of their entry into organized feminist movements in the mid-nineteenth century, with an assumption that between Mary Wollstonecraft and early Victorian forms of feminism, little happened other than a few hiccups on the Radical sidelines. It would be possible to construct this period rather differently and to see it as one in which a whole set of ideologies and social practices developed which saw middle-class women as essentially non-political beings, belonging to the private rather than the public sphere, having at most a supportive role to play in the rapidly expanding political world of their fathers, husbands and brothers. The ways in which such definitions were built into political institutions and related social practices ensured that the barriers against women thinking or acting politically were very extensive.

At one level the exclusion of middle-class women from the public world of politics is hardly surprising. After all, women never had been very involved in the political sphere. But neither had middle-class men. Their active involvement in the political process was a development largely associated with the late eighteenth and early nineteenth centuries. It was also an involvement of their own making, fought for and insisted upon in a society which had traditionally only legitimated the rights of the landed to be directly represented. After 1832 that legitimation was extended to all those men with sufficient property to ensure that their voices should be heard. It was in 1832 that for the first time the prefix 'male' was inserted into the act defining the right to a vote, thus making crystal clear something which had always been assumed previously, that in naming the propertied as those with the vote it was men of property who were being demarcated, not women. This process, of defining middle-class men as within the political arena and middle-class women as outside of it, did not simply happen by default. It is undoubtedly true that had a demand been made for the inclusion of women it would have been even more surprising, and certainly very much harder to achieve, than the demand on behalf of men. But many precedents were broken and assumptions challenged in the struggle by manufacturers, merchants, professional men and farmers to win the vote for themselves. The process whereby women were marginalized from that struggle needs explaining and documenting, rather than being assumed.

The late eighteenth and early nineteenth centuries marked a period of transition in English society when traditional values and beliefs were subjected to attack and criticism. Established social hierarchies were breaking down and common-sense notions being turned upside down. It was in this context that middle-class men articulated their new demand for representation. This was a demand which did not grow naturally by a process of evolution, but rather was forged out of the recognition that political influence was a necessary concomitant to their economic power. In the same way, there was nothing 'natural' about the process whereby women were not included in that demand. Certainly it coincided with custom. But middle-class men were busy challenging custom in other arenas. Customary patterns about gender divisions were reworked in this period of transition. It was in that reworking that men were firmly placed in the newly defined public world of business, commerce and politics; women were placed in the private world of home and family.

Wherever public power has been separated from private power, women have tended to be excluded from that public power.[4] As Rosaldo and Lamphere show in their anthropological work, those societies in which men and women inhabit the same domain tend to exhibit more egalitarian patterns of power and authority.[5] Historically the same patterns can be illustrated. In Roman society, for example, where there was a clear concept of public power, women were expressly excluded from it. In Carolingian times, however, there was scarcely any distinction between public and private power and consequently few restrictions on the power of women in any spheres of activity. It was landed families which were central to the exercise of power, rather than the state. Sons and daughters were able to share inheritance and some women were able to exercise considerable power. As the machinery of government was gradually developed and some control wrested from the aristocracy, so the influence of women declined. It was difficult for them to become part of the new state bureaucracies in the way men did.[6]

The early nineteenth century marked a point when the division between public and private became very highly demarcated. The notion of the division between public and private was an old-established one but it always has to be understood as historically specific and socially constructed.[7] In classical Greece, for example, the public or *polis* was seen as purely political; it was separated from both production and reproduction. Both production and reproduction were centred on the household, but political life was carried on by a small number of adult male citizens who depended on women and slaves to provide for their social and economic needs. The Greek household, with its many functions, was seen as the private sphere. Such a narrow definition of the public would have been mysterious to Victorian men and women who understood the public as including the world of business and commerce, the market, and the world of politics. The private, on the other hand, was the haven from the anxieties of the market, and was constituted around the home and family. This notion of public and private was itself significantly reworked from the late eighteenth century. Adam Smith, for example, conceptualized the market, governed as it was by freely made contracts, as part of the private, different from those public elements in life which were governed by the state.[8]

This reformulation of the public and the private was to do with making sense of a world which was changing very rapidly and in which pre-existing definitions and boundaries no longer fitted very well. Central to this was the development of the market and of wage labour and the subsequent decline of paternalism in its eighteenth-century form. The social relations of industrial capitalism were not easily contained within a pre-industrial mode of thought. Not surprisingly, however, the traditions of classical liberal theory remained very important in the struggle to establish new values and beliefs. The work of Hobbes and Locke, resting squarely as it did on the notion of theoretical individualism, at least in the public sphere, had marked the initial course. They were both concerned to critique and undermine the case made by Filmer for the divine right of kings – which rested on a notion of patriarchal power as natural and given by God. The line of command for Filmer passed from God to the king and then to the father in the household. He insisted on an analogy between kingly civil authority and husbandly familial power. There was no split between the public and the private – the family was politicized and the state familiarized. Hobbes and Locke both rejected familial authority as the paradigm for political authority and rejected divine sanction in favour of rationality.[9]

Locke saw the development of rationality as going together with a split between public and private. Reason was for him separate from passion. Reason existed in the public world, where individuals were free and equal and made contracts. Passion or desire survived in the private world, a world in which contracts and rationality had no place. In arguing against Filmer's case for patriarchy, Locke had presented women almost as men's equals for he claimed that both male and female parents had power over children. He claimed that the fifth commandment called for the child to honour his father and his mother and that the father should do nothing to discourage respect for the mother. But although he used parental equality to combat absolutism in the political realm he concluded elsewhere that there was a natural foundation to the customary and legal subjection of wives to their husbands. He assumed that fathers would represent the interests of their families in the wider society. For both Hobbes and Locke the fundamental subject matter of political philosophy was not the adult human individual but the male-headed family.

Locke's argument that women, by consenting to marriage, gave up their civil rights to their male protectors was mirrored by Rousseau's views on the distinctiveness of male and female characteristics.[10] And Rousseau was another powerful influence on late-eighteenth- and early-nineteenth-century thinking. Rousseau understood women as being defined by their natural procreative functions. He categorized man in terms of his limitless potential for rationality and for abstract thought. Women were seen as physical and sensual, deficient in rationality and incapable of rational thought. The nuclear family and patriarchy were both seen by Rousseau as natural. The sexes were complementary and man was free to become whatever he could or would whilst women were defined in terms of their capacity to bear children. Men were to do whilst women were to be, as Charlotte Brontë put it.[11] Rousseau had no notion of citizenship for women; their influence should be exercised through their husbands.

The assumption that women should be represented politically by their husbands or fathers, whether it descended from the classical English philosophical tradition or through the French, continued to govern thinking about the political position of women in the late eighteenth and early nineteenth centuries. Fox, the great Radical, when asked why it was that women should not have the vote, replied that nature and convention had made women dependent on men and, therefore, 'their voices would be governed by the relations in which they stand to society'.[12] This view, enunciated in 1797, was little different from that of Hannah More, whose conservative thinking was central to the emergence of Evangelicalism in the 1780s and 1790s as a powerful social and political force.[13] It was reiterated in 1824 by James Mill in his *Essay on Government:*

> One thing is pretty clear, that all those individuals whose interests are indisputably included in those of other individuals, may be struck off without inconvenience. In this light may be viewed all children up to a certain age, whose interests are involved in those of

> their parents. In this light also, women may be regarded, the interest of almost all of whom is involved either in that of their fathers or in that of their husbands.[14]

Mill's formulation caused considerable offence at the time but the position he enunciated was widely accepted. As the *Edinburgh Review* was to put it, women should be represented politically *in* their families.[15] The common-sensical character of the view that women should be represented by men is even reflected in Harriet Martineau's novel *Deerbrook* where the two sisters Hester and Margaret accept unquestioningly the political wisdom and principles of Hester's husband Edward, who by voting against the interests of the landlord in a county election finds himself ostracized and his practice as a doctor almost destroyed. They are proud to see Edward representing their principles for them.[16] As Harriet Martineau herself commented, 'I want to be doing something with the pen, since no other means of action in politics are in a woman's power.'[17] Such a view coexisted comfortably with the definition of women as exercising power through a beneficial moral influence over men – a view which was again held by both conservative and feminist thinkers. Hannah More, Mary Wollstonecraft and Harriet Martineau could all have agreed on the central importance of women's influence.

The issue of the vote for women was not a central political issue in this period; indeed it hardly surfaced until mid-century when the suffrage societies began to be organized. One explanation for the lateness of the emergence of this issue lies in the existing assumptions which have been mapped out here. Another important explanation, however, focuses on the activities of middle-class men and the ways in which they moved towards the struggle for the vote. Merchants, professionals and the 'middling sort' had, in the late seventeenth and the eighteenth centuries, tended to rely on influence and pressure on their MPs to get their views represented in Parliament. The City of London had its own representatives, as did the established boroughs. But in the rapidly expanding industrial provincial towns such as Birmingham, Manchester and Sheffield the commercial interests had to rely on the county members to make their voice heard. As the 'middling sort' became increasingly important, and as the old-established client economy gradually began to break down in the face of the broadening of the market and the growth of liquid forms of capital, so these commercial men began to seek more independence from the patronage and power of the aristocracy. 'Traders and merchants saw independence not as freedom conferred by landed property but as . . . freedom from the economic political control of the patricians', as John Brewer has put it.[18] Joseph Priestley, the Unitarian scientist and theologian, was one of the most influential voices articulating the new demands of the 'middling sort'. 'A sense of political and civil liberty', he wrote,

> though there should be no great occasion to exert it in the course of a man's life, gives him a constant feeling of his own power and importance, and is the foundation of his indulging a free, bold and manly turn of thinking, unrestrained by the most distant idea of control.[19]

The connections made here between political rights, power, control and manliness were to become part of the rhetoric of middle-class men's politics in the early nineteenth century.

The 'middling sort', who probably constituted roughly one-seventh of the English population, began during the eighteenth century to separate themselves both socially and politically from those above them and those below them. Crucial to this process of the establishment of an independent social and political identity were the clubs. There were clubs of every kind, from masonic lodges to clubs for drinking, for singing or for organizing the raising of capital. The economic and social functions of such clubs were always closely intermixed, since in a period before the development of a commercial and financial infrastructure arrangements for credit and other forms of economic support relied on family first, but second on friends. The existence of such clubs and voluntary societies gave their members a sense of collective identity such as they had not previously enjoyed. The power of this collective sense was well illustrated by the support for Wilkes, which relied heavily for its orchestration on the clubs. In less troubled times many of the societies 'boasted of the way in which they united Anglicans and dissenters, men from different trades, merchants and gentlemen, whigs and tories, in a common association, promoting unanimity and harmony where only conflict had previously existed.'[20] The atmosphere of these clubs is well evoked by a painting of 'Freeth's Circle', a group of Birmingham men who met regularly in the pub run by Freeth for a pint, a pipe and a chat. The twelve men are represented as sitting around the table with their drinks and tobacco, ready for any discussion. Such convivial evenings were characterized by being exclusively male; these were not the kinds of occasions at which women were welcome. James Bisset, a Birmingham japanner and member of Freeth's circle, recalled in his memoirs his membership of a whole range of groups of this kind:

> [We] used often to meet at 'The Poet Freeth's, as also at Joe Warden's and at 'The Fountains', where I very frequently attended, but my general evenings were spent at 'The Union', 'Shakespeare', or 'Hen and Chickens Tavern', then kept by Mrs Lloyd. I was president for many years of a debating society, and president also of Saint Andrew's Club, and in the Masonic Order, I was Provincial Grand Master for the County of Warwick.[21]

Bisset loved convivial evenings of this kind and being of a cheerful disposition, and always good for a song, he was greatly in demand. It was only in retrospect that he was sorry for leaving his wife alone so many evenings, after she put the children to bed, whilst he enjoyed himself with his friends. In later life he decided to give up this social round and devote himself more to the pleasures of domestic life, and this decision reflected a growing interest in domesticity amongst men of his class.

The fact that the location of so many of these clubs was in the tavern clarifies one reason for women's exclusion from them. Pubs were increasingly being defined as inappropriate settings for women who wished to maintain their gentility in the late eighteenth and early nineteenth centuries. At one time they had provided an easy and informal social space for both men and women.[22] But the attack on drinking habits associated with the rise of temperance, together with the general attempt which was spearheaded by the Evangelicals in the late eighteenth century to improve the manners and morals of the nation in an attempt to raise the moral tone of English society and fend off a social upheaval such as that which had afflicted France, made the pub increasingly a place where respectable women should probably not be seen, except perhaps behind the bar. But the pub remained vital to middle-class men, a central meeting place, though sometimes it was transformed into the more genteel 'hotel'. Eliezer Edwards, in his recollections of Birmingham in the early nineteenth century, stressed the importance of tavern life: 'As in the West End of London, every man has his club, so in Birmingham, about the commencement of the present century, almost every man had his tavern, where he regularly spent a portion of each day.'[23] The tavern was 'the exchange and news-room of the period'. Often the taverns were divided into separate rooms, with facilities for different classes. 'Commercial rooms', 'smoking rooms' and 'snuggeries' abounded, with the landlady often making herself responsible for preventing any breach of decorum.

'The Union', another Birmingham hostelry, had two special rooms for their most favoured clubs.[24] One was for the Bucks Society, or 'The Order of Bucks', which was devoted to the promotion of 'good fellowship, freedom of conversation and innocent mirth',[25] the other was for the Staffordshire Ironmasters who had been meeting regularly since the late eighteenth century to defend their interests and promote their trade.[26] Initially the ironmasters at their quarterly meetings had dealt with questions about prices and conditions of sale but very soon became involved with political issues too. Samuel Garbett, a prominent Birmingham ironmaster, having failed to persuade Burke 'to take the lead in considering our commerce as a subject of politics', decided that he would have to lead the way himself and played a significant part in the opposition to Pitt's excise scheme in 1784.[27] The iron trade was not an arena in which women could easily engage and the ironmasters' meetings were certainly no place for women. Richard Reynolds, a Quaker ironmaster, thought of the quarterly meetings as 'times of peculiar trial' and warned his son about the temptations he would encounter there. 'I will not say', he wrote,

> that the consideration of the dangers to which I was about to be exposed, and the desire that sometimes accompanied it for preservation from them, was always attended with that degree of watchfulness and circumspection which would have ensured the plaudits of my own conscience after it was over. For though I may say, with humble thankfulness, I hope my conduct did not bring any reproach on my religious profession . . . yet, when I reflected upon the levity of the conversation (to speak of it in the mildest terms) and how far I had contributed to it, or at least, countenanced it by sitting longer among them than was absolutely necessary, it has brought sorrow and condemnation on my part.[28]

The ironmasters' meetings were clearly times of excess and intemperance and by the early nineteenth century these meetings were taking place weekly at 'The Union' with a grand dinner after the main part of the business was concluded. 'Money was easily made, and freely spent in those days', recollected Edwards, and the share of the dinner bill 'was often a heavy sum, such as even such potentates as ironmasters would not care for their wives to know of'.[29]

Groups such as the Staffordshire Ironmasters, which started off with a commercial rationale but gradually became involved in more directly political matters as these impinged on their business, were responsible for much of the political education of men of the 'middling sort'. It was an education which women were excluded from. It was sufficient for family businesses to be represented by their male head at such gatherings, even when wives and daughters were actively involved in the running of the enterprise. When large public meetings were held the patterns of male conviviality tended to be maintained, with drinking and toasts. The General Chamber of Manufacturers, the first nationally organized expression of manufacturing opinion, was established in this sort of context. It relied on the activities of a group of men who were both friends and business associates. Its immediate trigger was the threatened lowering of the tariffs between Britain and Ireland but, as its founding document pointed out, it was high time that the manufacturers as a group should have their interests represented. 'It seems hitherto to have escaped the notice of the manufacturers', proclaimed their manifesto:

> That whilst the *landed* and the *funded interests*, the *East India* and other *commercial bodies*, have their respective advocates in the great council of the nation, *they* alone are destitute of that advantage; and it is probable from this source that many of their grievances have arisen – that they have repeatedly and perhaps inadvertently been oppressed by ministers unacquainted with their real interests, and misled by the designs of interested individuals.[30]

This Chamber of Manufacturers, which provided the basis for the Chamber of Commerce in Birmingham, played an important part in defining and articulating the interests of manufacturers and merchants. No women were ever listed in the press reports of those attending the meetings, nor were there any women subscribers. Yet it had been resolved at the founding meeting of the Chamber of Commerce, at Birmingham's Royal Hotel in 1813, that 'All persons interested in the manufactures and commerce of this town and neighbourhood subscribing a sum of not less than one guinea, be considered members of the society'.[31] 'Persons', from the point of view of the Chamber of Commerce, were clearly men. Similarly when the voice of the town of Birmingham was to be heard, it was the principal male inhabitants who collectively spoke.

The formation of the Chamber had been immediately preceded by the struggle nationally amongst manufacturers and the commercial interest to get the Orders in Council revoked which were having such disastrous consequences on trade. Birmingham, led by Thomas Attwood the banker, had been very prominent in this agitation which was widely understood as a triumph for the middle classes. As Castlereagh wrote gloomily to Wilberforce, 'Once does not like to own that we are forced to give way to our manufacturers.'[32] Those manufacturers were increasingly finding it necessary to instruct the governing classes on trading matters and to insist that their voices should be heard. It was this experience which fed directly into the demand for the reform of Parliament and for the vote for middle-class men. It was Attwood who led the Birmingham Political Union to their great victory in 1832, and it was he and his like who were extolled in the liberal poet Horton's poem about the town,

> The noblest men that dignify our age,
> The brightest names that live on history's pages.[33]

Middle-class men made their claim for direct representation on the grounds of the contribution which they were making to national wealth and prestige; it was their industriousness and their competence which meant that they had earned political recognition. It was clear that men and women wee not in the same place and would not expect to be treated in the same way. Thomas Wright Hill and his sons, who were running their school for boys at Hazelwood in Birmingham, and whose venture had gained fame through the publication of *Public Education* and the recognition of Bentham, were so committed to the fight for reform that it was decided that Frederick, one of the sons, should devote himself fully to activity in the Birmingham Political Union. This was a decision for the men of the family and was made at one of the family councils, which it appears that neither Mrs Hill nor her daughter Sarah attended, though they were both fully involved in the running of the school as a family enterprise.[34] Women attended the great political rallies organized by the Birmingham Political Union and were encouraged to wear blue garters inscribed with 'Attwood forever' but they played no part in the political discussions or decision-making.[35] They were *spectators* and *supporters* rather than being active in their own right and on their own behalf.

The Political Union was revived in Birmingham in 1837. There was a serious economic depression and Attwood revived his plans for currency reform in response. He had always been very enthusiastic about the reforming potential of currency policies but it was the vote, not currency, which had made him popular. This time the Union had little middle-class support, since the middle classes had fundamentally got what they wanted in the Reform Act, and the platform soon became universal male suffrage. Faced with an urgent need for support and a less genteel membership, a Female Political Union was formed. Part of the strategy for reform was that all taxed or excisable articles should be abstained from until the demands were won. Since tea was one of these it was thought by Titus Salt, one of the leaders, that the support of women was essential. He called upon the women of Birmingham to break their normal patterns and 'meddle with politics'; the 'whole family of the people' must unite.[36] The Female Political Union was established and its meetings were regularly reported in the *Birmingham Journal*, the paper of the reformers. The purpose of the Union was seen as to provide support for the men. Women should not be indifferent to politics but should be active on behalf of their men. Needless to say this was in itself a progressive position and would certainly not have been supported by conservative thinkers. The Radical/Liberal position was that women should participate in politics through men, using their moral agency. As the Whig *Edinburgh Review* trumpeted:

> we assume that it is never contemplated that the right of voting should be claimed for married women during their husbands' lives; or for unmarried women living under the protection of their parents. The divisions which would thereby be created in the heart of families, and the extensive injury consequent therefrom to domestic peace, are objections too obvious to require discussion.[37]

The male leaders of the Birmingham Political Union had no illusions about the supportive functions of their female counterpart. At a large tea-party held at the Town Hall, at which Attwood was the main speaker, all of the public speaking was done by men. Even the address from the Female Political Union which was presented to Attwood was read by a Mr Collins. As Scholefield, one of the town's first MPs, declared, 'it was gratifying to him to meet so many excellent and intelligent women, who, by their presence, showed very plainly that they took a lively interest in all that concerned the welfare of their husbands, fathers, brothers and sons . . .' and, he quickly added, 'which also deeply affected their own interests'.[38] He went on to argue for women's involvement in politics and cited their participation in the storming of the Bastille as an historic precedent of their engagement with the struggle for liberty. Mindful of the criticisms which had been made of the Union for encouraging women to desert their proper duties, he argued that he was 'far from wishing that politics should ever supersede the important duties of social and domestic life, which constituted the chief business of the female', but he still hoped that 'the women of Birmingham would never become indifferent to politics'.[39] Still it was clear that the leadership of the Political Union had a limited view of what the women could achieve. The women themselves sometimes had to insist on the part which they were playing. A meeting was reported in February, for example, at which Mr Collins spoke. In his address to the women he assured them that 'he could not but congratulate them on the glorious victory that had been that day achieved in the Town Hall by the men of Birmingham'. A 'female' present at this called out sharply, 'And by the women, Mr Collins; for we were there.' Mr Collins, chastened, 'was willing to admit the assistance the women had rendered.'[40]

This marginalization of the contribution made by the women, with its concurrent assumption that women were not really a part of the 'body politic', is nowhere better illustrated than in the ritual celebration of Birmingham's winning of borough status. This had been a long-drawn-out battle. Only the Liberals had been enthusiastic for incorporation in the wake of the Municipal Reform Act of 1835. The Whigs were neutral since their interests were well covered by the existing street commissioners, while the Tories were hostile. The charter was finally granted in October 1838 and in February of 1839 a dinner was held in the Town Hall to celebrate. This event was described in the *Birmingham Journal*, the wonderful decorations were enumerated, the atmosphere evoked . . .

> When to the effect of these very tasteful decorations, we add the attractions of the hall itself, with the blaze of light running along its extensive walls, the cheerful faces of not less than five hundred gentlemen at the tables below, and above all the blooming cheeks and bright eyes of nearly twice that number of elegantly dressed ladies in the galleries, the rich tones of the magnificent organ, and the pealing anthem swelling the note of praise . . .[41]

The symbolic importance of this occasion was clear to all – the town was now both represented in Parliament and had its own local government. But the presence of the 'blooming cheeks' in the galleries was less straightforward than it might have seemed. Those 'bright eyes' were only in the side galleries in 'consequence of many pressing applications'. Initially it had been intended to put them in either the grand gallery, where they would have been able to hear nothing, or in the side gallery, where they would have been able to neither see nor hear. As the editor of the *Journal* commented, however, their voices, usually gentle and low, became sharp when faced with this relegation and the seating arrangements had to be rethought.[42] This did not mean that the ladies were able either to dine or to drink, but they were able to enjoy a toast being drunk to them. The mayor, in his toast, made the traditional invocation to women as being above politics, and in that way morally superior to men:

> Gentlemen [he cried], we live in times of great political strife and exasperation. We sometimes forget in the animosity of our contentions, that differ as we will, we are still of the same kind and of the same country, kith and kin one of another, united by one common bond of mutual dependence and of mutual interest. We often forget this. Woman's gentle nature never forgets it. She knows no hatred, nor will let us know any, if we but appeal to her. Let us then, gentlemen, whenever we feel our hearts hardening towards each other, or towards our political opponents, let us fly for counsel to those whose province and whose dearest task it is to soften, to bless, and to purify our imperfect nature. Then, believe me, we shall ever find a store of charity, large as our deficiencies, and learn how easy a thing it is to conciliate, without the sacrifice of independence, and to contend without the bitterness of animosity.[43]

Those 'elegantly dressed ladies' could not have been told more clearly that they did not occupy the same political sphere as men. Those 'fit and proper persons' who had voted both nationally and locally and stood as candidates in Parliamentary and council elections relied on their women to soften, bless and purify their imperfect, and political, natures.

The marginalization of women in the political world has to be understood as part of a larger process whereby women were being marginalized from, or indeed excluded from, the public world generally. The debate over what part women should play in philanthropy illustrates this very clearly. As long as they were concerned with private philanthropic work, visiting people in their homes in particular, there was no problem.[44] The difficulties arose when they attempted to step outside of that domestic arena and take on a more public role. We can find the same pattern repeated in the churches; women were, again, at least amongst 'serious

Christians', encouraged to engage in visiting and tract distribution but anything more public, or indeed more official, was discouraged. The formalization of philanthropic and religious societies invariably marginalized women from the process of decision-making; their role was to support privately rather than engage publicly. Nevertheless, 'serious Christians', with their belief in spiritual equality, did provide women with some basis for trust in their own individual and independent judgement and their own moral sense. It was possible, if difficult, to argue that women's special moral sense should be interpreted in political terms and indeed that argument underpinned many feminist interventions in the later nineteenth century. But the move from spirituality and morality to politics was a difficult one to make.

One arena in which women had asserted their right to a political engagement was on the issue of anti -slavery. Here the line between philanthropic work and politics was hard to draw and it was this blurring which had made it a possible area for women. The female anti-slavery societies were mainly established by Quaker women, who had benefited from their traditions of autonomous organization. This in its turn stemmed from the Quaker belief in the spiritual equality of men and women. But the female anti-slavery societies never did the same kind of work as their male counterparts. Rather than lobbying Parliament or organizing demonstrations they relied on appealing to women as wives and mothers, preferably in their own homes. The Birmingham Female Society for the Relief of British Negro Slaves was established in 1828 and initially concerned itself with producing workbags, albums and portfolios to raise money for the relief of neglected and deserted negro slaves. In a discussion in their report of 1828 as to why more women had not got involved with their activities, they concluded that few realized how useful they could be. Female 'weakness and feebleness', they argued, far from meaning that women had nothing to offer, guaranteed them a special kind of strength. Women must use their special skills and gifts rather than pretending to be like men. The Birmingham Society appealed to women as consumers not to buy slave-grown sugar and to engage in house-to-house visiting in the town on this issue, saying:

> Is it for Christian females to be bribed by the greater *cheapness* of this, or the other articles of daily consumption, to lend themselves to the support of a flagrant system of blood-guiltiness and oppression, which cries to heaven for vengeance? – and can we think the

> cry will not be heard? The influence of females in the minor departments (as they are usually deemed) of household affairs is generally such, that it rests with them to determine whether the luxuries indulged in, and the conveniences enjoyed, shall come to them from *the employers of free men, or from the oppressors of British slaves.* When the preference is given to the latter, we see, therefore, with whom the responsibility must mainly rest; – we see at whose door the burden of the guilt must lie.[45]

Women should use their power as household managers to see that slave-grown sugar was not bought; this was the kind of political sphere in which they could have legitimate influence. Even this legitimacy was, however, contested. There were many men involved in the anti-slavery agitation, indeed Wilberforce himself, who were unhappy at this uncalled-for forwardness from ladies whom they preferred to think of as existing quietly in the domestic sphere.

The contestation over what were, and what were not, appropriate public arenas for women continued throughout the nineteenth century. It was not a contest which could be easily resolved since boundaries were open to change. Furthermore the debates over the nature of woman's influence and woman's mission embraced a wide number of issues. Politics, indeed, was rarely mentioned directly for it was assumed that it was not a sphere appropriate to women. What was 'political' was indeed partly defined by where the men were. Influential texts such as those by Mrs Ellis on the duties of the wives, mothers and daughters of England did not discuss the question of women's involvement in politics at all.[46] Mrs Ellis, like many others, believed that moral influence was the key. Nevertheless, on occasion the support of 'the ladies' could be very useful politically though this could lead to acute disagreements.

There was, of course, a well-established tradition of aristocratic ladies using what influence they could in support of their candidates. In Emily Eden's novel *The Semi-Attached Couple* Lady Teviot wanted to do what she could for her husband's candidate in an election. She acquired a poll book and went through it carefully to see whether any of her tradespeople were in it so that she might be able to exert some pressure. She and her mother

> drove into the town constantly, and seemed suddenly to have discovered that they were without any of the necessaries or luxuries of life, for the extent of their dealings with well-thinking trades-

> people was prodigious, and it might have been supposed that they were covertly sullying the purity of election; but, as they justly alleged, shopping was what every woman was born for, and could not, under any circumstances, be considered illegal . . .[47]

Undoubtedly there were middle-class versions of this kind of pressuring. George Eliot observed in *Felix Holt* that at a time when controversies between the Church and Dissent were very sharp, retailers who were Dissenters had to keep a strict hold on their tempers.[48] Tradespeople could not afford to be too sectarian. Similarly, Dr Hope's friends in *Deerbrook* assured him that no one would expect him to vote in a disputed election. 'You are quite absolved from interfering in politics', he was advised. 'Nobody expects it from a medical man. Everyone knows the disadvantage to a professional man, circumstanced like you, of taking any side in a party matter.'[49] No doubt well-to-do female customers and patients had ways of indicating their political preferences to those who provided them with services. But there was a marked difference between aristocratic and middle-class patterns when it came to the relation between women and politics. One aspect of the middle-class critique of aristocratic culture was that society hostesses neglected their families and their religious and moral responsibilities to their children in favour of more worldly pursuits.[50]

Sometimes this kind of 'behind the throne' influence was exercised more openly. The Anti-Corn Law League was quite prepared to utilize the support of middle-class women in their agitation for repeal. They were encouraged to run bazaars and fancy fairs as ways of raising money, capitalizing on the experience gained from such activities in the philanthropic world. The League was of course a Radical organization and as such took a more progressive position on the question of appropriate spheres for women than more conservative groups. They were happy to use lady collectors for the collecting of subscriptions and it was resolved by the Council of the League that 'in every town a committee must be formed, consisting of ladies and gentlemen, having a secretary and treasurer . . .'[51] Not surprisingly, however, these committees represented the highest echelons that ladies could reach. J. W. Croker in the *Quarterly Review* denounced the use that the League made of women as providing a clear indication of the Jacobin influences at work. 'It has been a frequent device of revolutionary agitators,' he asserted, 'to bring women forward as a screen and safeguard to their own operations.' He regarded the great bazaar held by the League with its stalls organized by women as 'a practice in our opinion equally offensive to good taste and good feeling, and destructive of the most amiable and valuable qualities of the female character'. Of a tea-party held with sixty lady stewardesses he commented:

> We exceedingly wonder and regret that the members of the Association and League [the *Councils* of these two bodies organized the bazaar], and still more that anybody else, should have chosen to exhibit their wives and daughters in the character of political agitators; and we most regret that so many ladies – modest, excellent and amiable persons we have no doubt in their domestic circles – should have been persuaded to allow their names to be *placarded* on such occasions – for be it remembered, this Bazaar and these Tea-parties did not even pretend to be for any *charitable* object, but entirely for the purposes of *political agitation.*[52]

J. W. Croker was right to be worried, for many of the daughters of Radicals who were involved in the agitation over the Corn Laws later became committed feminists. One thing could indeed lead to another! Many of the same objections had, however, been made to women's involvement in philanthropic bazaars, for, amongst other things, such occasions invited easy mixing between young men and women.[53] For many people amongst the respectable middle class there was a prohibition on genteel ladies appearing in public at all, except at church or chapel. The stress on the *private* definition of women made participation in the political world exceedingly difficult. For the political world was quintessentially a public world. The kinds of public recognition that were an essential part of political involvement were not accessible to women. Hobsbawm in his *The Age of Capital* tackles the question as to what defined the bourgeoisie as a class:

> the main characteristic of the bourgeoisie as a class was that it was a body of persons of power and influence, independent of the power and influence of traditional birth and status. To belong to it a man had to be 'someone'; a person who counted *as an individual* because of his wealth, his capacity to command other men, or otherwise to influence them.[54]

Such a definition is essentially male. There was no way in which women could be 'someone' in this sense. They did not have that kind of power or influence in either the world of business or in the sphere of voluntary associations. They were *private persons*, not *public someones*. As such they did not possess the necessary prerequisites for citizenship, nor indeed did they expect to occupy the world of political ideas. It was a source of acute amazement when a woman, Harriet Martineau, published a series on political economy, a subject not often associated with the 'fair sex'. When George Dawson, the influential preacher who inspired the 'civil gospel' which was taken up by Joseph Chamberlain and the Birmingham Liberals in the 1850s, fired his initial sally it was addressed to the 'Men of the Middle Classes'.[55] He would have been breaking with custom to have appealed to women as well, despite the fact that his church, with its large female congregation, provided the base for the civic gospel. He would also have been breaking with new social practices in relation to gender and politics which had been established in his own lifetime. Middle-class men had successfully established their pitch; middle-class women remained on the boundaries.

NOTES

1 Martha Syms, 'Letters and Reminiscences'. This manuscript was kindly lent to me by the late Margaret Wilson.
2 Dorothy Thompson, 'Women and Nineteenth-Century Radical Politics: A Lost Dimension', in Juliet Mitchell and Ann Oakley (eds), *The Rights and Wrongs of Women* (Penguin, Harmondsworth, 1976).
3 Barbara Taylor, *Eve and the New Jerusalem. Socialism and Feminism in the Nineteenth Century* (Virago, London, 1983).
4 Margaret Stacey and Marion Price, *Women, Power and Politics* (Tavistock, London, 1981).
5 Michelle Rosaldo and Louise Lamphere, *Women, Culture and Society* (Stanford University Press, Stanford, 1974).
6 J. A. McNamara and S. Wemple, 'The power of women through the family in medieval Europe: 500–1100', in Mary Hartman and Lois Banner (eds), *Clio's Consciousness Raised* (Harper, New York, 1974).
7 Jean Bethke Elshtain, *Public Man, Private Woman* (Martin Robertson, Oxford, 1981).
8 Adam Smith, *The Theory of Moral Sentiments* (Oxford University Press, London, 1976).
9 Susan Moller Okin, *Women in Western Political Thought* (Virago, London, 1980); Elizabeth Fox-Genovese, 'Property and Patriarchy in Classical Bourgeois Political Theory', *Radical History Review*, vol. 4, nos 2–3, 1977; R. W. Krouse, 'Patriarchal Liberalism and Beyond: from John Stuart Mill to Harriet Taylor', in Jean Bethke Elshtain (ed.), *The Family in Political Thought* (Harvester, Brighton, 1982); Gordon

Schochet, *Patriarchalism in Political Thought* (Blackwell, Oxford, 1975).
10 Okin, *Women in Western Political Thought.*
11 Mrs Elizabeth Gaskell, *The Life of Charlotte Brontë* (Dent, London, 1960), p. 123.
12 Quoted in R. Fulford, *Votes for Women* (White Lion, London, 1976), p. 23.
13 Catherine Hall, 'The Early Formation of Victorian Domestic Ideology', in this volume.
14 James Mill, *An Essay on Government* (Cambridge University Press, Cambridge, 1937), p. 45.
15 *Edinburgh Review*, vol. 73, 1841.
16 Harriet Martineau, *Deerbrook* (Virago, London, 1983).
17 Quoted in Ellen Moers, *Literary Women* (The Women's Press, London, 1978), p. 20.
18 John Brewer, 'Commercialization and politics' in Neil McKendrick, John Brewer and J. H. Plumb (eds), *The Birth of a Consumer Society: the Commercialization of Eighteenth-Century England* (Europa, London, 1982), p. 199.
19 Quoted in Roy Porter, *English Society in the Eighteenth Century* (Penguin, Harmondsworth, 1982), p. 274.
20 Brewer, 'Commercialization', p. 219.
21 James Bisset, *Memoir of James Bisset* (Glover, Leamington Spa, 1904), p. 76.
22 Marc Girouard, *Victorian Pubs* (Macmillan, London, 1975).
23 E. Edwards, *The Old Taverns of Birmingham* (Buckler Bros., Birmingham, 1879), p. 5.
24 Edwards, *The Old Taverns*, p. 5.
25 John Money, *Experience and Identity: Birmingham and the West Midlands, 1760–1800* (Manchester University Press, Manchester, 1977), p. 138.
26 T. S. Ashton, *Iron and Steel in the Industrial Revolution* (Manchester University Press, Manchester, 1951).
27 Ashton, *Iron and Steel*, p. 164.
28 Barry Trinder, *The Industrial Revolution in Shropshire* (Phillimore, London, 1973), p. 202.
29 Edwards, *The Old Taverns*, p. 77.
30 Ashton, *Iron and Steel*, p. 169.
31 G. H. Wright, *Chronicles of the Birmingham Chamber of Commerce 1813–1913 and of the Birmingham Commercial Society 1783–1812* (Birmingham, 1913), p. 54.
32 Clive Emsley, *British Society and the French Wars 1793–1815* (Macmillan, London, 1979), p. 160.
33 H. H. Horton, 'Birmingham' (Birmingham, 1851).
34 Frederick Hill, *An Autobiography of Fifty Years in Reform* (Richard Bentley & Son, London, 1893).

35 Carlos Flick, *The Birmingham Political Union* (Archon Books, Conn., 1978).
36 Titus C. Salt, 'To the Women of Birmingham', 16 August 1838.
37 *Edinburgh Review*, vol. 73, 1841, p. 203.
38 *Birmingham Journal*, 12 January 1839.
39 *Birmingham Journal*, 12 January 1839.
40 *Birmingham Journal*, 2 February 1839.
41 *Birmingham Journal*, 16 February 1839.
42 *Birmingham Journal*, 16 February 1839.
43 *Birmingham Journal*, 23 February 1839.
44 Anne Summers, 'A home from home – women's philanthropic work in the nineteenth century', in Sandra Burman (ed.), *Fit Work for Women* (Croom Helm, London, 1979); F. K. Prochaska, *Women and Philanthropy in Nineteenth-Century England* (Oxford University Press, London, 1980).
45 Female Society of Birmingham for the Relief of British Negro Slaves, 'Album', *c.*1828, Birmingham Reference Library, no. 361221.
46 Mrs Sarah Stickney Ellis, *The Women of England* (London Printing & Publishing Co., London, n.d.); *Mothers of England* (Peter Jackson Son & Co., London, n.d.); *The Daughters of England* (London Printing & Publishing Co., London, n.d.).
47 Emily Eden, *The Semi-Attached Couple* (Virago, London, 1979).
48 George Eliot, *Felix Holt, The Radical* (Dent, London, 1964), p. 226.
49 Martineau, *Deerbrook*, p. 183.
50 Leonore Davidoff, *The Best Circles: Society, Etiquette and the Season* (Croom Helm, London, 1973).
51 Norman McCord, *The Anti-Corn Law League 1838–46* (Allen & Unwin, London, 1958), p. 139.
52 *Quarterly Review*, vol. 71, 1842–3, p. 262.
53 John Angell James, *Female Piety, or, The Young Woman's Friend and Guide through Life to Immortality* (Hamilton Adams and Co., London, 1856).
54 E. J. Hobsbawm, *The Age of Capital* (Abacus, London, 1977), p. 286.
55 George Dawson, 'A Letter to the Middle Classes on the Present Crisis' (Birmingham, 1848).

8 Strains in the 'Firm of Wife, Children and Friends': middle-class women and employment in early-nineteenth-century England

If the stock of our bliss is in strangers' hands rested
The fund ill secured oft in bankruptcy ends,
But the heart is given bills which are never protested
When drawn on the firm of *Wife Children and Friends*.

Wolverhampton travelling salesman, 1811

In 1776 a baby girl was born to Captain Weeton and his wife in Lancaster. Her father regretted that she was a girl; 'unless a father can provide independent fortunes for his daughters', he argued, 'they must either be made mop squeezers, or mantua makers, whereas sons can easily make their way in the world'.[1] Miss Weeton never became either a mop squeezer or a mantua-maker, but her struggles to survive economically and socially, powerfully recorded in her journals and letters, vividly demonstrate the difficulties for middle-class women in living as independent persons in late-eighteenth- and early-nineteenth-century England. Her father was a sea captain, the son of a farmer. Her mother had been a lady's maid before her marriage and was the daughter of a butcher. She would take in lodgers during the Lancaster Assizes to provide a little extra money. In 1782 Captain Weeton died at sea and his widow was left with the little girl and her younger brother and only a small property on which to live.

In 1784 the three of them moved to the village of Up-Holland and there Mrs Weeton established a school with the help of her daughter who cooked, cleaned and sewed for the household, allowing them to manage without a servant. The son and heir, the focus of all the hopes and prayers of his mother and sister, was meanwhile sent to a clergyman's school as a dayboy and was articled at the age of fourteen in Preston. The two women suffered many deprivations and hardships for the sake of the boy, expecting that they would benefit in later life. As his sister acidly commented, however, 'it was a vain expectation, for like all his sex, when he was grown up, he considered what had been done for him was right; that he owed no gratitude to us, for we were but *female* relatives, and had only done our duty'.[2]

In 1797 Mrs Weeton died but Miss Weeton kept up the school to maintain her brother during his clerkship. Once finished he made a successful marriage with the daughter of a factory owner and was launched into the professional classes. Neither he nor his in-laws liked the idea of his sister running a village school for it was too public a display of her need for money. Nor did they want her to go governessing. The would have preferred her to take a few acres, keep a cow and a servant, and manage on her income.

In 1809 Miss Weeton gave up the school, left the village having let her cottage and bought the one next door as an investment, and for some time lived in lodgings on Merseyside. She invested some money in property in Liverpool without consulting her brother, and further asserting her independence she took a job in December 1809 as a companion and governess in the Lake District. Her brief was to act as improver and educator to the younger woman, previously a servant, who had married the gentleman son of a Preston banking family, and who needed training in the ways of gentility. 'My dear Tom', Miss Weeton explained to her brother,

> It is not mere education in language, manners, books, and work I have to attend to, but to persist in the proper direction and management of the servants and the household . . . if any rules of etiquette with which it is probable I may be unacquainted, should occur to you or Mrs Weeton, I should really be obliged to you to write them down for me, particularly at the dinner or supper table.[3]

Miss Weeton's initially favourable impressions of the Pedder household, Dove's Nest, did not last. She was shocked by the effects of marrying across ranks and commented on the innumerable humiliations Mrs Pedder suffered at the hands of her husband who 'seems to think that by lording it over two or three women he increased his own consequence'.[4] In her opinion Mr Pedder treated his wife worse than the servants, knowing that she could not leave him. It was perhaps her many discussions with Mrs Pedder as to her husband's autocratic ways that inspired her to write a short essay on women in which she argued that women are equal to men and 'ought to be treated as such in every respect'.[5]

In 1811 she left the Pedder household and after staying with friends for some months and holidaying on her own in the Isle of Man where she took long walks by herself (an unusual practice for a woman, as she knew), she went as a governess to a mill-owning family in Yorkshire. Here she experienced the social marginality which Charlotte Brontë was to evoke so powerfully with the image of Jane Eyre sitting on the edge of the 'company', there but not there. Two years in Yorkshire with the 'plodding, money-getting' manufacturers and farmers were enough for Miss Weeton and soon after leaving she married Aaron Stock, a cotton-spinner in Wigan.[6] Ten months later, when she was thirty-nine, a daughter, Mary, was born.

The marriage was a disaster. In retrospect she was convinced that Stock only married her for her small fortune, over which he gained complete control. In earlier years she had thought of marriage, tired of the contempt associated with being an old maid, of the strange looks and comments that were passed on her independence, and the restrictions that went with being a woman on her own, yet fearful of 'the conviction that one is merely addressed for the sake of the money one is worth'.[7] The reality of marriage she found unbearable, for she was cruelly treated both mentally and physically by her husband. In 1822 the couple separated. As a married woman Mrs Stock was at the mercy of her husband, with no rights either to her child or her property. The rest of her life she lived in lodgings, excluded from society as a separated woman with no money. She constantly struggled with her husband both to extract an allowance equal to the interest on her property and to be permitted to see her daughter. She found her main sustenance in reading, from Mme de Staël to Shakespeare and from Lady Mary Wortley Montague to the newspaper. She wrote bitterly:

> When man injures woman how can she defend herself? Her frame is weaker, her spirit timid; and if she be a wife, there is scarce a man anywhere to be found who will use the slightest exertion in her defence; and her own sex cannot, having no powers. She has no hope from law, for man, woman's enemy, exercises, as well as makes those laws. She cannot have a jury of her peers or equals, for men, every where prejudiced against the sex, are her jurors; man is her judge.[8]

Miss Weeton's life, spanning the years 1776–1844, gives us fascinating if disturbing glimpses into the working lives of middle-class ladies. Schoolmistress, lady companion, governess, wife, independent lady living in genteel penury, these were familiar routes for a middle-class woman in this period. In this chapter I attempt to explore the working world of middle-class women, to look at the kinds of work they did in the late eighteenth and early nineteenth centuries and the ways in which their work contracted and was redefined, while that of their husbands, fathers and brothers opened up. It is these changes which provide the context for the feminist demand in the 1850s for more training and employment for middle-class women, together with a change in the laws on married women's property. Miss Weeton's private cry of despair, that 'every female should know how to earn a living', was to become a rallying cry for England's first organized feminist movement.[9]

Brewer argues that 1 million out of a population of 7 million in eighteenth-century England can be described as of the 'middling sort' and claims that their numbers were expanding by the closing decades of that century.[10] This tallies with the estimates of historians of the early nineteenth century who are roughly agreed in their estimate of 20–25 per cent of the total population being middle class.[11] That middle-class world was peopled with farmers, merchants, manufacturers, tradesmen and professionals. Their fortunes rested on either the manufacture and sale of an immense variety of material goods – from Derbyshire stockings to Birmingham candlesticks, from Gloucestershire cheeses to Suffolk lawnmowers, from Yorkshire woollens to Kidderminster carpets; or the production and sale of material and cultural services – the clergyman tending the spiritual welfare of his flock, the dentist caring for their teeth, the physician and surgeon their health, the lawyer their property, the architect their buildings, the novelist and poet their imaginative fare, the essayist their moral and political diet. Within the sector, levels of income varied widely and a broad line of distinction can be drawn between the upper and the lower middle class with different styles of economic enterprise, different patterns of housing, different ways of organizing their inheritance and varieties of religious and political affiliation. A strong case, however, can be made for the creation of a cultural identity across these boundaries which drew together in some ways the disparate elements of the class.[12]

Estimates as to how many of the women within this class worked in the sense of 'gainful employment' are extremely hard to make. The fundamental difficulty lies in the ways in which the sources mask the work of married women since family enterprises are listed under the male head of household. Women appear in the trade directories, for example, as widows and single women running their own businesses, but the team of husband and wife almost never achieved formal recognition. Similarly, up to 1851 the census gives little help with women's work. Those of 1811 and 1821 focused on asking about the occupations of families, 'which question had entirely failed, from the impossibility of deciding whether females of the family, children, and servants were to be classed as if of no occupation, or of the occupation of the adult males of the family'.[13] This difficulty was resolved in 1831 by deciding to focus on adult males, a focus which gives us little help in establishing women's occupations. In 1841 both men and women were questioned and some evidence exists as to the work of single women and widows but the Registrar-General in his comments on the figures felt bound to explain the numbers of women without any occupation returned as consisting 'generally of unmarried women living with their parents, and of the wives of professional men or shopkeepers, living upon the earnings, but not considered as carrying on the occupations of their husbands'.[14] Such generalized assumptions tell us more about the values and expectations of the Registrar-General than the everyday lives of these women. The major occupations listed in 1841 which were most likely to be taken up by middle-class women included those in the retail trades, hotel- and innkeepers, dressmakers and schoolmistresses.[15]

By 1851 there was some recognition of the partiality of the previous figures and it was acknowledged that, 'Women ... in certain branches of business at home render important services; such as the wives of farmers, of small shopkeepers, innkeepers, shoemakers, butchers' and should be listed as such.[16] At the same time a major new category was introduced in the census, that of 'wife, mother and mistress of an English family', a category that gave formal status to the ideological construction of women as dependants of men.[17] This census, which revealed to the horror-struck nation that one in four wives and two in three widows were 'engaged in some extraneous occupation', also gave official status to the English wife and mother and argued that the 'proper duties' of women 'cannot be neglected without imminent peril to their children – to the nation of the next generation'.[18]

The economic activities of middle-class women were underpinned by a set of legal and property relations which crucially affected both expectations and possibilities. Widows and single women had independent legal status but married women had no separate legal identity, could not enter a partnership, could not make contracts, could not sue or be sued. Legally they were 'covered' by their husbands and could only operate in the market on behalf of their men.[19] Customary practice assumed that it was men who would be active in the world of commerce, women who would be provided for. A study of inheritance patterns, for example, amongst the Birmingham, Essex and Suffolk middle class in the period from 1780 to 1850, has shown that though sons and daughters tended to inherit equally the sons were given forms of property which they were expected to work with and which would provide a basis for expansion and accumulation. The daughters inherited forms of property which would provide an income and allow them to be dependent – a life assurance, an annuity, money in trust. The development of life assurance and the annuity are significant in that they allowed middle-class men who did not have land to provide in a secure way for their widows and daughters. The trust, a device heavily utilized by the upper middle class in the late eighteenth and early nineteenth centuries, allowed men to ensure an income for dependants while the capital in trust could be utilized by the overwhelmingly male trustees.[20] The law, together with such testamentary practices, ensured that women did not operate freely in the market. Their actual wealth, in urban properties, in bonds, in shares, was extensive – their potential to use that wealth in order to expand it was extremely limited. It is hardly surprising that amongst the first concerns of the feminists of the 1850s were the demands to change the law on married women's property and to educate middle-class women in the ways of business.

Miss Weeton's mother, the daughter of a tradesman, thought nothing of taking in lodgers or establishing a small village school in the 1770s and 1780s. In this she was simply following the pattern of the majority of middle-class women who would expect to contribute to the family income or, as widows, to provide in whatever ways possible. Considerable evidence has now been accumulated of the economic activity of middle-class women in the early modern period. This evidence suggests an extremely varied range of economic activities carried on in a world dominated legally, socially and financially by men.[21] Patterns of occupational segregation, so familiar in the twentieth century, are already apparent with the clustering of working-class as well as middle-class women in certain trades and sectors. In London there was a high concentration of women in spinning, laundering and nursing by the early eighteenth century.[22] In Oxford the businesses most often run by women were the food and drink trades, leather-working (specifically glove- and shoemaking) and clothing – sectors which clearly connected with women's domestic activities.[23] In the Midlands, women's activities as market traders were limited and were to become more so.[24] A study of the Birmingham Directories in this period, however, makes it clear that within the metal trades occupational segregation as we now know it was not yet clearly established. The late-eighteenth-century Directories, for example, reveal women agents, awl-blade makers, bell founders, bellow-makers, edge-toolmakers, iron founders, lock-makers, hinge-makers and platers. By the 1850s no women active in these sectors are recorded. Indeed the pattern of occupational segregation was by then far more fixed and the main women's trades listed by the 1830s and 1840s were the familiar ones of milliner, strawbonnet-maker, stay-maker, hosier and dressmaker, shopkeeper, innkeeper, lodging-house-keeper and schoolmistress.[25]

In the trades where women were active with men their opportunities and powers were restricted. In Oxford, as Prior's work has shown, those widows running businesses were tacitly excluded from office in the guilds and there is no evidence that they attended regular meetings of the guilds and companies. The common law allowed single women and widows to trade but borough custom made it difficult. Some guilds, as for example the tailors, did not encourage widows to maintain their husbands' businesses and actively discouraged them by only allowing them to take one apprentice. Furthermore, the form of apprenticeship undertaken under the supervision of a woman inevitably neglected some aspects of training which only a man could do.[26] Women seem to have taken small numbers of apprentices generally and usually the apprenticeship deeds appear in the name of the couple.[27] In the southern and eastern counties, as Snell has shown, there was a high level of apprenticeship for girls in as wide a variety of trades as boys.[28] But the differential meaning of apprenticeship for the two sexes may well have been considerable. Lantz's research on eighteenth-century Essex and Staffordshire suggests high levels of apprenticeship for girls but with strictly limited thresholds both in skill and training.[29] The training in most trades included the learning of feminine values and behaviour just as young men learned the symbols and meanings of masculinity through the rituals and games of apprenticeship and its rites of passage.[30]

A major field of women's economic activity in the eighteenth century was as wives, daughters, mothers and sisters active in family enterprises. In farming, as Pinchbeck argues, 'it was still customary for the wife of a large farmer to take an active share in the management of the household'.[31] This could involve the production of food, in the large kitchens beloved of Cobbett; a good deal of the clothing would also be provided for the household by the mistress in the intervals between the care of the dairy, the calves, pigs and poultry, the garden and orchard. It was the dairy which was the most productive aspect of the work of farmers' wives and 'on all but the largest farms, the mistress superintended every stage of the business and performed all the more difficult operations herself'.[32] She would also be responsible for the business side of the dairy, taking her butters and cheeses to market herself or dealing with the relevant tradesmen, and training and managing the young women who helped her. It was perfectly acceptable for a widow or daughter to carry on a farm if a farmer died without a male heir, as Young's frequent mentions of women farmers make clear.[33]

The same pattern can be found both in traditional trades and in new areas of manufacture. Family enterprises were informal partnerships between husband and wife in which the labour of both was essential. The wives of retailers were responsible for running the large households with their children, apprentices, paid workers and servants, as well as minding the shop when necessary and looking after business affairs when their husbands were away.[34] Their services could include anything from doing the books to mending the apprentices' socks, from checking the credit-worthiness of customers on the gossip networks to entertaining regular customers with 'open house' on market days.[35] Daughters would be expected to help in whatever ways were most useful. Sarah Robinson, for example, the younger daughter of a Birmingham cooper and his wife, born in the town-centre home and shop in 1767, helped in the retail side of the business.[36]

The essential contributions made by wives were extremely varied. Jedediah Strutt, the son of a farmer and maltster in Derbyshire, was apprenticed at the age of fourteen to a wheelwright and fell in love with the daughter of the house, Elizabeth.[37] She went into service with the master of the dissenting academy in the town, and then to London as the servant of a Nonconformist divine, a Dr Benson, who became very attached to her and was so horrified at the idea of her getting married that he offered to make her financially independent at his death. The courtship between Jedediah and Elizabeth lasted for seven years and they finally married in 1755. Jedediah started in business as a wheelwright but turned to farming, having been left some stock. He then invented a process of making ribbed stockings by machine. Elizabeth, contributing in whatever ways she could, investigated the possibility of her late employer, the doctor, lending them some capital but she was unsuccessful in this. She visited London and canvassed among relatives and Nonconformist friends for orders for her husband and her brother who was working with him. She also checked out possible sources of supply. She was always active and well informed as to the business and her letters reveal details of the ins and outs of ribbed stockings as well as the relative values of different kinds of thread. She was a 'partner in herself', as the family biographers describe her, but without the legal appurtenances of partnership since these were denied to married women.[38] As the business grew, turning from hosiery production to the establishment of a silk mill before moving into cotton in partnership with Richard Arkwright, it provided sustenance for Jedediah's younger brother as well as Elizabeth's brother and their children. Elizabeth's eldest daughter helped in the warehouse while the three sons all entered the business. By the time the younger daughter was growing up the family was wealthy and well established and Martha perhaps was more in favour of trips with the Arkwrights (as in 1775 when she went with them to Birmingham, dressed like Miss Arkwright in a 'genteel riding dress' and provided with 'pen and ink and Memorandum Books that they may see which writes the best journal') than with checking stock or managing the household.[39]

The contribution of middle-class women to family enterprise remained extremely significant throughout the early nineteenth century for family enterprise was at the heart of economic organization.[40] It was only late in the century that companies with limited liability (which had been introduced in mid-century) came to dominate over single-person enterprises and partnership. Partnership was the major way for businesses to expand in the early nineteenth century, for a partner could provide much-needed capital, skills and labour. The informal partner, as we have seen, was often the wife. Wives may have had no legal rights but the informal partnership between husband and wife was the starting point for many enterprises, for a marriage meant two sources of capital, two sets of hands, two lots of skills, two sets of relatives and friends.

Many women brought capital into their marriage, as did Rebecca Smith whose father provided five hundred pounds for her on her marriage and another five hundred pounds a year later when she was twenty-one. This capital was crucial to her husband Archibald Kenrick, who had been a buckle-maker in Birmingham, suffered from the decline of that trade, and was able to set up as an iron founder in 1791. Subsequent Kenrick men benefited in similar ways from their marriages which opened up possibilities of loans and sources of credit as well as the lump sums which might be given as a wedding settlement.[41] Among the lower middle class, women's resources were constantly used to start off small businesses and provide credit. The death of a wife's father was often a time at which further capital could be invested in the business and provide for expansion, or simply help out at a time which might otherwise have been disastrous, for bankruptcy always lurked around the corner for middle-class households in this period of acute economic instability. Indeed a wife's inheritance could provide sustenance in face of bankruptcy, but such settlements were the exception rather than the rule and great care had to be taken over the legal arrangements. A Birmingham Methodist button-maker in the 1780s recorded the unfortunate case of the Gardner family, who were members of his chapel. Mr Gardner was declared bankrupt and the carelessness of Mrs Gardner's trustees meant that her property was not safeguarded. A Mr Guest had been 'the principal manager in all the business', conducting the Commission of Bankruptcy:

> It was he who found a flaw in a lease of some premises recently erected by order of some trustees to a sum left for the use and at the disposal of Mrs Gardner; this money had been lent by her consent to her husband. She at length agreed to it being laid out in some building; and as the original trustees lived at a distance in Cheshire, they desired Mr Charles Nevill and Mr Gardner's eldest son, Richard Gardner, not only to overlook the management thereof, but likewise to have the lease of the land made out in their name. All this was done: but for want of a legal transfer of authority from the former trustees to those deputed to act in their stead, Mr Guest was of the opinion (as did the other Commissioners appear to be) that

> the interest if any in the lease in question belonged to the private creditors of Mr Gardner. Mr Barker, the attorney, made the lease, whose fault it was in making this capital error, whereby Mrs Gardner and her family are likely to be great sufferers.[42]

Women brought their own contacts and skills into an enterprise as well as their capital. In addition their relatives and friends might provide useful connections, lines of supply or further sources of expertise. Their brothers and husbands might go into partnership, their nephews might be educated and trained by them in the family business. Mrs Strutt used her contacts in London, as we have seen, to build up their hosiery business in its early days. George Dawson, the well-known preacher and protagonist of the 'civic gospel' in Birmingham in mid-century, married into the established merchant family of Crompton. One Crompton son had gone into the ministry, another was a doctor; Susan (Dawson's wife) and her sister Sarah were intellectual women, writers and teachers, friends of Harriet Martineau in whose house in the Lake District the Dawsons enjoyed their honeymoon. Susan edited her husband's sermons and prayers for publication while Sarah was the superintendent of the Sunday school at her brother-in-law's Church of the Saviour, and wrote numerous children's books, seeing it, as so many middle-class women did, appropriate to their sphere to write for younger readers. Together they pioneered the 'Evening Schools for the Education of Women' in Birmingham in the 1850s, schools for working-class wives which aimed to train their pupils in 'the womanly habits of civilised life', including reading, writing and domestic economy, which were written up by Martineau in *Household Words* and achieved considerable attention. George, Susan and Sarah shared a belief in their educational responsibilities as middle-class people, they brought their different skills to bear on the problems of ignorance, inactivity and misunderstanding between classes. In the name of improvement they were ready to 'sacrifice themselves and their pleasures to the claims of the times'. Together they made a formidable team, an extended family enterprise.[43]

The contribution of wives to the enterprise did not stop at capital, contacts and skills. Their labour was also vital. Sometimes they were directly involved, as was Annie Gillott, whose brothers were in the steel-pen trade. She married Joseph Gillott and together they worked in the manufacture of steel pens in Birmingham, an enterprise which became extremely lucrative.[44] Similarly, the wives of shopkeepers continued to serve in the shop, the wives of farmers to organize the dairy, the wives of innkeepers to supply food and drink. Other women provided indirect support for an enterprise: the doctor's wife who took messages, the bank manager's wife who cleaned the bankhouse, the town missionary's wife who was available to work with women and girls when delicacy required it. Meanwhile all wives were engaged in the work of managing the household for the provision of food, the supply and maintenance of clothes, the upkeep of standards of cleanliness and tidiness, the education and training of small children, the management of servants, the care of apprentices, pupils or trainees; all this had traditionally been part of women's work and continued to be so. When workplace and home were the same, as was so frequently the case in the late eighteenth and early nineteenth centuries, this could be a very substantial responsibility. The schoolmaster with living-in pupils, the surgical-instrument maker with his apprentices, the land agent with his living-in clerk, all relied on the mistress of the house to feed them, clothe them, darn their socks and iron their neckerchiefs, order the fires laid and the water heated.

Furthermore, women had the vital task of bearing children, a labour riven with significance in a predominantly Christian middle-class culture. That culture regarded children as a blessing and sorrowed for those who did not have them. Until the 1860s and the beginning of the decline in family size, middle-class women, who like their husbands married relatively late, could expect to spend a large portion of their married lives pregnant, child-bearing or breast-feeding.[45] Take Martha Gibbins, the wife of a Birmingham button manufacturer and banker, who married young in 1778 when she was twenty and her husband twenty-two and had seventeen children between 1779 and 1806, thirteen of whom survived. Or, Sarah Lea Hill, the wife of the schoolmaster and founder of the well-known Benthamite school, Hazelwood, who married in 1791 when she was twenty-six and her husband twenty-eight and had eight children between 1792 and 1807. When her last daughter was born in 1807 Sarah had five children under nine and three in their teens while Martha in 1800, when baby Sarah was born, had an infant of one, a toddler of two, a little boy of four, one of seven, one of eight and one of nine in addition to the five boys and girls in their teens and the three who were still to come. The responsibilities involved were unending.[46]

Wives indeed were indispensable. It was difficult for a man to operate alone in many fields of business as Julius Hardy, the

Birmingham button manufacturer, found to his cost in the late 1780s. His house was next to his business in the centre of the town and he employed between thirty and forty men, women and boys. One of his workmen and his wife lived with him rent-free in exchange for the wife's cooking and domestic help. She was assisted by a servant girl. The workman, however, was sacked and Hardy seriously considered marriage at this point, but felt the need of 'much deep and long consideration' on 'so momentous an affair'. His worries on the subject were brought to a head when he discovered that the servant girl was pregnant and he feared that he would be blamed. He summarily dismissed her and decided it was his 'duty' and 'interest' to marry. It was not possible to run a decent and trouble-free household without a wife.[47]

In a different sector of the middle-class world, clergymen found it difficult to do their parochial work properly without a wife, and indeed part of a Protestant minister's duty was to marry, for celibacy was dangerously associated with Catholicism. For the serious Christians of the early nineteenth century, inspired with religious passion by Evangelicalism, that wife must have the love of Christ as her 'spring of action'. Only a properly Christian woman could make a good clerical wife. Husband and wife together would make 'the welfare of his [*sic*] flock an object of *primary* solicitude'. This would inevitably involve the loss of much domestic enjoyment but that loss would be as nothing compared with the pleasure in doing one's Christian duty. The Revd John George Breay, Anglican Evangelical and minister of the new Christ Church, especially built for the working classes in Birmingham's town centre in the early nineteenth century, found in Miss Phillis Peyton 'the chosen partner of his future life'. John and Phillis shared a commitment to serious Christianity and a certainty of their mutual duty to create a new moral world. On their wedding day in 1827 the money usually spent on a wedding cake was instead given to poor widows in the vicinity of Haddenham, the Revd Breay's first living. Before her marriage Phillis had devoted much time to philanthropic and religious causes together with the two women friends with whom she had lived. As a clergyman's wife she immediately helped to set up a Sunday school and train the necessary teachers, while running the household which consisted of herself and her husband, four pupils whose fees made a substantial contribution to the household economy, and her old friend Miss Lamb, whom she had lived with before her marriage. One of the special responsibilities of 'the ladies' was to organize the clothing club which provided respectable clothing for the poor and they helped to found the various schools for both adults and children which Breay, in his untiring Evangelical enthusiasm, had inspired. In 1832 the family, now with three young children, moved to Birmingham and again Phillis launched into Sunday schools, clothing clubs and schools of industry, as well as being personally involved with the new Birmingham Magdalen Asylum. In 1837 a new schoolroom was built, able to cater for one thousand children, a monument to the joint endeavours of the Breay family enterprise. Phillis's efforts, however, were never directly remunerated. Just as the married woman was 'covered' by her husband in law, so she was 'covered' by his stipend or salary. In 1839 the Revd Breay caught scarlet fever from one of his sons and died, leaving his widow with five young children. His congregation, recognizing their plight, raised £3,000 to be invested for them and Phillis stayed in Birmingham for the rest of her life, bringing up her children and working for varied philanthropic causes.[48]

Marriage was a partnership, a partnership without legal guarantees but nevertheless the basis of most successful family enterprises. It was wife, children and friends who made the venture of life worth while, who could be relied on for support in a shifting and dangerous world. A Wolverhampton salesman, writing to his loved one during their courtship, captured this spirit in a poem he quoted to her:

> If the stock of our bliss is in strangers' hands rested
> The fund ill secured oft in bankruptcy ends,
> But the heart is given bills which are never protested
> When drawn on the firm of *Wife Children and Friends.*[49]

Assumptions as to the nature of women's involvement with the 'firm of Wife Children and Friends' were, however, changing – changing in ways which were to lead to a crisis over the question of middle-class women's employment by the 1850s. The increased specialization and more advanced division of labour characteristic of agrarian and industrial capitalism affected the middle classes as well as their employees. The varied tasks of the eighteenth-century attorney became the specialized professions of solicitor, surveyor, estate agent, auctioneer or stockbroker; the iron founder who had lent some money on the side became a fully fledged banker; the producer and retailer turned either to manufacture or to his shop. Such specialization meant the need for more training and of different kinds: the 'sound commercial education' so sought after by the English middle classes for their sons, which would enable them to operate in the increasingly complex world of business. A young stockbroker, for example, needed not only numeracy and literacy, a grasp of the financial market and its dealings (which middle-class women were extremely unlikely to have), but also the social skills and contacts to operate within the market. In the early nineteenth century those contacts were informal but middle-class men worked hard to develop the infrastructure of their commercial world. They organized committees of manufacturers and chambers of commerce to articulate and represent their interests. They built market halls and exchanges to centralize their dealings and codify their practices. Their clubs were for men only, their purpose-built buildings designed for the male commercial world. Women were increasingly marginalized and excluded from this world, both formally and informally.

Let us take farming, where the traditional responsibilities of the farmer's wife, or daughter, were under attack. In the dairy more scientific methods of cheese-making combined with more specialized and large-scale organization to marginalize women. They had relied on traditional skills, handed down from mother to daughter, skills which could not compete with the increasingly approved methods of empirical observation and experiment. 'By 1843', as Leonore Davidoff points out, '*the Royal Commission on Women and Children in Agriculture* announced that the patience, skill and strength needed to produce cheese made this work unsuitable for women'.[50] Those women who tried to go on farming independently found themselves operating in an increasingly specialized market. More capital investment was needed to survive but this presented difficulties since women were seen as less creditworthy than men both by their kin and by the country banks which helped to sustain middle-class lines of credit.

Women who were actively engaged in family business when home and workplace were the same found their patterns of daily life significantly different when, and if, the two were separated. By the 1830s and 1840s such separation was becoming more common amongst both the upper-middle and sections of the lower-middle classes as suburban housing was more extensively developed.[51] Often it was a relief, particularly for the mothers of young children, to be away from the 'business house', with its noise, its dirt, its associations with the dangers of a town centre. As the daughter of a Birmingham retail chemist wrote about her mother,

> When our dear mother was first married, she went to the business house in Bull St . . . there were several young men resident in the house, and many callers and visitors to be provided for, and my mother has sometimes told us that the two or three years before the removal to Camp Hill were years of considerable trial. At Bull St. it was a noisy thoroughfare in the centre of the town, our mother went to her brother's house in Gt. Charles St. when the two elder of her children, Anna Mary and Ellen were born.[52]

Later the family moved to a small house about two miles from the business and a few years afterwards to Edgbaston, Birmingham's premier suburb. Similarly, the Best family, manufacturers of lamps in Birmingham in the early nineteenth century, lived close to the town centre for many years in a Georgian house with a small factory built in the yard next door. In 1858 they also moved to Edgbaston, concerned that their neighbourhood had been 'going down' and no doubt enjoyed their view of the Botanical Gardens rather more than the factory outlook they had lived with for so long.[53]

The separation between workplace and home was undoubtedly connected in part with the increased desire amongst sections of the middle class to demonstrate their gentility by ensuring that their womenfolk had nothing directly to do with productive enterprise. While economic activity gave men dignity and worth, it threatened women's femininity which was primarily assured by being a wife and mother. Such ideas, articulated most powerfully in the writings of women such as the Evangelical Hannah More in the 1780s and 1790s and the ubiquitous Mrs Sarah Stickney Ellis in the 1830s and 1840s, depended on the notion of 'separate spheres' for the two sexes and assumed that men's and wonen's natures and interests were fundamentally different.[54] By mid-century it was deemed unladylike and ungenteel for a middle-class woman to be seen to be economically active. One indication of this is in the slightly embarrassed way daughters and granddaughters, in memoirs and letters, explained to themselves and their friends that their mothers and grandmothers had been involved in business. Ann Bassett, who had taken over from her brother as a saddler, collar- and whip-maker in central Birmingham in the 1780s, relied on her two nieces and a foreman to help her with the shop and workshop. One of the nieces 'often remarked that saddlery was a very unsuitable trade for ladies'.[55] When her aunt died in 1811 the business was sold and eventually the two sisters moved to Edgbaston.

It was necessity that drove middle-class women to make money and necessity was likely to hit widows and single women hardest, though a husband's lack of success or illness could mean that wives too had to become the main source of support within a family. It was necessity that drove Mrs Weeton to start a school and necessity that drove a Yorkshire woman, the youngest daughter of a minister, to take over her brother-in-law's haberdasher's shop in Halifax. She had gone to live with him and look after his motherless children when her sister had died. Two years later he died and she had to take responsibility for the shop as well as the children. When she herself married fifteen years later, three of her nieces continued to run the shop for another sixteen years until their retirement.[56]

The demands of necessity could on occasion provide a welcome escape from the monotony of a genteel life. Harriet Martineau recognized that her father's death and the failure of the family business were a blessing in disguise as far as her writing was concerned. Her family came to accept the idea of her earning money and even offered her some grudging recognition.[57] Sometimes it was some kind of breakdown that offered an escape route, as in the well-known cases of Florence Nightingale or Isabella Bird, the veteran lady travel writer. Isabella came from the heartlands of Evangelical Anglicanism. Her father, a Birmingham clergyman in the 1840s, was related to the Wilberforce family and was himself a prominent fighter for the Evangelical cause. Her mother was active in the parish while her Aunt Mary and Cousin May both became well-known missionaries. Isabella taught Sunday school, trained the choir, and engaged in philanthropic work. From her early adulthood, however, she suffered from aches and pains, from lethargy, insomnia and backache, and her doctor in desperation eventually prescribed a long sea voyage. Her first trip was to America and in later years she travelled to Hawaii, the Rockies and Japan. Her *A Lady's Life in the Rocky Mountains* was immensely successful. Abroad she was able to climb mountains and volcanoes, ride, sleep out, live rough and generally be 'privileged to do the most improper things with perfect propriety'.[58] Harriet Martineau, Florence Nightingale and Isabella Bird, however, were the success stories, and all came from families where confidence and ambition were part of their stock in trade. Behind them clustered the shadowy forms of seamstresses and governesses whose plight was to become public and who were to inspire the first organized feminist attempts to improve economic opportunities for middle-class women.

As early as 1792 Mary Wollstonecraft, in her *Vindication of the Rights of Woman*, commented on the lowly status of the middle-class milliners, mantua-makers and governesses who were scarely fitted for the humiliating situations into which they were forced by necessity. Like Mary Wollstonecraft, Miss Weeton had also longed for the day when 'honest, independent women' would be able to fill 'respectable stations' as physicians, farmers and shopkeepers, able to stand erect, 'supported by their own industry' rather than reduced to dependence.[59] By the 1840s the possibilities of women filling those 'respectable stations' looked ever more remote and the first wave of publicity over the pathetic conditions of elderly governesses was to be reinforced with the evidence from the 1851 census of the numbers of women who were employed, in official terms, and the revelations as to those half-million 'redundant women' who were not married and therefore had no proper place. It was in this context that the subject of middle-class women's employment became a matter of public debate and concern.[60]

For commentators such as W. R. Greg the 'redundant woman', as Vicinus has argued, provided a potent symbol of the wider social disorders associated with industrialization and urbanization.[61] Unattached women could have no rhyme or reason in their lives since Greg's concept of true womanhood (one which was widely and publicly shared) was being supported by and ministering to men. But a growing number of middle-class women, especially those who were single, were becoming more vocal in their search for economic opportunities, both because they needed them and because they wanted them. The injunctions on middle-class fathers to provide for their dependants could often not be met and many unmarried daughters were left without resources in a world where working for money meant loss of gentility. Widows could find themselves desperately in need of employment and wives could discover that their husbands were less than adequate providers. At the same time, some women confined to a life of gentility longed for the independence and interest which could be associated with employment and the status and power which went with certain kinds of labour. Florence Nightingale's passionate demand for some greater meaning in her life, some sphere where her intellect and moral sense could be exercised, was echoed by many others, not just in the privacy of their diaries and journals but also on an increasingly public stage.[62] In beginning to articulate the limitations of their 'separate sphere' women had to reflect on, and make sense of, the new conditions which confronted their class and their sex in mid-century England.

Take Barbara Leigh Smith, one of the first group of students at the Ladies' College in Bedford Square, who in 1854 wrote the pamphlet on women and the law which was to act as a focus for the agitation on married women's property and the subsequent founding of the *English Woman's Journal*.[63] Barbara Leigh Smith came from a wealthy Radical and Unitarian mercantile and landed family. Her grandfather had been the leading parliamentary spokesperson for the Dissenters in the early nineteenth century, a strong protagonist of the repeal of the Test and Corporation Acts and heavily involved in the anti-slavery movement with his childhood friends, but political antagonists, the Wilberforces and the Thorntons. He was a close friend of the well-known Unitarian Thomas Belsham and a strong believer in the importance of reason and the necessarian doctrine, propounded by Joseph Priestley, that the moral and natural universe worked according to laws set in motion by God, that these laws were inevitable but that man, by using reason, could understand the laws and conform to them. It was man's positive duty to do this and to advance the divine plan. Each man was the maker of his own fortune.[64] Barbara's father, Benjamin, who restored the family fortunes in time of trouble with his successful distillery, also became a Member of Parliament and a well-known philanthropist. In 1823 he met Anne Longden, a milliner's apprentice, with whom he lived and who had five children before she died. Barbara, therefore, was illegitimate, undoubtedly a considerable social stigma at the time and one which placed the Leigh Smiths beyond the pale for some of their relatives. Indeed, Mrs Gaskell attributed Barbara's unconventional feminist opinions, to which she was not sympathetic, to the taint on her birth.[65]

Barbara's own thinking was shaped by this Radical, Unitarian, slightly unconventional world to which she belonged.[66] She was used to a stress on improvement and progress, she had learned an optimism about the human capacity to grow and change, she trusted in the power of reason. Unitarians, with their commitment to rationality and intellectual inquiry, were usually serious in their consideration of girls' education – though the female pursuit of knowledge took place within narrower boundaries than that of the male. Unitarians were used to criticism and disapproval, to being rebels (though after the 1830s they were substantially represented in local government), to being linked with dangerous ideas such as deism and Owenism, to the assumed link between their theological doctrines and reforming politics.[67] Indeed, the *Monthly Repository*, under the editorship of W. J. Fox, advocated the emancipation of women and the liberalizing of divorce laws, a stance which many Unitarians could not stomach and which provoked heartfelt complaints that the journal could no longer be left on respectable sideboards. Fox's sexual politics, including his separation from his wife and living openly with another woman, led to his expulsion from the association of Unitarian ministers, for Unitarian Radicalism in politics and religion was rarely matched by a radicalism on familial relations.[68] However, their faith, in its encouragement of the rational pursuit of knowledge and its belief in individual responsibility, provided a space within which women could challenge assumptions of male superiority.

Mary Wollstonecraft, Harriet Martineau and Barbara Leigh Smith all had connections with Unitarianism. But they did not stand alone. In Unitarian congregations across the country women had claimed the right to organize activities for their sex, whether girls' Sunday schools or female Schools of Industry. They had long been accustomed to involvement in mixed discussion groups for young adults, sometimes they were even privileged to cast a vote in chapel meetings when a new minister was to be appointed.[69] But such rights could not be assumed. They were constantly fought over and contested, with the heavy weight not only of conventional conservative thinking about sexual difference but also the new doctrines of separate spheres ever present.

It is in this context that Barbara Leigh Smith published her book *Women and Work* in 1857. On the title-page she quoted St Paul's Epistle to the Galatians,

> There is neither Jew nor Greek, there is neither bond nor free, there is neither male nor female: for ye are all one in Christ Jesus.

This text had long been a critical one for Christian women since it asserted women's spiritual equality with men. Drawing on the debates as to women's place within the church or chapel which had been a prominent feature of the previous decades, as women claimed the right to be active as philanthropists, Leigh Smith extended this claim and insisted on women's social equality. Women were God's children equally with men, she argued, a theory which was proclaimed in Christian society but not lived in practice. As the necessarian doctrine had taught, all are God's tools, sent into the world to forward progress. No human being, whether male or female, had the right to be idle. Women *wanted* to work.[70]

Leigh Smith's claim for social equality and the right to work reflected the middle-class insistence on the dignity of labour. For middle-class men, faced with the aristocratic and gentry code which maintained that true gentility depended on the capacity to live on the labour of others, a central issue was their demand that there was no disrespect associated with the counting-house, the stockroom or the office.[71] Indeed, progress and improvement depended on the reason and action of men like them who would steer the great engine of expansion with their quills, their theodolites and their bibles. It was they who stood at the prow of the good ship British Enterprise. It was not uncommon for middle-class people to explain mechanization and industrialization in terms of the rise of their class, as did Harriet Martineau in her powerful intervention 'On female industry' in the *Edinburgh Review*. For her it was the rise of the middle class which brought with it the need for, and supply of, female industry, an indication of the sense of power and agency which entrepreneurship bestowed.[72] Women like Barbara Leigh Smith and Harriet Martineau wanted to share that potential – not to work meant serfdom, as Elizabeth Barrett Browning had so eloquently written in the lines that Leigh Smith quoted next to St Paul,

> The honest earnest man must stand and work;
> The woman also; otherwise she drops
> At once below the dignity of man,
> Accepting serfdom.[73]

That same year John Duguid Milne, an eloquent friend of feminism, in his discussion of the *Industrial and Social Position of Women in the Middle and Lower Ranks* echoed these sentiments. He argued that it was a waste for middle-class women to live such purposeless lives and that, although it was exhausting to work, such work carried the satisfaction of being useful and interesting, quite apart from that of making money. Despite the difficulties of operating ethically in the market, industry could have good moral influence since it demanded honesty and honour. 'The moral culture of an upright man of business', he suggested, 'cannot but exceed far what is possible in a sedentary life or in affluent leisure':[74] an astonishing belief in a society which was used to the argument that women, by nature, and by virtue of their seclusion in the home, were more moral than men.

Women like Barbara Leigh Smith and her great friend Bessie Rayner Parkes had the *class* confidence which allowed them to speak in a society in which the bastions of inherited power had been successively broken down by their fathers, their grandfathers and their great-grandfathers. Their sense of themselves as ladies who should be publicly silent was broken by the tensions between the aspirations of their class and their sex. Middle-class men, in claiming rights for themselves, had claimed the right to support, protect and represent their womenfolk. But some of those womenfolk, surrounded by the discourses of power yet condemned by their sex to social and political marginality, broke the boundaries of genteel femininity and transformed the languages with which they were familiar, the languages of Christian duty and individual fulfilment, into weapons for themselves.

The language of liberal individualism was clearly present in the writing of Bessie Rayner Parkes. Her great-grandfather was the famed Radical, Unitarian theologian and chemist Joseph Priestley, whose necessarian doctrines influenced successive generations of Unitarians and the example of whose exile at the hands of a 'Church and king' mob was a potent reminder of the dangers associated with Radical politics. Her father, the Radical Utilitarian lawyer Joseph Parkes, had been active in the Benthamite initiatives in Birmingham since the early 1820s, was heavily involved in the struggle for the Reform Act in 1832, and soon after moved to London to work on the Municipal Corporations Commission. Both the Reform Act and the local government acts enfranchised and empowered middle-class men while for the first time formally excluding women. When the Parkes family moved to London they lived above the offices of the Municipal Corporations Commission, 'a great convenience' for Parkes and an arrangement which must have familiarized young Bessie with the ways of the political world.[75] By the time she was writing her articles on women's work for the review she co-edited, the *English Woman's Journal*, she had lost her father's faith in the hidden hand of the market. The market could not be left entirely to itself, she argued, to sort out the problem of middle-class women's work. Active intervention was needed if women were to claim their rightful place as workers. As long as families educated daughters only to be wives and mothers the opportunities associated with an ever-expanding economy could not be taken up. Prejudices would have to be tackled and attitudes changed, unrestricted production could not be seen as the only good. Even such modest criticisms of the orthodoxies of political economy as those offered by Parkes were greeted with severe disfavour, by her father as well as by other commentators.[76]

For those feminists such as Harriet Martineau and Bessie Rayner Parkes who had been heavily influenced by Utilitarianism with its belief in the potential benevolence of the market, there was a deep confidence in the economy's capacity to expand. Men's 'monopolising spirit', their fear of the threat to their jobs and conditions of work if women were allowed in, their jealous protection of their exclusive crafts and skills, were castigated on the grounds that there could be openings for all and that the exclusion of women from large sectors of the economy meant that their 'powers' and 'industry' were wasted. Harriet Martineau quoted the ironic case of the British watchmakers who refused to allow women into the trade with the result that Swiss watches were being imported which had been made by men and women. Her central argument was that there must be a proper recognition of the reality and extent of women's work. This reality had been demonstrated in the census of 1851 with its revelation that 'three millions out of six adult English women work for subsistence; and two out of the three in independence'.[77] Changes in the law were not necessary – it was changes in attitude that were required. The assumption that all women were supported by men was patently not true. A recognition of the reality of women's work in agriculture, in fishing, in domestic service, in the retail industries, in manufacturing or as landladies was a necessary first step in exploding masculine fantasies that the market was not big enough for both the sexes and the popular myth that all women were dependent. The liberal feminist case for the right of all individuals to fulfil their full potential had to be built, in the time-honoured Utilitarian tradition, on empirical investigation and a proper statistical base. Women were already in employment, in large numbers. The world should stop pretending they were not, recognize the value of that work and provide more openings, especially for middle-class women.

For the ladies of the *English Woman's Journal*, the issue of the restricted employment possibilities available to middle-class women occupied them greatly. They wrote about it, organized around it, set up practical initiatives to try and change it. They were mainly born in the decades of the 1820s and 1830s so their mothers were the generation whose engagement with the family enterprise was likely to have been reduced as the business world became more organized around men. They had moved into the suburbs or modernized their farms with parlours and front doors; they learned to be professional wives and mothers. Their daughters demanded the re-entry of women into family enterprises and the education of women in the ways of the business world. They did not challenge the importance of the profession of wife and mother but argued forcefully that 'the middle class is at the mercy of a thousand accidents of commercial or professional life, and thousands and thousands of destitute educated women have to earn their daily bread'. Most *Journal* readers, they thought, would have a female relative or intimate friend who had been affected by trade failures, by death or by the 'exigencies of a large household'.[78] Some of these women could be absorbed into family businesses but others had no conveniently placed relatives.[79] Such women needed either salaried positions, or to be able to set up in business themselves.

Bessie Rayner Parkes bemoaned the lack of available capital for women. 'Girls never have any capital, they hardly know what it means,' she wrote and, reflecting on the commonplace assumption that the financial world was not a world that women needed to know anything about, she argued that girls needed to be taught, just as boys were, 'how to make capital reproductive, instead of merely how to live upon its interest'.[80] It was the property laws in part which had encouraged such assumptions and it is hardly surprising that the demand for economic opportunities for women went hand-in-hand with the demand for a change in the laws on married women's property.

The importance of an active engagement with the world of business was recognized in the financial organization of the *English Woman's Journal* itself. Middle-class women had long been used to the organization of philanthropic committees, of church and chapel auxiliary societies. Barbara Leigh Smith had herself been actively involved in the establishment of a school and had set up a women's discussion group, where members showed each other their artistic productions. She and her friends took these established skills along different routes. They set up a committee to agitate on married women's property, they even established a joint-stock company themselves. The *Journal* was set up on joint-stock principles though

Leigh Smith actually bought most of the initial shares with the independent income her father had settled on her.[81] Joint-stock was seen as a way forward for women, for if they would cooperate they could establish a business even with very limited capital. 'If twenty ladies in any town,' wrote Bessie Rayner Parkes, 'would club together £5 a piece, they might open a stationery shop in which, if they gave all their own custom and tried to get that of their friends, they might secure a profit after employing a lady as manager, and if the business increased female clerks also.'[82] If joint-stock represented the financial organization of the future, women must not be afraid of it and must learn to make use of it.

Jessie Boucherett, an early enthusiast for the *Journal* who became actively involved in setting up the Society for Promoting the Employment of Women, was so shocked by the recognition that the possibilities for women to work in shops were partly limited by the fact that they could not add up properly that she set up a school to train them.[83] Her enthusiasm for the genius and benevolence of a capitalist economy spread to life assurance, that instrument designed specifically to deal with the problem of financial dependants, usually women. Rather than criticizing such a form, she saw it as 'one of the positive duties of women to foster and disseminate an elastic principle which if carried out to its fullest extent would nearly banish poverty from our land'. It was a part of woman's mission to talk to people about this 'beautiful system' and life assurance needed the powerful aid of female influence. She set out to explain the benevolent principles of life assurance in simple terms without using the technical jargon which made it so particularly inaccessible to women. She proposed the establishment of a woman's life assurance mutual society, enrolled under the Act of Friendly Societies or registered under the Joint Stock Act, in which women could be trained to serve as clerks. Initially it would have to have male directors and a male secretary but she looked forward to the time when 'vital economics', mathematics and statistics would not be 'deemed improper subjects for female instruction'.[84] Indeed, even the agents to the company could be women, conveniently combining such work with their domestic duties. In this utopian dream women would raise the capital, they would act as clerks and agents, they would secure incomes for themselves and benefit the whole society. The New Jerusalem of the middle-class feminists of the 1850s was peopled with female insurance agents, female accountants, female doctors, female lawyers, female photographers, female designers and female artists as well as the more traditional female teachers and dressmakers. Their Jerusalem would recognize women as active subjects, treat them as independent persons legally, encourage and develop their skills and capacities, give them the opportunity to thrive in the world as businesswomen or as wives and mothers.

Such a dream provoked a deep sexual antagonism. The feminists, like most of their class and their generation, believed in the immense potential of the British economy. But they also knew and experienced men's fears, jealousies and 'monopolising spirits'. A group of Birmingham women in the 1850s established a 'Maidens' Club' that would have warmed the heart of Miss Weeton. The society consisted of young unmarried women who were committed to remaining single and to restricting their relationships with the male sex to their relatives. They held weekly discussion meetings at a clubroom in the town centre where they discussed such issues as whether men should be allowed to enjoy their men-only clubs. One week the question for debate was 'Are men the competent subjects they assume to be?'[85] Whatever their conclusions, both the society and its subject matter were another indication of a new willingness amongst some middle-class women to voice their grievances, make new claims as independent persons and speak for their sex.

NOTES

1 N. Stock, *Miss Weeton's Journal of a Governess 1811–25*, 2 vols. (David & Charles, Newton Abbot, 1969), vol. 1, p. 6. Miss Weeton's story is all drawn from this source. Subsequently only direct quotes are noted.
2 Stock, *Miss Weeton*, vol. 1, p. 23.
3 Stock, *Miss Weeton*, vol. 1, p. 211.
4 Stock, *Miss Weeton*, vol. 1, p. 259.
5 Stock, *Miss Weeton*, vol. 1, p. 312.
6 Stock, *Miss Weeton*, vol. 2, p. 72.
7 Stock, *Miss Weeton*, vol. 1, p. 78.
8 Stock, *Miss Weeton*, vol. 2, pp. 376–7.
9 Stock, *Miss Weeton*, vol. 2, p. 396.
10 John Brewer, 'Commercialization and Politics', in Neil McKendrick, John Brewer and J. H. Plumb (eds), *The Birth of a Consumer Society: The Commercialization of Eighteenth-Century England* (Europa, London, 1982), p. 24.
11 For estimates of the size of the middle class see, for example, John Foster, *Class Struggle and the Industrial Revolution* (Weidenfeld & Nicolson, London, 1974), p. 74; John Burnett, *A History of the Cost of*

Living (Penguin, Harmondsworth, 1979), p. 77; Leonore Davidoff and Catherine Hall, *Family Fortunes: Men and Women of the English Middle Class 1780–1850* (Hutchinson and Chicago University Press, London and Chicago, 1987), pp. 18–28.

12 The lines of division were, of course, always fluid and flexible. For this argument, see Davidoff and Hall, *Family Fortunes*, pp. 18–28; see also the work of Robert J. Morris, particularly *Class, Sect and Party. The Making of the British Middle Class, 1820–1850* (Manchester University Press, Manchester, 1990).

13 Parliamentary Papers, *The Population Returns of 1831*, London, 1832, p. 2.

14 Parliamentary Papers, *Occupation Abstract of the Census Returns, 1841*, London, 1844, p. 9.

15 See the useful appendix on women's occupations in 1841 in Ivy Pinchbeck, *Women Workers and the Industrial Revolution 1750–1850* (Frank Cass, London, 1969).

16 Parliamentary Papers, *Census of Great Britain 1851*, Population Tables, Report and Summary Tables, pt 2, vol. 1, London, 1854, LXXXXVIII.

17 Parliamentary Papers, *Census, 1851.*

18 Parliamentary Papers, *Census, 1851.*

19 Erna Reiss, *Rights and Duties of Englishwomen* (Sherratt & Hughes, Manchester, 1934); Lee Holcombe, *Wives and Property: Reform of the Married Women's Property Law in Nineteenth-Century England* (Martin Robertson, Oxford, 1983).

20 Davidoff and Hall, *Family Fortunes*. Ch. 4 is a discussion of gender and property and this paragraph draws heavily on it.

21 For a discussion of this literature, see Maxine Berg, 'Women's Work, Mechanisation and the Early Phases of Industrialisation', in Patrick Joyce (ed.), *The Historical Meanings of Work* (Cambridge University Press, Cambridge, 1987); see also Maxine Berg, *The Age of Manufactures 1700–1820* (Blackwell, Oxford, 1985). For a helpful discussion of feminist approaches to women's employment, see Veronica Beechey's introduction to her *Unequal Work* (Verso, London, 1987).

22 Kay Lacey, 'Women and Work in fourteenth and fifteenth century London', in Lindsey Charles and Lorna Duffin (eds), *Women and Work in Pre-Industrial England* (Croom Helm, London, 1985).

23 Mary Prior, 'Women and the Urban Economy: Oxford 1500–1800', in Mary Prior (ed.), *Women in English Society 1500–1800* (Methuen, London, 1985).

24 Wendy Thwaites, 'Women in the Market-place: Oxfordshire 1690–1800', *Midland History*, 9.

25 A sample of Birmingham Directories was taken from 1767–1852.

26 Prior, 'Women and the Urban Economy'.

27 M. Roberts, 'Images of Work and Gender', in Charles and Duffin (eds), *Women and Work.*

28 Keith Snell, *Annals of the Labouring Poor* (Cambridge University Press, Cambridge, 1985).
29 Deborah Lantz, 'The role of apprenticeship in the education of eighteenth-century women', unpublished paper in *Warwick Working Papers in Social History – Workshop on Proto-Industrial Communities*, 1986. I owe this reference to Maxine Berg.
30 For some discussion of the ways masculinity was learned in the workshop, see Keith McClelland, 'Time to work, time to live: some aspects of work and the reformation of class in Britain, 1850–1880', in Joyce, *The Historical Meanings of Work*.
31 Pinchbeck, *Women Workers*, p. 8.
32 Pinchbeck, *Women Workers*, p. 11.
33 See *Annals of Agriculture, and Other Useful Arts*, collected and published by Arthur Young, 1784–1815, 46 vols.: vol. 6, p. 123; vol. 8., p. 82. Quoted in Pinchbeck, *Women Workers*, p. 10.
34 For an account of one such family business, see 'The Butcher, the Baker, the Candlestick-maker' in this volume.
35 See the fictional account of the Furzes, ironmongers, in Mark Rutherford, *Catherine Furze* (Hogarth, London, 1985).
36 I. Southall, William Ransom, Margaret Evans (eds), *Memorials of the Families of Shorthouse and Robinson and Others connected with them* (privately published, Birmingham, 1902).
37 Robert S. Fitton and Alfred P. Wadsworth, *The Strutts and the Arkwrights 1758–1830* (Manchester University Press, Manchester, 1958).
38 Fitton and Wadsworth, *The Strutts*, p. 111.
39 Fitton and Wadsworth, *The Strutts*, p. 77.
40 For a much longer discussion of the family enterprise and the character of men's and women's work, see Davidoff and Hall, *Family Fortunes*, especially pt 2.
41 Archibald Kenrick, unpublished MS diary 1787–89, Birmingham Reference Library, no. 110/24; Mrs W. Byng Kenrick (ed.), *Chronicles of a Nonconformist Family: The Kenricks of Wynne Hall, Exeter and Birmingham* (Cornish Bros., Birmingham, 1932); Roy Church, *Kenricks in Hardware: A Family Business 1791–1966* (David & Charles, Newton Abbot, 1969).
42 Unpublished diary of Julius Hardy, Buttonmaker of Birmingham, 1788–93, transcribed and annotated by A. M. Banks, 1973, Birmingham Reference Library, no. 669002, p. 8.
43 Wright Wilson, *The Life of George Dawson 1821–76* (Percival James, Birmingham, 1905); Ernest P. Hennock, *Fit and Proper Persons: Ideal and Reality in Nineteenth-Century Urban Government* (Edward Arnold, London, 1973); Sarah Crompton, *Evening Schools for the Education of Women* (Tonks, Birmingham, 1852); Harriet Martineau, 'The New School for Wives', *Household Words*, no. 107, 1852.

44 Eliezer Edwards, 'Joseph Gillott', in *Personal Recollections of Birmingham and Birmingham Men*, reprinted from the *Birmingham Daily Mail* (Midland Education, Birmingham, 1877).
45 For a longer discussion of this, see Davidoff and Hall, *Family Fortunes*, especially pt 3.
46 Emma Gibbins, *Records of the Gibbins Family, also Reminiscences of Emma J. Gibbins and Letters and Papers relating to the Bevington Family* (Cornish Bros., Birmingham, 1911); Thomas Wright Hill, *Remains of the Late T. W. Hill* (privately published, London, 1859); Frederick Hill, *An Autobiography of Fifty Years in Time of Reform*, edited with additions by his daughter Constance Hill (Richard Bentley & Son, London, 1893); Rosamund and Florence Davenport-Hill, *The Recorder of Birmingham. A Memoir of Matthew Davenport Hill* (Macmillan, London, 1878); Rowland and G. H. Hill, *The Life of Sir Rowland Hill and the History of Penny Postage*, 2 vols (Thomas de la Rue, London, 1880).
47 Unpublished diary of Julius Hardy, pp. 36, 55.
48 Revd John George Breay, *Memoir of the Rev. John George Breay Minister of Christ Church, Birmingham*, 5th edn (Beilby, London, 1844), p. 124. References to Mrs Breay's activities in later life have been found in charitable records.
49 Shaw Letters, Birmingham University Library, no. 4.
50 Leonore Davidoff, 'The role of gender in the "First Industrial Nation": Agriculture in England 1780–1850', in Rosemary Crompton and Michael Mann (eds), *Gender and Stratification* (Cambridge University Press, Cambridge, 1986), p. 204. This paragraph is heavily dependent on this article.
51 Leonore Davidoff and Catherine Hall, 'The architecture of public and private life: English middle-class society in a provincial town 1780–1850', in Derek Fraser and Anthony Sutcliffe (eds), *The Pursuit of Urban History* (Edward Arnold, London, 1983).
52 Southall et al. (eds), *Memorials of the Families of Shorthouse*, p. 68.
53 Richard D. Best, *Brass Chandelier. A biography of R. H. Best by his son R. D. Best* (Allen & Unwin, London, 1940).
54 See, for example, Hannah More's best-selling novel, *Coelebs in Search of A Wife.* (R. B. Seeley and W. Burnside, London, 1809); Mrs Sarah Stickney Ellis's series *The Women of England, The Wives of England, The Daughers of England, The Mothers of England* was immensely popular in the 1830s and 1840s.
55 A. W. Matthews, *A Biography of William Matthews, Expositor of Gas and Water Engineering* (privately published, London, 1899), p. 5.
56 John Wilson, 'Mrs William Rawson and her Diary', *Transactions of the Halifax Antiquarian Society*, 1958. Thanks to Dorothy Thompson for this reference.

57 Harriet Martineau, *Autobiography with Memorials by Maria Weston Chapman*, 3 vols (Smith, Elder & Co., London, 1877).
58 Pat Barr, *A Curious Life for a Lady: The Story of Isabella Bird, Traveller Extraordinary* (Penguin, Harmondsworth, 1958), p. 185.
59 Mary Wollstonecraft, *A Vindication of the Rights of Woman*, new edn (Penguin, Harmondsworth, 1985), p. 262; Stock, *Miss Weeton*, vol. 2, p. 396.
60 For an account of the emergence of the debate, see Ray Strachey, *The Cause: A Short History of the Women's Movement in Great Britain*, new edn (Virago, London, 1978); Lee Holcombe, *Victorian Ladies at Work: Middle Class Working Women in England and Wales 1850–1914* (David & Charles, Newton Abbot, 1973); for the most famous 'naming' of the redundant women, see William R. Greg, 'Why are Women Redundant?', in *Literary and Social Judgements* (London, 1869); for an interesting discussion of Greg, see Judy Worsnop, 'A re-evaluation of "the problem of surplus women" in nineteenth-century England, in the context of the history of gender' (unpublished MA dissertation, University of Essex, 1983).
61 Martha Vicinus, *Independent Women: Work and Community for Single Women 1850–1920* (University of Chicago Press, Chicago, 1985), p. 3. See ch. 1 for Vicinus' account of 'The revolt against redundancy'.
62 Florence Nightingale, 'Cassandra', reprinted in Strachey, *The Cause.*
63 On Barbara Leigh Smith who became Barbara Bodichon, see Hester Burton, *Barbara Bodichon 1827–91* (John Murray, London, 1949); Sheila R. Herstein, *A Mid-Victorian Feminist, Barbara Leigh Smith Bodichon* (Yale University Press, New Haven, 1985); Jane Rendall, 'A "Moral Engine"? Feminism, Liberalism and the *English Woman's Journal*', in Jane Rendall (ed.), *Equal or Different: Women's Politics in the Nineteenth Century 1800–1914* (Blackwell, Oxford, 1987).
64 On necessarian doctrines, see Robert K. Webb, *Harriet Martineau: A Radical Victorian* (Heinemann, New York, 1960).
65 Herstein, *A Mid-Victorian Feminist*, pp. 15–16.
66 Barbara Leigh Smith was taught for some time by an Owenite; see Burton, *Barbara Bodichon*, and Barbara Taylor, *Eve and the New Jerusalem: Socialism and Feminism in the Nineteenth Century* (Virago, London, 1983), ch. 9.
67 On Unitarianism and middle-class culture, see John Seed, 'Unitarianism, political economy and the antinomies of liberal culture in Manchester 1830–50', *Social History*, vol. 7, no. 1, January 1982; John Seed, 'Theologies of power: Unitarianism and the social relations of religious discourse 1800–1850', in Robert J. Morris (ed.), *Class, Power and Social Structure in British Nineteenth Century Towns* (Leicester University Press, Leicester, 1986).
68 Francis E. Mineka, *The Dissidence of Dissent: The Monthly Repository 1806–38* (University of North Carolina Press, Chapel Hill, 1944).

69 For a longer discussion of church and chapel government and the relative places of men and women, see Davidoff and Hall, *Family Fortunes*, ch. 2.
70 Barbara Leigh Smith, *Women and Work* (Bosworth & Harrison, London, 1857).
71 On the dignity of work see, for example, Thomas Carlyle, *Selected Writings* (Penguin, Harmondsworth, 1971).
72 Harriet Martineau, 'Female Industry', *Edinburgh Review*, vol. 109, no. 222, 1859.
73 Quoted on the title-page of Leigh Smith, *Women and Work*; Elizabeth Barrett Browning, *Aurora Leigh*, new edn (The Women's Press, London, 1978); see the Introduction by Cora Kaplan.
74 John Duguid Milne, *Industrial and Social Position of Women in the Middle and Lower Ranks* (Chapman & Hall, London, 1857).
75 Jessie K. Buckley, *Joseph Parkes of Birmingham* (Methuen, London, 1926), p. 118.
76 Rendall, 'A "Moral Engine" ', documents Joseph Parkes's criticism of his daughter for her ignorance of political economy, fn 66.
77 The phrases are those of Harriet Martineau, 'Female Industry', pp. 333, 335.
78 Bessie Rayner Parkes, *Essays on Women's Work* (Alexander Strahan, London, 1865), p. 76. Most of the material in this book was reprinted from the *English Woman's Journal*. On the question of attitudes to married women and work, see Moira Maconachie, 'Women's Work and Domesticity in the *English Woman's Journal*: 1858–64', in Sally Alexander (ed.), *Studies in the History of Feminism 1850s–1930s* (University of London, Dept. of Extra-Mural Studies, Work in Progress, 1984).
79 Milne took up this point particularly, *Industrial and Social Position*.
80 Parkes, *Essays on Women's Work*, pp. 143–6.
81 On the business arrangements behind the *English Woman's Journal*, see Burton, *Barbara Bodichon*; Herstein, *A Mid-Victorian Feminist*; Rendall, 'A "Moral Engine" '.
82 Parkes, *Essays on Women's Work*, pp. 143, 146.
83 On the varied enterprises associated with the *English Woman's Journal*, see Holcombe, *Victorian Ladies at Work*; Alexander (ed.), *Studies in the History of Feminism*.
84 'J.B.', 'Life Assurance', *English Woman's Journal*, nos 2, 11, 1859, pp. 310–11, 316–17.
85 'Newspaper Cuttings Relating to Old and New Birmingham 1864–1905', collected by J. Macmillan. Thanks to Doug Reid for this reference.

PART III

Race, Ethnicity and Difference

9 Missionary Stories: gender and ethnicity in England in the 1830s and 1840s

In the 1990s nationalisms and national identities have become key political issues. The collapse of the Cold War and of the Soviet Union, the reunification of Germany, the re-mapping of Europe and the planned increased economic and political integration of EEC member countries in 1992 all raise critical questions about the nation state, national sovereignty, national 'belonging' and forms of citizenship. In this context national identity has emerged as a crucial issue in British politics.

But what does it mean to be British? National communities are, as Benedict Anderson has argued, 'imagined communities'.[1] Whilst sometimes appearing natural, they have always been constructed through elaborate ideological and political work which produces a sense of nation and national identity, but a sense which can always be challenged. For there is no single national identity – rather, competing national identities jostle with each other in a struggle for dominance. 'Britishness' and 'Englishness' are continually contested terrains in which meaning is not given but discursively constructed and reconstructed in conditions of historical specificity.

English national identity is a subject which has received relatively little attention.[2] In England the recognition that Englishness is an ethnicity, just like any other, demands a decentring of the English imagination. For ethnicities have been constructed as belonging to 'others', not to the norm which is English. A recognition that Englishness *is* an ethnicity, just like any other, necessitates, therefore, its own relativization of the West.[3] This essay is about English ethnicity – but it is centrally preoccupied with exposing the relations of power involved in that ethnicity and problematizing the relation between centre and margin. Ethnicities do not only belong to those on the margins – every culture has its own forms of ethnic identity. How, then, has Englishness been constructed as a national identity and what have been its historical specificities? What white ethnic identities were available, and what dominant, in the England of the mid-nineteenth century?

I use *English* rather than British advisedly but I would argue that Englishness marginalizes other identities, those from the peripheries, the Welsh, the Scottish and the Irish. In constructing what it meant to be English, a further claim was constantly being made – that Englishness was British, whereas those on the margins could never claim the right to speak for the whole. A Welsh identity could never be anything other than distinctively Welsh: an English identity could claim to provide the norm for the whole of the United Kingdom, and indeed the Empire.

In writing about the construction of white English ethnicity, the trap of participating in the 'morbid celebration of Englishness', castigated by Paul Gilroy recently, has to be avoided.[4] In recent decades a celebration of Englishness, of England's heritage in her rich history, her country houses, her Empire, her once assured place as the first industrial nation, has provided one response to post-colonialism, the collapse of Britain as a world empire and the challenge to white British identity constituted in the emergence of black and Asian British identities within the urban communities of the 1980s and 1990s.

In working on the English middle class in the period from the 1830s to the 1860s, the time when England could securely claim to lead the world in industrial and economic development, in empire-building and the development of democratic political forms, and when the English middle class was effectively challenging aristocratic power not only within the bastions of the national and local state but also within the hearts and minds of the English people, I aim not to celebrate those stories which we have been told and have told ourselves about nation, empire and civilization. Rather, I aim to deconstruct those English identities which were constructed in the mid-nineteenth century, to unpick the stories which gave meaning to the national and the imperial project, and to understand the ways in which English identity was constructed through the active silencing of the disruptive relations of ethnicity, of gender and of class. My project is not to reconstitute Englishness but to uncover the contingency of that construction in its historical specificity – to look at the dependencies, inequalities and oppressions which it hid in its celebration of national identity.

That national identity was powerfully articulated by middle-class men in this period: men who claimed to speak for the nation and on behalf of others. Those men, however, lived in a society cross-cut by complex social and political antagonisms, not only those of class which they thought, spoke and wrote about most forcibly, but also of gender (which they silenced) and of race and ethnicity. Their search for a masculine independence, for a secure identity, was built on their assertion of their superiority over the decadent aristocracy, over dependent females, over children, servants and employees, over the peoples of the Empire, whether in Ireland, India or Jamaica, over all *others* who were not English, male and middle class. But this identity was rooted in an ever shifting and historically specific cultural and political world, where the search for certainty and stability, 'I know who I am and I know how and why I have power over you', masked conflict, insecurity and resistance. In attempting to open up the contradictions within this middle-class identity, to demonstrate the shifting sands upon which an apparently secure sense of nationality was constructed, I hope to investigate a complex set of articulations in which class, gender and ethnicity are all axes of power, sometimes mutually reinforcing each other, sometimes contradicting each other. Cultural identity is always complexly constituted within a field of power and never depends upon any single dimension. To understand the construction of a national identity we need an analysis of the interrelations between class, gender and ethnicity as axes of power.

In the England of the 1830s and 1840s religion provided one of the key discursive terrains for the articulation of these axes and thus for the construction of a national identity.[5] The Evangelical revival of the late eighteenth century provided middle-class men and women with a language redolent with certainty – the certainty of religious conviction. The experience of conversion, so central to Evangelical belief, and the consequent commitment to a new life governed by faith, gave men the confidence to insist on their truths, even when this meant fundamental challenges to received wisdoms. Religious belief provided a vocabulary of right – the right to know and to speak that knowledge, with the moral power that was attached to the speaking of God's word. One of the issues on which they spoke was what it meant to be English.

My investigation of national identity is based on the argument that the English can only recognize themselves in relation to others. My project, therefore, is concerned with English representations of Jamaica and its peoples between the 1830s and the 1860s. For in characterizing, defining and identifying those others, they characterized, defined and identified themselves. Englishness was what the planters were not; the freed slaves might be, the freed slaves were not. In the turbulent decades between emancipation (1833) and the rising at Morant Bay in 1865 the changes in English perceptions of Jamaican blacks and the debates about those perceptions not only revealed changing attitudes to blacks but also to 'whiteness' itself and what it meant to be English. By the early 1830s an emancipationist position was effectively an orthodoxy within respectable middle-class society in England – only the paid lackeys of the planters would publicly defend slavery. The famous anti-slavery slogans, 'Am I not a man and a brother? Am I not a woman and a sister?', and the icon of the kneeling slave seeking British help, represented the belief in the civilizational equality of the negro, the potential of the negro to be raised from the state of savagery, through childhood to manhood, which characterized the cultural racism of the anti-slavery movement.

That cultural racism, with its paradoxical conviction that slaves were brothers and sisters, all God's children, but younger brothers and sisters who must be educated and led by their older white siblings, was most clearly articulated by the middle-class vanguard of the anti-slavery movement, in the forefront of which in the crucial years of 1831–3 were a group of Baptist missionaries from Jamaica.[6] These men were among those who were central to the organization of the public campaign, the petitions, the pamphlets, the lecture tours, the questioning of parliamentary candidates, which ensured that the first substantial piece of legislation from the reformed Parliament of 1832, elected by large numbers of middle-class voters who were exercising their right for the first time, was the emancipation of the slaves. Behind the men, never in the public forefront but absolutely central to the struggle, were large numbers of women whose activities until very recently have been seen as unimportant.[7] In 1833 the dominant definition of Englishness included the gratifying element of liberator of enslaved Africans.

By 1865, when in the wake of Morant Bay Jamaica once again occupied centre-stage in English politics, the situation had changed. English middle-class discourses on Jamaican blacks had by this time become much more explicitly racist. The failure of the public campaign spearheaded by John Stuart Mill and a group of Liberal intellectuals, to censure Governor Eyre for his brutal acts of suppression in the wake of the events at Morant Bay, and the success of the oppositional campaign, led by Thomas Carlyle, in celebrating Eyre's actions and narrating him as an English hero, revealed the extent to which the cultural racism of the 1830s, with its Liberal and progressive attachments, had been displaced by a more aggressive biological racism, rooted in the assumption that blacks were not brothers and sisters but a different species, born to be mastered.[8] This biological racism with its conservative structures of thought encoded an Englishness which celebrated hierarchy and difference, and relied on military power to enforce its superiority.

In the debates over slaves or freed blacks, English men and women were as much concerned with constructing their own identities as with defining those of others, and those identities were always classed and gendered as well as ethnically specific. Furthermore, their capacity to define those others was an important aspect of their own authority and power. English national identity, in other words, cannot be understood outside of England's colonial dependencies. Jamaica, a small island in the Caribbean, may never have been seen by the majority of the English population yet it occupied a place in their imaginary. Their ethnic identity as *English* was rooted in a series of assumptions about others.

This essay is concerned, then, with examining a particular colonial discourse, not primarily to extricate the history of those 'others' who the missionaries and their allies aimed to contain in their narrative strategies, but rather to investigate those English ethnicities which were in play. The regime of knowledge constructed by the abolitionists was to fix the relations of dominant and subordinate – the construction of the dominant 'gaze' was as central a preoccupation as the suppression of resistant 'others'. In their public interventions the missionaries and their allies were constructing their own identities and writing their own histories. Their mutual celebration of their effectiveness in Jamaica was important in confirming and sustaining English middle-class confidence in their capacity to check Old Corruption in whatever form it took – whether English aristocrats or Jamaican planters.

The missionary story that this paper is concerned with deals with a particular group of Baptist missionaries in Jamaica in the 1830s and 1840s. It has been widely argued that British missionaries of all persuasions were a powerful force in defining the imperial project in the nineteenth century and that anti-slavery discourse, which informed much of their practice and to which they made an important contribution, played a significant role in generating and consolidating British imperialist attitudes.[9] But missionaries from varying denominations are characterized as much by difference as by their similarities. Different discourses jostled for power amongst different missionary groups, and between those groups, and missionaries were themselves positioned very differently in different colonized societies. Some missionaries relied on a close partnership with the elite of the society in which they worked, others had a more contentious and marginal position.

This small group of Baptist missionaries in Jamaica, radicalized by their encounter with slavery, allied themselves with the slaves and put themselves in the forefront of the struggle for emancipation in England in the 1830s. Through their public speaking and writing on the anti-slavery and missionary circuits they were able to claim that their special knowledge of Jamaican society and of the institution of slavery gave them a right to be heard. In the most immediate and dramatic ways they evoked the horrors of the plantations: the whips, the cries, the instruments of torture, and worst sin of all, the denial of revealed religion. They represented themselves as the conscience of England, and indeed Britain.

Between the 1830s and the late 1840s they were able to build on this heritage and significantly intervene in public debate in England on questions of race and ethnicity. They articulated gendered representations of the 'other', of Jamaican black men and women, which significantly reduced the distance between themselves and their subjects, though that distance was never obliterated.[10] As colonizing subjects they saw themselves as privileged narrators, those who represented others, the leaders, the guides, the parents of the universal imperial Christian family. In constituting their own subjectivity they also constituted their subjects as manly men and domesticated, virtuous women rather than suffering and victimized slaves; the characteristics they sought to clothe them with were a version of those which they sought for themselves and which expressed their national identity.

Jamaica provided the test case for the great British experiment with emancipation, since it was the largest and the richest of the British West India islands. For the anti-slavery movement, and especially for the missionaries, it was vital that the experiment should work. Missionary dependence on the British public did not end with emancipation. It soon became clear that apprenticeship was in effect slavery by another name and that the historic work was unfinished. Furthermore, once apprenticeship was abolished, the planters tried other means to secure an unfree labour force. The missionaries engaged in unceasing efforts to secure the success of what they defined as the project of a free Jamaica, to make the island into a Christian, civilized, capitalist, free-labour economy with democratic institutions; in other words, into a country based on their version of the British model. This task occupied them without rest until the late 1840s when their optimism began to weaken, their faith in their own power became more limited. Between the public campaign of 1832–3 and the late 1840s there was a never-ending flow of words and people between England and Jamaica, attempting to secure the on-going politics of emancipation. Reports in the missionary press and in the anti-slavery press, public meetings, lecture tours, fund-raising campaigns, books, pamphlets, private letters designed to be read in part at missionary prayer meetings or abolitionist gatherings, all fuelled the fires of the emancipatory public and kept the issue of Jamaica at the forefront of the public conscience.

A series of substantial reports and memoirs were published between 1837 and 1849 which together marked a strategic intervention in this politics.[11] Their authors were those who claimed authority to write on Jamaica and the Jamaicans, missionaries such as Thomas Burchell and James Mursell Phillippo who had lived there for many years, established British middle-class figures including the well-known Birmingham philanthropist and businessman Joseph Sturge and the eminent Quaker banker and public man, Joseph John Gurney, who visited the island in order to investigate the *true* state of the island, both for themselves and for the British public. These texts referred to, and relied upon, each other, establishing what Edward Said calls a 'strategic formation' within the culture at large through their density and referential power.[12] The authors quoted each other, were reviewed favourably in the same journals and newspapers, provided reference points for the same section of the public. Their particular version of colonial discourse, their strategic creation of a space for subject peoples through the production of knowledge and exercise of power and surveillance, was abolitionist discourse, organized around the notion of 'negroes' (their terminology) as younger brothers and sisters.[13]

These texts explicitly concerned the category black, what it had meant and what it could mean; implicitly they suggested a preoccupation with whiteness, a category which was masked because it was seen as normal.[14] Whiteness, in the discourse of the Baptist missionaries and their allies, should mean order, civilization, Christianity, separate spheres and domesticity, rationality, modernity and industry. Those moments when whiteness meant something quite other were terrifying, as, for example, when white Anglican clergymen and planters, some dressed up as women, joined forces to burn down chapels and mission stations and lynch, tar and feather missionaries themselves.[15] Whites then became 'savages', with all the characteristics of the planter stereotype of the black. As Thomas Burchell wrote of his experiences in 1832 on his return to Jamaica in the wake of the slave rebellion of 1831, a rebellion that terrified white Jamaicans and was responsible for the winning of emancipation in England:

> the most furious and savage spirit was manifested by some of (what were called) the most respectable white inhabitants, that ever could have been discovered amongst civilised society. They began to throng around me, hissing, groaning and gnashing at me with their teeth. Had I never been at Montego Bay before, I must have supposed myself among cannibals, or in the midst of the savage hordes of Siberia, or the uncultivated and uncivilised tribes of central Africa . . . I am fully persuaded, had it not been for the protection afforded me by the coloured part of the population – natives of Jamaica – I should have been barbarously murdered – yea, torn limb from limb, by my countrymen – by so-called *enlightened*, RESPECTABLE! CHRISTIAN BRITONS![16]

In writing and publishing these texts, and in their lecture tours and campaigns in Britain, the missionaries and their friends were empowering themselves, deriving authority from their capacity to speak for others. Slaves spoke through and by virtue of a particular male, middle-class, English imagination, to paraphrase and adapt the views of Said. In that process the slaves themselves were partially silenced. William Knibb, in his most famous speech on abolition delivered at Exeter Hall in London, that Jerusalem of Evangelicals (a speech that was printed and widely circulated), to a packed audience whose response was tumultuous, opened with these words:

> Next to the heartfelt satisfaction of being instrumental to the conversion of the ignorant to the knowledge of the truth as it is in Christ Jesus, there is nothing more delightful than to stand forward as the advocate of the innocent and persecuted; and, when I consider

that on the present occasion I appear before an assembly of my countrymen on behalf of the persecuted African, I find in the fact a reward for all the sufferings in character and person which I have endured in the cause, as a missionary, for the last eight years.[17]

At a public meeting in Newcastle Knibb opened in similar vein:

There is nothing more delightful and interesting than to plead the cause of the injured, the degraded and the oppressed. This, under any circumstances, is peculiarly delightful; but it is especially so when the speaker finds himself surrounded by so large a number of his fellow-Christians, who he feels assured never hear of misery but they endeavour to remove it; who never hear of sorrow, but they are anxious to dry the mourner's tears; and who never hear of oppression, but every feeling of their heart rises up in just and holy indignation against the person who inflicts it.[18]

Here the pleasure which Knibb incited, to use Homi Bhabha's definition of colonial discourse, was the pleasure of speaking for the oppressed, than which there was nothing 'more delightful'.[19] Especially pleasurable was the capacity to speak for those who were doubly oppressed – female slaves:

I ask, in the presence of ladies, what Englishman could stand by, what Englishman could even contemplate the flogging of females without a flush of indignation? . . . Must I not therefore plead for women? . . . if I must speak at all, I must speak the real sentiments of my mind, and those sentiments must, to my latest moment, be uttered against slavery – slavery of every kind – but, above all, slavery of woman.[20]

Whiteness at this moment meant pity and care for lesser peoples, the authority through public campaigns to exercise that concern, to challenge existing power relations in Britain, challenge the West India interest, and insist on emancipation as a moral and political imperative. That definition of whiteness, however, was subject to constant attack itself. When planters behaved like savages and freed coloureds saved whites from their fury, what did it mean to be white and what distinctions could be made between black and white?

Such denunciations of the planters, and the doubts their conduct cast on the nature of a supposedly English and Christian brethren, were taken up with vigour by the rhetoricians of the anti-slavery movement. Sir Thomas Fowell Buxton, the Parliamentary leader of the movement after the retirement of William Wilberforce, relied heavily on missionary information for his speeches and reports. Horrified by the tales of missionary persecution in the aftermath of the 1831 rebellion, he contrasted the 'savage' behaviour of the Jamaican planters with the expectations as to how a supposedly Christian grouping should conduct themselves.

> Hereafter we must make selection among our missionaries. Is there a man whose timid or tender spirit is unequal to the storm of persecution? Send him to the savage, expose him to the cannibal, save his life by directing his steps to the rude haunts of the barbarian. But, if there is a man of a stiffer, sterner nature, a man willing to encounter obloquy, torture and death, let him be reserved for the tender mercies of our Christian brethren and fellow countrymen, the planters of Jamaica.[21]

Emancipation meant that the politics of racial equality came closer. As the reality of blacks as brothers and sisters loomed larger it became increasingly important to denote the differences between black and white. At the heart of the Baptist missionary enterprise was a profound ambivalence – a belief in brotherhood and spiritual equality combined with an assumption of white superiority. This contradiction, which so closely echoed the fraught ambivalence of Evangelical discourses on gender, destabilizes missionary discourse and ensures that there is never a single clear-cut utterance. Rather they are complex and ambivalent, with gender and racial contradictions erupting from the text, carrying the uncertainties and confusions of a particular definition of white identity, whilst attempting to present certainty and confidence, maintaining a fiction. By the late 1840s the fiction of the Englishman as defender of grateful Africans, which had continued to dominate respectable British middle-class opinion from the early 1830s, was much less secure. Conflicting colonial discourses with different rhetorical strategies were increasingly displacing and challenging the abolitionist voice, and the ambivalence of the missionaries themselves threatening to blow apart their dream.

As part of the British Empire Jamaica was nominally a Christian country and had an established Anglican presence. No attempts were made to Christianize the slaves, however, until the mid-eighteenth century when Moravian missionaries settled in the island.[22] The planters were extremely suspicious of missionary activity and many of them were actively hostile to it. The

Moravians were followed by some Wesleyans in 1791 and then by black Baptists in the wake of the American Revolution. In 1813 the Baptist Missionary Society (BMS) finally decided to send a missionary to Jamaica to establish their first white station there. All the missionary societies insisted on political neutrality and instructed their employees not to involve themselves with political questions. This, however, as Mary Turner has documented so well, proved impossible, since the 'serious' religion of the Evangelical enterprise was inevitably at odds with slavery. Planter toleration for missionary activity was at best uneasy and, in periods of political tension, broke down. The missionaries depended for their survival on the protection of the imperial government. This in turn meant that the imperial government had to be constantly petitioned and pressured to defend Nonconformist missionaries, hardly a likely group for the Colonial Office to concern themselves with. Inevitably, therefore, the missionaries depended on public support in England and the activities of their societies, not only to fund their work but to be able to do it at all.

The BMS had its roots in the Evangelical revival of the late eighteenth century, that re-emergence of vital, serious or real Christianity as compared with the nominal and empty forms which had come to dominate Christian worship and experience. Both Nonconformists and Anglicans were inspired by the revival and shared a common body of doctrine which at times allowed them to overcome the division between church and chapel and work together on missionary endeavours both at home and abroad. They shared a common insistence on the centrality of individual sin and the conversion experience, on the individual's capacity to be born anew and to construct a new Christian identity, whether as man or woman, built around their particular relation to the Christian household; and on a close monitoring both by the individual and by his/her pastor and his/her congregation of each soul and its progress towards salvation.[23]

Many Nonconformists shared the conviction of William Wilberforce and Hannah More, key ideologues of the Anglican Evangelical revival and leaders of the movement to abolish the slave trade and slavery on the grounds that they were deeply immoral and irreligious, that the real struggle which Christians must engage with in the wake of the French Revolution and the growth of English Radicalism, was the struggle for the hearts and minds of those heathens at home and abroad who did not understand that the fight was with the Devil and with sin; the army that was required was the army of God. The BMS, in the words of its contemporary historian the Revd F. A. Cox, was born of this conviction. The French Revolution had had disastrous effects,

> infidelity eclipsed the glory of truth, and spread its pestilential atmosphere amidst the moral darkness and confusion. The nation became warm in politics and cold in religion.[24]

Disturbed by this state of affairs, a small group of Baptist ministers met for an anniversary meeting in Kettering, Northamptonshire, and decided, under the inspiration of William Carey, to 'act together in society for the purpose of propagating the gospel among the heathen'.[25] Carey, a Baptist minister in Northamptonshire, had been preoccupied for some time with the importance of this work and wrote his *Enquiry into the Obligations of Christians to use Means for the Conversion of the Heathens* to convince others of the desperate need for this project abroad. 'It has been objected', he wrote,

> that there are multitudes in our own nation . . . who are as ignorant as the South-Sea savages, and that therefore we have work enough at home, without going into other countries . . . (but) . . . Our own countrymen have the means of grace, and may attend on the word preached if they chuse it . . . faithful ministers are placed in almost every part of the land, whose spheres of action might be much extended if their congregations were but more hearty and active in the cause: but with them the case is widely different, who have no Bible, no written language . . . no ministers, no good civil government, nor any of those advantages which we have. Pity therefore, humanity, and much more Christianity, call loudly for every possible exertion to introduce the gospel amongst them.[26]

The first field of activity for the BMS was in India and Carey ('this new Columbus (who) beheld a yet undiscovered world of heathenism') established with William Ward and Joshua Marshman the station at Serampore which was to dominate Baptist missionary endeavours for the first years.[27] In 1814, after pleas from the black Baptists established in Jamaica for support, and correspondence between Dr Ryland, the Baptist divine, and William Wilberforce, the BMS sent John Rowe out as their first emissary to the West Indies. The centre was reaching out to the peripheries, sending its forms of knowledge and civilization in the person of a young Englishman. His instructions from the committee, secure in their ethnocentric assumption of British superiority, impressed on him that he must not despise the slaves on account of 'their ignorance, their colour, their country, or their enslaved condition'.[28] The first years in Jamaica were dogged by ill-health, death and political problems for the missionaries but in the early 1820s the general revival of British interest in anti-slavery affected the Baptists too and they committed more resources to Jamaica. Three of the men who were to be most influential both in the island and at home went to Jamaica at this time – William Knibb, Thomas Burchell and James Phillippo.

The BMS venture remained on a relatively modest scale. By 1827 there were eight Baptist churches with approximately 5,000 members; by 1831 there were twenty-four churches with 10,000 members and 17,000 inquirers (that is, people who were seeking membership and being observed by the missionary and his auxiliaries); by 1835 this had increased to fifty-two stations with 13,795 members, and for some years these figures were to rise steadily as the missionaries benefited from the conviction amongst blacks that they had been crucial to the ending of slavery and apprenticeship.[29] Most Baptist missionaries came from artisanal families, some from the borders of the middle class. Baptists in England tended to occupy these class positions and had much less solid middle-class support than the Independents or Anglican Evangelicals, nothing like the wealth and status of Quakers or Unitarians. From the very beginning the missionaries had to contend with planter contempt, derision and harassment, but they were used to being laughed at for their faith, used to a society in which they were discriminated against and in which they had to fight to make their voices heard, used to being part of the army of God, outfacing sin in whatever manifestations it appeared. Their struggle both at home and abroad, as they conceptualized it, was with the forces of evil, reaction, 'dark savagery', heathenism and superstition – all of which could as easily be met in the back streets of Birmingham, in the markets of Calcutta or in the plantations of Jamaica. Sin, however, had its own special horror in the colonies, whether in the form of Hindoo superstitions or West Indian slavery. As William Knibb described it to a friend soon after his arrival in Jamaica in 1823,

> I have now reached the land of sin, disease, and death, where Satan reigns with awful power, and carries multitudes captive at his will. True religion is scoffed at, and those who profess it are ridiculed and insulted . . . The poor, oppressed, benighted, and despised sons of Africa, form a pleasing contrast to the debauched white population.[30]

Thomas Burchell, who came from a solidly middle-class mercantile background and was used to being treated with respect, for his status if not for his religion, was shocked, despite all preparation, at the contempt with which he was treated by planters and officials in Jamaica. On one occasion he was summoned to court with a verbal message from a 'common constable'. 'Thus a slave would be called to appear before a court of magistrates', he commented in a letter to England, 'but no Englishman, except a missionary, would be treated with so much contempt'.[31] Similarly, Phillippo noted that even an invitation from the Governor to meet him did not save him from the disdain of Jamaican whites. He found himself 'in a large room filled with planters and others of the ruling class, including the rector and curate of the parish. I was treated with superciliousness and contempt.'[32] As many have noted, the missionaries were placed in a highly ambivalent position – white, yet allies of the slaves and freed blacks, white, yet for the most part from a very different class background to that of the planters and the Anglican clergy.

The contempt they faced could be offset, however, with the influence which they established with the black population. Missionaries were consistently impressed with the 'hunger' which they found for Christianity amongst the blacks, which contrasted so sharply with the situation in England. Lee Compere, one of the earliest missionaries on the island, was much quoted in later years for his depiction of eager blacks seeking British Christian guidance:

> here are many souls continually heaving a sigh to England, and in their broken language continually crying out, 'O buckra, buckra, no one care for poor black man's soul! Buckra know God in England. O buckra, come over that great big water, and instruct me, poor black negro.'[33]

Mary Ann Hutchins, the wife of a missionary, wrote to her brother in similar vein in 1834:

> The thirst for knowledge amongst the blacks and coloured people is very great; many of them are asking for books to read, and the anxiety they evince, is very pleasing. I was much pleased one of the Sabbaths I was at Montego Bay, to see a Chapel pretty well filled with communicants, and instead of two – *fourteen bottles of wine* were used at the Sacrament. Oh! when in my dear native land will a scene like this be witnessed?[34]

The missionaries delighted in sending home computations of the numbers they had baptized, the numbers of their members and inquirers – a scientific demonstration of the power of the Word amongst the heathen.

Since real religion depended on a conversion experience, all missionaries had gone through this watershed (not always experienced as a blinding moment, but always as a fundamental turning point) usually in their late adolescence or early manhood. For Thomas Burchell, the son of a wool stapler, conversion meant freedom from sin, the only true freedom there was; 'his captivity was exchanged for freedom, and his mourning turned into joy'.[35] William Knibb, the son of a tradesman, described the growth of his conviction to the congregation at his baptism:

> Having enjoyed the unspeakable advantages of a religious education, and of being trained under the care of a pious and affectionate mother, I was early taught my state as a sinner, and the necessity of flying to Jesus Christ as the only hope of escape from that punishment which my sins had deserved.[36]

Conversion brought with it the need for action, for Christian manliness was defined through action. As the Revd Isaac Taylor, a popular Evangelical preacher and writer of manuals on Christian practice had taught, 'A man must act'.[37] It was through his action in the world, his assertion of his independence, that he recognized himself as a man and was recognized by others. For Evangelical Christians the action of combating sin, of enlisting in the army of God, provided a worthy arena within which they could prove their manhood. For aspirant artisans or lower-middle-class men, missionary work abroad offered an exciting opportunity; indeed it proved to be a great deal more exciting than working as a minister in England where congregations were pitifully small and the Word went mainly unheeded; in Jamaica, converts came in their thousands to those who survived (the assault of ill-health and death meant that the average length of service was less than three years), and the influence of the missionaries appeared to be profound. Furthermore, the encounter with the heathen 'other' gave an intensity, laced with ambivalence, to the work, which may have been hard to maintain in the mean streets of Manchester.

The desire to become a missionary often closely followed conversion. Joshua Tinson was inspired by an overwhelming pity for those who were 'ignorant and wretched'.[38] Thomas Knibb,

William's brother who preceded him to Jamaica and whose death determined William to go, looked forward with delight to missionary work:

> I thought that, however Christians were separated during the short time allotted to human life, they all reached the same home; and that it would be far more delightful, more honourable, to go to heaven from a heathen country than a Christian one.[39]

Some of the missionaries recorded that they had been preoccupied since childhood with stories of heathens as, for example, Thomas Burchell, who as a young man had loved to read conversion stories in the missionary press. This was a dissenting version of Martin Green's argument about the place of Empire in the British imagination. Imperial adventure stories were, Green argues, 'collectively the story England told itself as it went to sleep at night; and in the form of its dreams, they charged England's will with the energy to go out into the world and explore, conquer and rule'.[40]

For missionaries, such stories were of the glories of the conversion of the heathen against all odds, their dreams concerning sin and its defeat rather than money or conquest. After some years in Jamaica William Knibb, amongst others, became preoccupied with the idea of a mission to Africa. He was especially enthusiastic that this should be the first task of native missionaries. When it came about, he wrote in great excitement to a friend in England, 'a beloved brother, one of the despised, traduced, black Christians, an African by birth, has left this island . . . has worked his passage to Africa, and . . . is now on the spot from whence he was stolen as a boy, telling his fellow-countrymen the name of Jesus.' He implored his friend to plead for Africa,

> think of Africa, her wrongs, her sins, her openings. O my heavenly Father! work by whom thou wilt work, but save poor, poor, benighted, degraded, Europe-cursed Africa! my affection for Africa may seem extravagant. I cannot help it. I dream of it nearly every night, nor can I think of anything else.[41]

Such dreams inspired Bernard Barton, the Quaker Evangelical poet, when he was invited to write some introductory verses for Cox's *History of the Baptist Missionary Society*. Barton celebrated the men who went to the colonies not for the more traditional prizes of wealth, or land, not for excitement or because they wanted to be tourists enjoying the wonders of nature; rather their noble task, commanded from above, was to save sinners, they were the tools of the living God:

> For they went forth as followers of the Lamb,
> To spread his gospel-message far and wide,
> In the dread power of Him, the great I AM,
> In the meek spirit of the Crucified, –
> With unction from the Holy Ghost supplied,
> To war with error, ignorance and sin,
> To exalt humility, to humble pride,
> To still the passion's stormy strife within,
> Through wisdom from above immortal souls to win.[42]

Burchell's reading of the missionary press made him long 'to tread their shores, to mingle with their swarthy people, and to unfurl in their midst the banners of salvation'. As he became 'more acquainted with their barbarous atrocities and superstitious rites, together with their sanguinary and obscene abominations' he was increasingly convinced that he could find the strength to give up home. As he declared at his ordination, 'All my thoughts were occupied on missionary themes, and my chief happiness was associated with solicitude for the heathen'. His dreams were of India, for this was where Baptist missionaries were then active. 'India', he wrote in a letter in 1820, 'I long to place my foot on thy polluted shores. I long to enter the field of action as an ensign in the army of the Saviour, bearing the banner of his cross. I long to exert myself in the glorious revolution now talking place.'[43] James Phillippo meanwhile, the son of a master builder who was converted in young adulthood, felt an increasing desire to be useful, 'especially among the far-off nations lying in darkness and in the shadow of death'. He read missionary publications with avidity and trained himself in skills which he thought would stand him in good stead: medicine, brick-making, house-building, cabinetwork, agriculture, and the production of food and clothes. As he expressed his philosophy to his parents, 'This world is not a place of repose for a faithful soldier of the Cross'.[44]

Entry into missionary work meant applying to the BMS committee as a suitable candidate. Once accepted, the young men would undergo some training either at one of the dissenting academies or in the home of a Baptist minister deemed suitable to take in a small group for preparation. Most of the trainees had a very limited educational background, having left school to go into trade at the age of twelve to thirteen. This lack of a 'proper' education provided another source of derision from their class superiors both at home and abroad. Ordination followed the training and the ritual of 'setting apart' the missionaries for their work, usually performed by a group of established ministers, some of whom would have personal connections with the ordinand. Many of the Baptist missionaries in Jamaica were trained together and 'set apart' together, often with senior missionaries officiating, thus affirming the existence of a 'mission family', which it was a primary objective to sustain. The BMS committee decided where missionaries were to go and each missionary was responsible to the committee for his actions. In the hostile circumstances into which so many missionaries went, support from home was a necessary part of survival and there was a constant flow of letters between England and Jamaica. Missionaries were always at least partially dependent on money from home to finance their activities as well as needing committee intervention with the Colonial Office at times of acute tension.

The final 'necessary preparation' before sailing was marriage, for it was assumed that a married missionary would be more use than a single one.[45] Furthermore, Evangelical horror at the debauchery, as they saw it, of planter society, with its acceptance of concubinage, made Jamaica a dangerous place in which to be a man alone. Time and again in the biographies of missionaries their marriages are seen as secondary to their act of faith. For women this was rather different; those Baptist women who were seized with the missionary spirit could not themselves become preachers in the early nineteenth century. Indeed, the claim that women should be engaged in missionary work at all was one that had to be contested and won, just as the right to do philanthropic work was continually fought over. Women were not only needed to accompany men, it was argued, but women's missionary work was crucial to the heathen for it would be impossible to have access to many heathen women without workers of their own sex. It was widely believed in early-nineteenth-century England that Western women owed their superior position to Christianity, for it was Christianity which had raised society from its superstitions and freed women from the degradations associated in the English mind with heathenism, in particular the practice of 'sati' in India. It was proper, argued the protagonists of a special missionary sphere for women, that the daughters of Eve, first in transgression, should be the first in restoration.[46] There was no question, however, of accepting women as trainees or granting them equal access with men. Marriage, therefore, offered a possible route into the work for those women who wanted to do it. Accompanying an unmarried brother was also occasionally possible and by the 1830s a small number of women were going out as teachers.

Mary Ann Chambers, for example, experienced conversion at the age of twenty while her brother was training to be a missionary. 'What a noble cause,' she wrote to him, 'to be employed in teaching Jesus to the poor heathen . . . My soul does indeed long to be with the poor heathen.' She pined to go abroad with him. 'I do indeed love the missionary cause; it is nearer my heart than anything else; my soul seems in the work.' She was terrified that he would leave her behind. Through a friend she then met the Revd James Coultart who was about to go to Jamaica as a missionary. Her contemporary biographer explains that 'Her elegant person and accomplished mind at once engaged his heart; while she regarded the whole affair as the gracious leadings of Providence.'[47]

Mary Ann Middleditch, the daughter of a Baptist minister, also suffered from envy of a brother who trained to be a minister and who, under her influence, eventually became a missionary for a short time. Baptized in 1830, she became heavily involved with the struggle for emancipation and fascinated by Jamaica. On first leaving home to work in a school she greatly missed the missionary news that she had had access to at home. 'Let me know all that you can about the missionary meetings,' she wrote to her parents in 1833. 'Is Mr Knibb to be there? Oh! that I had the wings of a dove . . .' In a pious correspondence with a woman friend she discussed the hardship of their not being able to be missionaries abroad but argued that they must do all that they could in the mission field at home. 'I long to go as missionary, more and more,' she wrote to her friend. 'I think I speak advisedly, when I say, that I would rather go to Jamaica than dwell in England.' She attended missionary prayer meetings, read missionary books ('I have had a great treat this week, in reading Stathams's *Indian Recollections*. I have almost fancied myself there . . .'), eagerly awaited the day when schoolmasters and schoolmistresses would be sent out to teach the 'emancipated negroes'. Eventually her route was through marriage but in her letter to her parents explaining her decision to go it was love of Christ which was emphasized, not of her husband-to-be.

> Could your Mary Ann be happy, think you, if she refused to devote herself to Missionary work? Dare I, then, indulge the hope that I love Christ more than Father or Mother, if I refused to relinquish

> the pleasure of their society for His sake? No, my dear parents, duty calls, and great as is the sacrifice, your child must go . . .[48]

In the discourse of Evangelical Christianity there was plenty of space for imagination and adventure but little for the idea of romantic love as the key to marital choice.

Faith was at the heart of the missionary endeavour. In his letter of application to the BMS, James Phillippo made a brief statement of his faith:

> I believe in the total depravity of all mankind; in the absolute necessity of a change of heart; in man's inability to accomplish this work; that it is effected by the Holy Spirit, through the use of means; that Christ is the only way of salvation; the necessity of personal holiness. I recognise also two Ordinances: Baptism, administered to adults on a profession of faith in Christ; and the Lord's Supper. I believe in the final salvation of believers, and the final destruction of unbelievers.[49]

This statement would have been heartily endorsed by most Baptists. The sect was marked off by the belief in adult baptism but in all other respects was very close to other Evangelical dissenters. Individual sin and the conversion experience were at the heart of their Christianity, the loss of self and the being born anew in Christ. This rebirth of the Christian man and Christian woman, embedded in the Christian household, the finding of a new sense of self in Christ, was central to the Evangelical project. The abandonment of self, the conviction that men and women were but 'worms' in God's service, the most abject creatures at his command, has to be held together, however, with the powerful sense of self which both sexes derived from their beliefs. Thus, William Knibb, writing to his wife during a very successful visit to England in 1840 when he achieved all that he had hoped and was being celebrated at large public meetings all over the country, commented, 'When I look at the results of my mission to England, I am both thankful and humbled. O what a condescending creature God must be, to employ such an instrument in his service.'[50] He then went on to document his achievements concluding with, 'O this is a mercy and God shall have all the glory.'

Similarly, Thomas Burchell, described by many visitors as a patriarch, a gentleman, dispensing hospitality in ample style from his very comfortable country residence, wrote to the secretary of the BMS committee after establishing successfully a series of new stations, 'I do not wish to mention anything boastingly, I feel my own nothingness, and my anxious desire is to be found at the foot of the cross.'[51]

The strength of the missionaries was in their righteousness combined with their weakness ('worms' in the face of God), their isolation, their persecution, their oft-invoked spirit of Protestant martyrdom, their commitment to the voluntary principle and, therefore, their conviction that it was only through the agency of men and women such as themselves that the new moral world would be created. The savagery and barbarism, as they constructed it, of the societies they went to, justified their intervention. In bringing Christianity they were bringing civilization, for the two were equated in their discourse. The contest over slavery was a contest with Christianity – freedom meant the light of the word of God, the chains of bondage were infidelity and ignorance. In the 'contest for empire' between Christianity and slavery, the light had triumphed and Satan was defeated.[52] The missionaries were the 'messengers of mercy' as Phillippo described it:

> (They) have gone forth singly and at intervals, almost unperceived, while by their seeming weakness they have excited the pity and contempt rather than roused the opposition of foes . . . By residing among cruel savages and effeminate idolaters till, by their blameless lives and disinterested efforts, they have conciliated their respect, by introducing the useful arts of civilised society, or imperceptibly infusing the spirit of Christian truth . . . they have prepared the way for the Lord.[53]

The missionaries seem to have suffered little from doubts as to the absolutism of their faith, or rather, perhaps, they struggled not to acknowledge those doubts for in their isolation they needed to keep their fears at bay. This apparent absolutism was built on a faith rooted in an ethnic superiority; by virtue of being white and European they 'knew' and had the right to teach others. Whatever the inadequacies of their own education as perceived in England – for Baptist missionaries were denounced as low mechanicks and tradesmen – they did not hesitate to scoff at their rivals in Jamaica. They were possessed of the one truth, the one correct reading of the gospel. Those first missionaries who had to establish themselves on the basis of the work done by black Baptists found much to contend with. James Coultart often had to deal with those who thought they were Baptists but had been, in his view, very badly taught. His task was 'to separate the precious from the vile, to correct what was erroneous, to instruct the ignorant, to humble without offending the conceit and pride of the self-sufficient and out of these elements to form a Church according to the New Testament of our Lord Jesus Christ'.[54]

Thomas Knibb was shocked at the presence of 'pretend preachers' in the island who claimed to teach the gospel:

> There are many persons who profess to be teachers, who are as ignorant of the gospel as a Hindoo or Hottentot. They preach to, and live upon the people, and tell them tales that are as ridiculous as they are irreligious . . . Some of the black people go about the island *preaching* and baptising. They generally have a book to preach out of, but sometimes mistake a spelling-book, or a dictionary, for a Testament, and sometimes preach with it upside down.

It did not apparently occur to him that difficulty in understanding 'the negroes' when he first arrived might be to do not with their inadequacies, but with his own. 'Their understandings are very limited,' he wrote in patronizing vein to an English friend, 'exceedingly so with field negroes, so that we find the greatest difficulty in understanding what they mean.'[55] James Coultart noted with satisfaction that 'abundant evidences appear both of the power and progress of religion' amongst the blacks. The 'sublime character and the sanctifying energy of the gospel flash', he observed, 'like brilliant beams of sunshine amidst parting clouds, through the broken forms of negro language'.[56] The truth would out, even with these broken forms.

The construction of a New Jerusalem depended on the ceaseless industry and activity of the little band of missionaries, who had set themselves the task of converting the heathen. Their enterprise was rooted in the 'mission family' which they worked hard to create and sustain. The Baptist missionaries came from a society in which family enterprises were at the heart of economic, social and cultural life.[57] They were used to a world which was physically organized around the family enterprise, to which men, women and children all contributed in the 'properly' gendered ways – men as the public and legal front, women as the informal partners. In the world of tradesmen, small proprietors and merchants, artisans and ministers from which they came, it would have been unthinkable for women not to have contributed to the family enterprise in innumerable ways. Men provided the driving force and the public face but women were the source of capital, labour and contacts, they were the mothers who bore children to carry on the family business and to reproduce it in its daily life. Missionary wives, it was assumed, needed no training to know how to do any of this, it was their vocation.

But the family enterprise was only the starting point for the mission family. Mission stations provided the basis for what became an extended family stretching across the island. The family was defined not only by blood but also by religious brotherhood; 'friend', 'brother' and 'sister' were all terms whose meanings crossed blood relations and ties of friendship. Stations might begin with only one couple but would hope to bring in others as their work extended and the numbers of chapels under their care grew. When new stations were established they kept in close touch with their 'parent' stations and relied on them for succour and support. A Jamaica Baptist Association was formed in 1824 to link the missions across the island. Family was indeed a many-layered concept in this context for there was the family of origin, the family of marriage, the family of the chapel, the mission family, the family of Baptists at home and the family-to-be in the skies – this last providing the key to the overarching spiritual nature of the Christian family. Without a religious family, individuals would be hard-pressed to maintain their faith – the family was a bulwark, a defence against the immorality of 'the world', a haven in which Christian morality was practised.

The overlapping family networks provided a series of settings in which people could live their daily lives and enjoy a promise for the future to come. As Mary Ann Hutchins (née Middleditch) put it in the last letter that she wrote to her parents before she left England, the pain of parting was lessened by her great desire that they might 'form a family anew, unbroken in the skies'.[58] Once in Jamaica she found that the mission family treated her just like a daughter and that Thomas Burchell and his wife took her into their home as if she were their child. Indeed, the months of her last illness and early death were spent with them. For these Baptists, like their Evangelical counterparts in England, the terrible pain of the loss of children was alleviated by the presence of the family in heaven. In 1843, William Knibb wrote to his wife Mary while she was in England telling her that he had preached from

> 'the whole family in heaven'. It is a delightful subject, and I hope I feel it to be so. In that family *there are an innumerable company of children* . . . our five sweet cherubs are there; but Oh! the loneliness they have left.[59]

The mission family was literally tied by a web of cross-cutting relationships. Many of the missionaries came from Baptist families and carried their fathers' and grandfathers' activities into another field. They married into Baptist families, named their children after Baptist luminaries and friends, saw their children marry missionaries or become missionaries themselves. Thomas Burchell's grandfather was a Baptist minister, his wife's sister married another Jamaican Baptist missionary, Samuel Oughton, his daughter married a missionary, Edward Hewett.[60] William Knibb's brother was a missionary, his nephew, left orphaned, was cared for by him and returned to Jamaica to work as a schoolteacher in the new village of Kettering which he had established, named after his home town in Northamptonshire; one of his daughters married a minister who took over the church in Kettering and their son was a minister; Knibb's sister's son also became a missionary. Two sisters, the Misses Drayton, who came to Jamaica in the 1840s as teachers, both married missionaries. Missionaries who were widowed married relatives of their extended mission family, widows often remarried other missionaries or ministers.

Naming patterns confirmed these connections and friendships. Two of William Knibb's sons were named after missionary friends, James Coultart and Thomas Burchell – the latter was originally to have been named Augustus Africanus but they changed their minds, a significant indicator of where primary identifications lay. Knibb's first son was named Andrew Fuller, after the celebrated Baptist divine from Kettering, whose chapel he had been connected with and whose son he had been apprenticed to. James Phillippo sealed a friendship for life with a Baptist brother when they were both undergoing their missionary training – they exchanged names and each took the other's surname as a middle name; he became James Mursell Phillippo.

Like all families, this extended mission family was subject to acute tensions and conflicts as well as providing support for each other. There were tensions between London and Jamaica over many issues: most notably over slavery and open political commitment in 1831–2 when the BMS committee was reluctant to abandon its insistence on political neutrality but was propelled into this by the weight of Baptist opinion mobilized by Knibb and his friends; and in 1841 over issues about Baptist missionary conduct in Jamaica which some saw as smacking dangerously of Africanism. This debate was to push the missionaries in Jamaica into the decision to become entirely self-supporting, a decision taken in even more contentious circumstances at Serampore in 1837, and one which several of the Jamaican missionaries, including James Phillippo, were not happy with.[61] The subject of the development of a native ministry was also divisive. Both in India and Jamaica many Baptist missionaries were convinced that one of their most important tasks was to educate and train a native ministry who would be able in time to take on the work. What period of training and apprenticeship was necessary was, however, a matter of dispute in both places. In 1837 Burchell had serious reservations about native agency. He argued that

> It is not to the men, but to their present want of fitness that I feel compelled to object. So far as the free coloured people are concerned, in consequence of their very defective and partial education, they were till lately deemed ineligible to the office of clerks or book-keepers. With respect to the slaves, they could be instructed only by stealth or in the Sunday school. Their acquirements, therefore, are very, very meagre indeed. Yet, this is no reflection upon them, but rather upon that accursed system under which they have so long laboured and suffered . . . This is not the age of miracles; and it is scarcely reasonable to expect that the negro churches can grow from infancy to manhood in a day.

His cautious words, however, went unheeded; a disregard that was to be regretted by the BMS later when they admitted that, in utilizing the example of the East Indies, they had not taken 'into full consideration the difference which existed in the mental development of the partially educated Hindoos and the utterly untutored children of Ham'.[62]

A very serious division occurred within the mission family in Jamaica when Phillippo visited England for a lengthy period because of ill-health and on his return found that Dowson, the 'native agent' who had been looking after his congregation in Spanish Town, now claimed the chapel as his own. On the death of one of Dowson's followers, Phillippo refused permission for a burial in the chapel cemetery. Enraged by this, Dowson's supporters stormed the cemetery at night and were attacked by a group of Phillippo's allies. Only the calling out of the militia quelled the violence.[63] Several years of dispute and litigation followed which severely taxed all concerned.[64] On the whole, however, the beleaguered position of the missionaries and their need for mutual support ensured the cohesiveness of the little community, whatever the untold costs. 'We have been a happy and united family,' wrote Burchell, 'we have generally consulted each other in our concerns.'[65]

The structure of the mission family, as with the early-nineteenth-century English family from which it was derived, was strictly patriarchal. It was the missionary who was appointed by the BMS and who had all formal responsibilities. It was most unusual for there to be any direct correspondence, for example, between the BMS and a missionary's wife. All dealings with the authorities in Jamaica went through the missionary and his wife was understood to be his helpmeet and junior partner, covered by him in law. The missionary's role in the family enterprise was in part defined by his fatherhood – head of household, father of the family, father of the congregation, father of the children in his schools. The range of his activities was immense, his working hours extensive. In a letter to his mother in 1828, James Phillippo described his working day, and indirectly the ways in which it intersected with that of his wife:

> I rise every morning at five o'clock, spend an hour in my study, pass another hour in my garden, or walking about to inhale the freshness of the morning air. I then return to my study, and remain there till eight. Breakfast; conduct family worship, including any persons who may happen to be on the premises. We afterwards go down into the school, which is on the floor beneath us, and which we superintend, and there remain until other engagements require attention. At two o'clock, when at home, I again visit the school, and remain till it is over for the day, concluding as it was begun, with singing and prayer. About half-past four we dine, then get ready for chapel, class-meetings, singing classes, leaders' meetings, evening adult school, or meetings of some kind or another in town or country every day of the week. They usually commence at six o'clock and continue for an hour and a half. We then take tea, have family prayers, and at nine or half-past retire for the night.

On Sundays there were of course the services and the Sunday schools, there were visits to the sick, monthly meetings with members and inquirers, 'experience meetings', church meetings, the settlement of disputes, marriages, burials, baptisms, meetings with other missionaries, encounters with officials and all the other myriad responsibilities of the pastor. By 1841, Phillippo had been taking care of the district of Spanish Town 'alone', as he put it, for seventeen years. He was responsible for eight stations, some of them twenty miles away from his base, all of which required services and meetings. He superintended eight schools, was building three new chapels and enlarging another. His congregations were between 2,000 and 3,000 and as father of his churches he kept a sharp eye, or as sharp as he could given the numbers, on their practices. He managed the budget of this entire enterprise, receiving some money from England but raising much of it from his members.[66]

In his conception of his duties, Phillippo was typical of the missionaries. As William Knibb pointed out in a letter to the treasurer of the BMS, discussing the differences between England and Jamaica:

> Here we are obliged to be everything – everything religiously, politically, civilly, and (if I may coin a word) buildingly. While our brethren at home have deacons who can manage the temporal affairs of the church, and collect the necessary moneys, we must be responsible for all, and manage all. While there are laymen to whom the poor can go for advice, and even for legal advice, here ours is the only appeal. Every disagreement, domestic or civil, comes before us; by our advice they go to law, or by our advice abstain. It is just the same in political matters; not a step will they take, nor an agreement will they sign, without asking us.[67]

Phillippo and his brothers all relied heavily on their wives to support them in whatever ways were appropriate. Mrs Phillippo lived above the school in which she worked alongside her husband. She taught the girls while he taught the boys – a division of labour firmly established in Evangelical schools, whether Sunday or day schools, from the late eighteenth century. In addition she ran the household, bore nine children, five of whom died, and suffered extreme ill-health. As a missionary's wife she would be expected to run a household in which hospitality was always available, receive callers and visitors on all the occasions when her husband was not there, visit sick and poor women and children, question female applicants for church membership.

This last activity became a source of serious attack from some quarters in the early 1840s. At a time when the influence of the Baptist missionaries was at its height there was considerable envy from the missionaries of other denominations who resented their success. Accusations were published in the press which included a critique of the practice whereby female inquirers, who sought baptism and membership, were dealt with by missionary wives rather than by the pastors themselves. This was seen as a dangerous dereliction of duty, for how could untrained and unordained women treat inquirers with the proper rectitude? Knibb was sent to England by the Jamaica Baptists to defend the record both to the BMS and to the British public. He was aggressive in his defence, linking it to the propriety of women working with women, a favoured discourse amongst Evangelicals and one that was widely used to justify women's intervention in spheres that might have been deemed unsuitable:

> I know that a great deal of the examination of females for church-fellowship devolves upon our wives; but it is not necessary for me to state the reasons why females should be thus employed, when we think of the former state of Jamaica. It is right that this should be done by females who, though unobtrusive, are well qualified to form a judgement, and who know what the female mind of Jamaica is; who in their humble walk never slacken, though seldom praised, but are doing a work which angels will admire, and Jesus approve. I say, if we are wrong to take the testimony of our wives to the competency of those in scriptural knowledge who wish to come into our churches, being females, then we are wrong and shall be wrong still.[68]

He added that he always spoke to the inquirers afterwards himself, thus confirming the female judgement.

The appalling relations of men and women under slavery, in the eyes of the missionaries, made the task of raising women to a Christian state a particularly crucial one. 'Like the inhabitants of all uncivilised nations, the men treated the women as inferior in the scale of being to themselves'; every woman was a prostitute, every man a libertine.[69] Even after the abolition of apprenticeship Knibb saw the young girls on the estates as prey to seduction. 'I wish I could interest the females of Birmingham' (where, as noted, there was a very strong women's anti-slavery society), he wrote to an English correspondent in Birmingham, no doubt hoping that the hint would be passed on, 'in the situation of the young girls on the estates, most of whom are the prey of the seducer. I want to establish separate schools for them, under female teachers . . . I know full well, that until the female character is raised, we shall never far advance in civilisation and virtue.' He welcomed signs of domesticity amongst his congregations and measured civilization and freedom by 'the cottager's comfortable home, by the wife's proper release from toil, by the instructed child' – by the English middle-class family model, in other words[70] One of the missionaries' proudest claims was of the thousands that they had married in the years after emancipation, a claim that gave them the opportunity both to count numbers, a favourite early-Victorian activity, and to provide proof of an improvement in morality; for 'those who are married', wrote Phillippo, when going to church on Sundays, exhibit 'the truly civilised and social spectacle of walking arm in arm'.[71]

Missionary wives received none of the public praise which was heaped on their successful husbands in the heady years of the 1830s and 1840s. The public funerals, the public meetings, the obituaries, the memorials and biographies were not for them. They had to be satisfied with a quieter form of praise. 'I assure you, my dear girls,' wrote Knibb to his daughters, 'that I attribute most of my success in my missionary career to your excellent mother, while we are mutually impressed with the truth that we owe all to sovereign mercy, and feel that we have been unprofitable servants.'[72] If wives died before husbands, daughters took on the task of providing help and support. The family enterprise was defined by being a family – the family under God the father and the father/head of household. The pressure to conform with this was immense. Sons or daughters who did not move in a clear line towards adult baptism and a life of service were pressured, prayed for, publicly urged to identify themselves with Christ. Those children who died young were sometimes mythologized for their love of freedom and of the Saviour, as in the case of young William Knibb, the only son left in the family:

> The destroyer of our race had left him but one son, a noble boy of twelve years of age, intelligent, pious, and enthusiastically interested in the negro's welfare. No sooner was the manumission of the apprentices in his father's church determined, than the heart of William leaped for joy; and, hastily bounding away, he sketched a British ship in full sail, with the word 'liberty' on her flag, chasing two slavers, who were in the act of striking their colours. On the pendant was written, 'slavery must fall'. The excitement brought on a fever in the night, in the delirium of which, his rambling words showed a mind filled with ideas of negro emancipation, and the triumphs of humanity, law, and religion.[73]

Since, during slavery, the plantation provided the major community to which the slaves belonged, one of the essential tasks of the missionaries, both before and after emancipation, was to build an alternative community around the chapel. The chapel could potentially provide a place of belonging, a source of identity, a social life. Much of the strength of dissenting congregations in England derived from this sense of community, the cohesion of the chapel world, with its voluntary principles and its clear rules of conduct. The missionaries worked to develop equivalent structures in Jamaica. In order to extend their supervision and build up a band of responsible helpers outside the immediate family but within the family of the Church, missionaries made use of the pattern of leaders established within the Wesleyan Church and of the appointment of deacons, a feature of all Nonconformist churches in England. Teachers, deacons, helpers, all were trained by the missionary and delegated by him. He sat at the centre of this web of surveillance, managing and organizing. 'The characteristics of this organisation,' wrote Phillippo, 'are union, division of labour, and classification, combined with the most vigilant pastoral direction and supervision.'

Each church was divided into classes, each class superintended, and fuelled with the 'holy ambition' to surpass their brothers in duty. Each individual was encouraged to see himself as part of the whole and there were frequent social meetings to foster a sense of union and mutual effort. The agents 'instructed inquirers, visited the sick, sought after backsliders, superintended funerals, and reported cases of poverty and distress throughout their respective districts'. Each member of the church thought of himself as his brother's keeper; together they were one family. 'Bound closely to each other by mutual knowledge, intercourse, and love, "there is neither Jew nor Greek, there is neither male nor female, there is neither bond nor free, but all are one in Christ Jesus",' wrote Phillippo, quoting St Paul and failing to recognize the ways in which equality was hardly the central characteristic of this system, for at the centre, 'planning, improving and directing all its movements,' was the pastor himself, the patriarch.[74]

If gender hierarchy was inscribed at the heart of the missionary enterprise, so was that of race. Missionaries arrived in the island with their heads full of images of 'poor Africans', 'savages', 'heathens'. The welcome they met softened the notions of savagery and heathenism, which are, indeed, increasingly found attached to the planters in missionary discourse, and intensified the emphasis on pity. As Mary Ann Hutchins put it to a friend, 'I wish you could hear the artless way in which we are welcomed by the Negroes. – poor things! – they are interesting creatures.'[75] Here the language of chatteldom, 'poor things', and of difference, 'interesting creature', specimens to be observed, are clearly in play. Mary Ann identified herself more and more with these 'poor things', however, and in her letters home, probably designed to be read at the missionary prayer meetings that she had so missed when she first left the parental nest, she tried to identify her parents with the project of brotherhood. After her husband's first baptismal service she wrote to her mother describing the glorious scene, 'a song of praise, a fervent prayer, and then nine of *our* – yes *your* black brethren and sisters buried in the stream ...' Similarly she described to them the immensely moving scene when Burchell returned to the island after the 1831 rebellion and his persecution. One of those who welcomed him was 'a fine looking black man' who was completely overcome:

> big tears rolled down his manly face, and he was obliged to retire to give vent to his feelings. He lifted up his hands, and could thank God only with tears! – *This is a specimen of that tribe between the monkey and the human species, who are quite destitute of feeling.*

In his *Memoir of Mary Ann Hutchins*, articulating her last thoughts on race and difference, her father thought it appropriate to quote these lines, celebrating brotherhood across cultures:

> Afric's emancipated sons
> Shall join with Europe's polish'd race,
> To celebrate in different tongues,
> The triumphs of Redeeming grace.[76]

Poetic effusions on the brotherhood of man were a favoured form for the missionaries. In Phillippo's discussion of the race question in his book on Jamaica, written for an English audience, he quoted approvingly these lines:

> Children we are all
> Of one great Father, in whatever clime
> His Providence hath cast the seeds of life, –
> All tongues, all colours! Neither after death
> Shall we be sorted into languages
> And tints – white, black, and tawny, Greek and Goth,
> Northmen and offspring of hot Africa;
> Th'all-seeing Father – he in whom we live and move –
> He, th'indifferent Judge of all – regards
> Nations, and hues, and dialects alike;
> According to their works shall they be judged.

Phillippo undoubtedly believed with one part of himself that all nations and hues were equal under God, just as he thought that 'neither male nor female, we are all one in Christ Jesus'. Slaves, he argued, were the hapless victims of a revolting system; they were

> men of the same common origin with ourselves, – of the same form and delineation of feature, though with a darker skin, – men endowed with minds equal in dignity, equal in capacity, and equal in duration of experience, – men of the same social dispositions and affections, and destined to occupy the same rank with ourselves in the great family of man.

This family of man, however, was like all families internally ordered. Jostling with the language of equality in Phillippo's mind was the language of hierarchy, undercutting that very equality he claimed to espouse. There was an evolutionary ladder, he believed, at the top of which were Europeans and up which, when things were going well, freed blacks would climb. As the free coloureds rose, there was a 'corresponding improvement' amongst the more respectable blacks:

> The latter have advanced to that degree in the scale of civilisation and intelligence, formerly occupied by the people of colour, and the former to that previously held by their more favoured white brethren. In no respect do these now differ from the middling and lower classes of tradesmen and others in England. Their eyes have long been open to the disgrace and sin of concubinage, and marriage among them has become common. The eye of the Christian is now delighted, especially on the Sabbath, by the spectacle of multitudes of these classes with their families walking to and fro from the house of God in company.[77]

Blacks, in other words, proved that they were the same as whites by aspiring to behave like them.

Phillippo declared in his Preface that he had tried to make his book more interesting for English readers by the inclusion of anecdotes and dialect. The black voices, both male and female, which were encoded in his text told a story of accommodation, piety and respectability. Few disruptive moments surfaced in his stories of negro gratitude and affection. Similarly the Revd Cox, in his account of missionary activities in Jamaica, was at pains to quote the testimony of negroes to demonstrate their loyalty and affection to the English. Negroes were thus constructed by the missionaries and their friends, both for themselves and for an English audience, through the filter of a set of assumptions as to what post-emancipation society should be like – a set of assumptions which seesawed on the ambivalence of racial difference: blacks were, and were not, equal.

Black inferiority was further encoded in the language of the family. Blacks were the 'sons of Africa', 'babes in Christ', children who must be led to freedom, which meant adulthood. The missionaries were the parents who would act as their guides, teaching them, admonishing and reproving them, congratulating them when they did right. 'They are willing to be taught,' wrote Knibb, 'and where there is sympathy with them, they love those who instruct them.' At the same time he baulked at including them in his own immediate family. He disliked, for example, having to employ a black wet-nurse when his wife was too ill to feed one of their children: 'I feel at having a black person for this purpose, but there is no remedy.' He was also entirely comfortable, on occasion, with using the epithet 'blackey' and with stereotyping negro characteristics. 'The little dears leaped for joy when I entered,' he wrote to a friend about a visit to a school, 'and many could not refrain from dancing, for a negro must express his joy.'[78]

Emancipation, for the missionaries, meant black entry into manhood, for masculinity in their world meant freedom from dependence on the will of another.[79] To be subject meant a loss of male identity, whereas for women one form of subjectivity, that of the female slave dependent on her master, was ideally exchanged for another, that of the freed woman on her husband. Marriage and domesticity was the desired status for women. 'Emancipation,' wrote Knibb in 1839, 'is a glorious triumph of Christianity. The insulted African has, by his calm propriety of conduct, fully vindicated his claim to be a man.'[80] Once again this hierarchical conception of racial difference was cross-cut with a more egalitarian rhetoric. 'The same God that made the white made the black man', Knibb preached on the anniversary of the end of apprenticeship, 'the same blood that runs in the white man's veins, flows in yours'.[81] The old characteristics of 'the negro', it was concluded, were disappearing as the legacy of slavery was destroyed by a Christian culture and Christian education:

> That cunning, craft, and suspicion – those dark passions and savage dispositions before described as characteristics of the negro, if ever possessed in the degree in which they are attributed to him, – are now giving place to a noble, manly, and independent, yet patient and submissive spirit.[82]

Those respectable English visitors who came to the island in the wake of abolition to inquire into apprenticeship and its aftermath and write their definitive and authoritative reports on 'the negro', shared these sets of assumptions. They came to Jamaica to look at a species, were impressed by the potential which they saw, but 'raising the native mind', in the words of Joseph John Gurney, raising the native mind to European standards, was the key to their project.[83] Joseph Sturge and Thomas Harvey put great stress on the promise of their objects of study; 'their conduct and their character are full of promise for the future,' they wrote, 'full of tokens of their capacity to become, when free, a well-ordered, industrious and prosperous community.'[84] 'The negroes', John Candler thought three years later, in 1840, were like children:

> The Negroes now they have got freedom like to show that they have it, and cannot bear to be told that if they want a day to themselves they must ask their master to let them have it. They wish to work, and to intermit work as they please, and think they have a right to do so. This we know is perplexing to the master; but the Negroes, with all their shrewdness, have much of the child about them, and need to be humoured.[85]

Gurney, while attempting to convince both himself and his readers throughout his text of the respectability and seriousness of blacks, ended on a hopelessly optimistic note as to the rapid disappearance of distinctions of colour in the West Indies – an argument which his own writing belied.

For these visitors, subaltern voices in the text are occasionally disruptive in ways which suggest their deep uncertainties as to the relations of black and white. Candler and Gurney both tell the story of an encounter with a myalman. In Candler's account:

> The doctor, a black young man of about twenty, very fashionably attired, came in with the easy manners of a perfect gentleman, and taking his seat, called for a glass of water, which was brought him with haste and reverence by one of the company. At first he only professed to cure diseases by the administration of simple medicines, suited to the disease complained of; but, on being pressed further, told us that he was qualified to hold discourse with good spirits of the dead, who intimated to him all the secret and hidden evils of the human body, such as no human eye could penetrate, and that by this means he could effect cures which no white man could perform. We asked the people whether they believed this; they said with one voice, 'We do believe it', and seemed astonished at our

> incredulity. J. J. Gurney spoke to them on the folly of such superstition; and some of them, in return, before we went away, hoped that God would open our eyes and make us see clearer.

Gurney's account concludes optimistically: 'We were sorry to observe the obstinacy of their delusions, but such things will be gradually corrected by Christian instruction.' The unspoken worry was that they would not be. For anxious readers he adds the rational note that it was because the negroes were deprived of medical help that they inevitably resorted to quacks.[86]

Part of what was in play here was an articulation of class difference as well as racial difference. If men such as Phillippo and Knibb had stayed in England as Baptist ministers, they would have been assured positions within the middle class. With modest stipends they would have occupied the lower end of that class economically, whilst deriving status from their profession. They would never, however, have been able to compete with an Anglican clergyman. Some Nonconformist ministers in England were able to achieve solid middle-class positions by virtue of the success of their chapels and attached ventures such as taking in pupils or writing books. The most comfortable often owed that comfort to a well-made marriage once they had achieved status as preachers. In Jamaica their prospects were much better. As George Bridges, Anglican clergyman, scourge of all dissenters and founder of the Colonial Church Union, acidly commented in his *Annals of Jamaica*, 'a cloud of itinerant preachers' had 'hastened to exchange a parish pittance in England, for a lucrative profession in the West Indies'.[87]

In Jamaica, despite the contempt of the established white population, white missionary skins gave authority, an authority confirming that derived from faith, an authority to command. The Baptist missionaries saw it as a part of their historic task to create an industrious, respectable, free working class in Jamaica. In class terms as well as in racial terms they only partially believed in equality. Spiritual equality might be one thing. Economic and cultural equality were entirely another. Despite the suspicions of the planters, less blinkered contemporaries were convinced of the missionaries' commitment to the construction of a genuinely free labour market by their tireless efforts to convince the blacks that they must fulfil their side of the bargain. 'A fair day's work for a fair day's wage' was their maxim.[88] In line with this, they were delighted to see women becoming respectable domestic servants as the terrible vestiges of slavery were abandoned, for if women had to work outside the home they believed that the best possible work was that of a domestic kind. For respectable English middle-class men, the spectacle of women working in someone else's home was far less damaging to their concept of femininity than to see them working, sometimes in mixed gangs, on the estates. Conveniently forgetting the complaints about servants which were part of the stock in trade of the English middle class, Phillippo wrote with great smugness:

> Domestic servants are beginning to be eminently trustworthy; and, when properly treated and confided in, do not suffer by a comparison with the great bulk of the same class in England.

This was indeed a sign of 'society advancing to that high moral standard which is fixed in the great Christian code'.[89]

There were complicated issues at play, however, in the class relations of missionary and church member, for the missionaries became increasingly financially dependent, as were their counterparts in England, on their congregations. Some money came from the BMS but after the abolition of apprenticeship an increasing proportion of the income came from the membership. This necessarily meant a shift in power. Missionaries might be the fathers of their children, their guides and leaders; yet their physical comfort and security rested on them. Take the case of the building of a new home for William Knibb, a story which was widely reported in England because of the attack in 1841 on the luxurious way of life of some of the Baptists. In a public speech at Exeter Hall, Knibb told the tale and defended his actions:

> When I laid a report before the members of my church, and read the title deeds of the chapels – that all those chapels that are out of debt were vested in trustees – and when they found that the house in which I lived, the bed on which I reposed, and the furniture which I used, was not my property, but theirs, and belonged entirely to the church, they said, 'Minister, have you took care and got a house for your wife?' I said, 'No: do you think that I would take your money without your leave, and buy a house for Mrs Knibb?' They replied, 'If you have not got one, it is time you had. You go to Kettering, to the land left that belongs to you, and you build a good house there, and we will pay for it.' I took them at their word . . . for Edward Barrett (a deacon) said, 'Set about it soon, minister; you may cut' – that is, I might die; 'and we cannot bear the thought that your wife should go home; let her stop here.' I built the house and it cost 1,000

> sterling; and, as soon as it was completed, I assigned it over to Mrs Knibb and our dear children, determined not to hold property there. In Kettering House she is now . . .

Knibb claimed that none of the Baptists that he knew in Jamaica lived in houses that were more 'costly or commodious, or better furnished, than any individual with a family, who has been used to move in respectable life, is fairly entitled to'.[90] There was a certain naivety in this; it is unlikely that any Baptist minister in England had had a thousand-pound house built for him by this congregation, furnished, furthermore, with a two-hundred-pound library. Knibb's status and power were secure in post-emancipation Jamaica, but in the end depended, as he put it himself, on the generosity of the blacks. Building a large house for your minister was one way of showing him his dependence on you – a reversal which figures little in missionary discourse.

In the wake of the abolition of apprenticeship it soon became clear to the missionaries that the planters would do everything in their power to drive down wages and construct new forms of unfree labour. The missionary response to this proved to be their most ambitious venture in Jamaica – the establishment of free villages.[91] Yet in those villages racial, class and gender hierarchies were literally built in. Faced with the planters' refusal to rent houses and provision grounds at a reasonable rate, a group of missionaries headed by Knibb, Phillippo and Burchell started to raise money to buy land themselves, establish new villages and then sell the plots mainly to their trusted church members. Joseph Sturge was a key figure in supporting this venture in England. He had established close friendships with several of the Baptist missionaries during his visit to Jamaica, led the efforts to bring the apprenticeship issue to the front of the public conscience in England, and was the driving force behind the Jamaica Education Society which provided money for new schools. He was entirely in favour of a project which he saw as promoting negro welfare and set up the West India Land Investment Company to buy up bankrupt plantations. As the prospectus put it, the point of the Company was 'to transfer the control of West India property gradually from those who have systematically opposed the advancement of the Negroes in civilisation, knowledge and christianity, to such men as would really promote their moral and religious welfare . . .'[92] Between

1838 and 1844, 19,000 freedmen and their families settled in these free villages, possibly 100,000 people in all.[93]

The villages were imagined as missionary utopias; designed and planned by missionaries, they were built around the church, mission house and school. Free peasants could buy their plot of land, sometimes paying it off in instalments, thus securing their manhood, not only with the possession of property but also with the vote that it carried. The lots sold were designed to contribute to a family enterprise in which men would continue to work on the estates but the family would be able to grow provisions, both to feed themselves and to sell on the local market. Phillippo hoped through the establishment of these villages to give 'his' people 'a relish for the comforts and conveniencies of civilised life', to improve their domestic economy, and to 'convince these simple-minded people that their *own* prosperity, as well as that of the island at large, depended on their willingness to work for moderate wages, on the different properties around them'. He had personally first purchased the land, then

> surveyed and laid out the allotments, superintended the construction of the roads and streets, directed the settlers in the building of their cottages, and cultivation of their grounds, supplied them with their deeds of conveyance, formed societies among them for the improvement of agricultural operations . . .[94]

Phillippo's early estimation of the multiple skills necessary for the missionary had indeed come to fruition! The towns were named after the heroes of the anti-slavery movement: Sligoville, Clarkson Town, Wilberforce Ville, Sturge Town, later to be renamed Birmingham after Sturge's home town, Buxton, Gurney, Albert and Macaulay. Even one heroine of the movement, a Quaker feminist Anne Knight, sister-in-law of John Candler, had a village named after her, Knight's Ville.[95] Knibb named one village in his area Kettering after his birthplace and it was here that the commodious Kettering House was built and legally placed in the names of his wife and children so that, in his eyes, his position as pastor was not impugned.

In Sligoville, named after the Marquis of Sligo, one-time Governor of Jamaica who had been supportive of missionary efforts, the houses were significantly named too: Victoria, Happy Home, Content, Comfort Castle, Industry, Happy Hut, Happy Grove, Content My Own, Paradise, Liberty Content, Comfortable

Garden, Happy Retreat, the names expressing both the meaning for freed slaves of owning a place of their own and the definitions of home and domesticity which were inscribed in these properties. Phillippo proudly described a typical cottage in Sligoville, where he himself had a 'a neat but commodious country house'[96]; they were thatched or shingled, plastered or built in stone or wood, some had a porch with shutters or glass and there was a sitting room in the middle, a bedroom at each end.

> . . . many of the latter contain good mahogany bedsteads, a wash-handstand, a looking glass, and chairs. The middle apartment is usually furnished with a sideboard, displaying sundry articles of crockery-ware, some decent-looking chairs, and not unfrequently with a few broad-sheets of the Tract society hung round the walls in neat frames of cedar.

There was a kitchen at the back and a place for stock. Sometimes the gardens at the front were decorated in European style with rose-bushes and other flowering shrubs. All in all they were a perfect setting for a domesticated family life. As Phillippo commented, 'On returning from their daily labor the men almost uniformly employ themselves in cultivating their own grounds or in improving their own little freeholds, and the women in culinary and other domestic purposes.'[97] Visitors to the villages were impressed, though Gurney was concerned about the evidence of too much love of luxury amongst the negroes and hoped they would soon learn to be more frugal. In Sligoville he was delighted that 'The people settled there were all married pairs, mostly with families, and the men employed the bulk of their time in working for wages on the neighbouring estates.' Overall the scene was one of contentment, industry and piety; all under the eye of James Mursell Phillippo.[98]

These villages represented the perfect society for the Baptist missionaries: Knibb in Kettering and Hoby Town, named after a Birmingham Baptist minister and friend in England; Burchell in Bethel Town and Mount Carey, named after William Carey; Phillippo in Sligoville, Sturge Town, Clarkson Town; Clark in Wilberforce Ville and Buxton, all had the opportunity to create a new moral and material world in which Christianity and freedom reigned, where the chief benefactor was the missionary and the very structure of the town embodied his beliefs about the right ordering of the races, the classes, the sexes. This potentially perfect dream, of model villages, of a more ordered England in the

Caribbean, offset the fears and anxieties of the missionaries themselves as they tried to live their lives between two cultures. Of course, the missionary stories give us very limited access to the meanings which those communities held for the black residents – to uncover that would require a different kind of research. What the missionary tales do tell us about, however, is the ways in which English dreams and aspirations were expressed through the construction of these Jamaican villages.

The missionaries suffered from troubling uncertainties as to where they really belonged – uncertainties that are highly evocative in the 1990s. They always thought of themselves as English, British, and saw England and the abolitionist public as their ultimate source of support. But they also suffered from feelings of shame about their 'race', as they constructed it, and were engaged in a constant polemic to ensure that their definition of what it meant to be English should be the dominant one. When contemplating slavery, Knibb felt 'ashamed that I belong to a race that can indulge in such atrocities'.[99] In his campaign of 1832–3 he constantly called upon his audiences to be 'patriots', which in his terms meant to be opposed to slavery – this was the true nature of the English, and therefore to his mind British, love of freedom. After abolition, when apprenticeship became the issue, Knibb despaired of Jamaican whites and declared that, 'from English patriots must come, if it come at all, the Magna Charta of Africa's rights'.[100] Similarly, Phillippo bemoaned the ways in which the planters' behaviour impugned the national honour; it was not English to persecute blacks and despise other races and he was particularly ashamed on one occasion when a French official visitor observed the planters' vituperations.[101] Abolitionist activists all assumed that England must do what had to be done. Since the whites in Jamaica would not take their responsibilities to their race seriously, and the prospect of the blacks taking decisions into their own hands was too horrifying to contemplate except at moments of extreme stress, it was up to the *right kinds* of English people to assert *their* conception of what it meant to be English and to ensure that appropriate legislation was passed for 'our colony'.[102]

In England the missionaries spoke for the afflicted, whether as slaves or freed men being denied their proper opportunities, and begged the English, primarily the middle class since these were the people they predominantly addressed at their meetings and in their writings, to show their kindness, their generosity, their pity for those less fortunate than themselves, to exercise their power and influence and free the slaves, give money for their education, raise them to full personhood through the building of proper villages, with proper homes, schools, churches and jobs.

In a series of grand celebrations of abolition, of the ending of apprenticeship and of subsequent anniversaries of these historic events, of the BMS jubilee, of the Jamaican missionary jubilee, England and the English were ritually constructed as the benefactors, those who had given the slaves freedom, those to whom the freed slaves must demonstrate their worthiness, their manhood, their domesticated femininity. In renderings of 'God save the Queen' and 'Rule Britannia', in the banners which celebrated the English heroes of the anti-slavery movement, just as the names of the villages did, in their portraits which were hung in the chapels, in the 'Freedom Flag' with the Union Jack in the corner, in the posters proclaiming 'England, land of liberty, of light, of life' and 'Philanthropy, Patriotism and Religion have under God achieved for us this glorious triumph', in the marble memorial in Knibb chapel at Falmouth celebrating the death of slavery, in the English hymns which were sung, England was celebrated as the land of the free and the giver of freedom.[103] Listen to the reported witness which was invited from respectable black (male) deacons in Knibb's chapel at the ending of apprenticeship and then recorded in the British missionary press with all the accompanying insignia of proper forms of address and English names:

> Mr Andrew Dickson: 'I do truly thank God for the light of the everlasting gospel. I present my thanks to the people of England for the gospel.'
>
> Mr William Kerr: 'We bless God, we bless the queen, we bless the Governor, we bless the people of England for the joy we have.'
>
> Mr Edward Barrett: 'My good friends, we are meet together here to show our gratitude to a certain gentleman and the people of England, who felt for us when we did not feel for ourselves. We have been made to stand up and see our wives flogged, and we could not help them. The people of England did not see us, but God see us, and God stir up their hearts to get us freedom, and now we are all free people![104]

Among the celebrations to invoke England's greatness and magnanimity was that held in Birmingham in 1838 to mark the contribution which Joseph Sturge, the town's renowned citizen, had made to the ending of apprenticeship. The festivities lasted two days, 1st and 2nd August. The first event was a gathering of four to five thousand Sunday school scholars in the Town Hall, addressed by Baptist ministers and other dignitaries and attended by Daniel O'Connell, that emancipator of another British colony. The speeches were followed by a meal of British bread and beef and a procession through the town to the site of a new school, the Negro Emancipation School, the foundation stone of which was laid by Sturge himself. An inscription hailed Sturge as 'the friend of the negro, the friend of the children, and the friend of man' so distinguishing, if ambiguously, between negroes and men. The children, who would undoubtedly have been predominantly working class, sang 'Rejoice the Saviour Reigns' and 'The Trump of Freedom Sounds', rejoicing, in theory at least, that their Saviour reigned in the colonies as well as at home and that their betters had given freedom to their inferiors in Jamaica.[105]

Thus one England, the middle-class, Nonconformist-influenced, patriarchal England, identified herself for herself and her multiple 'others'. As the greatly loved abolitionist poet Montgomery put it:

> Thy chains are broken: Africa be free!
> Thus saith the Island-Empress of the sea;
> Thus saith Britannia – Oh, ye winds and waves!
> Waft the glad tidings to the land of slaves![106]

In 1840 the considered opinion of James Stephen, the powerful Permanent Under-Secretary at the Colonial Office with an unrivalled knowledge of colonial affairs, was that the influence of the Baptist missionaries would steadily increase and 'make them masters at no very distant time of the fortunes of Jamaica'. 'The tendency of things in Jamaica,' he wrote, 'appears to be towards the Establishment of a sacerdotal Government, exercised by narrow-minded men over a Body of docile, grateful, and affectionate Disciples. All things considered I doubt whether this is a just subject of regret.'[107] His judgement, however, on this matter was substantially wrong. Missionary influence was to be steadily weakened in subsequent years.

In June and July 1842 the jubilee of the BMS was celebrated in Kettering, England, and Kettering, Jamaica, with Knibb participating in both events. In England the services were attended by more than five thousand people and one of the texts was, 'The Lord hath done great things for us, whereof we are glad'.[108] In Jamaica, where there were also huge celebrations with tens of thousands of people, Knibb addressed five hundred deacons and leaders 'on the important position they occupied'.[109] On the second day, after a prayer meeting, he spoke to the assembled multitudes and pressed them to do a fair day's work for a fair day's pay. 'The eyes of the world are upon you', he warned them,

> and every slave who moaning clanks his chain, expects by your conduct to have it smitten from his manacled body. By the woes of bleeding Africa, by you to be hushed; by the hopes of the American slaves, by you to be realised; by all the great and eternal principles of justice; by all the past mercies you have received; by the present momentous position in which you stand! – do, I implore you, use the influence you so justly possess, to maintain on fair and equitable principles, Jamaica's welfare.[110]

Now it was Knibb's turn to 'implore' the negroes to behave as England thought they should, to show their gratitude for all that England had done for them by being good wage labourers and responsible citizens and fathers. But the times were becoming less auspicious for missionary dreams.

In September 1842 an alarming irruption took place at Salter's Hall Baptist chapel in Jamaica where Walter Dendy had been the missionary for more than ten years. At that time,

> a fearful spirit of delusions came over many persons who resided on estates near Ironside-by-the-Sea . . . Some of the members and inquirers became affected with it, and seemed fascinated as by a spell. On the 25th December they entered the chapel at Salter's Hill, in the time of Divine Service. They ran about like mad persons, jumped on the benches, began to speak wildly, and interrupted the worship. [Mr Dendy asked the congregation to keep calm, the Myal men and women were removed and the deacons guarded the doors.] Mr Dendy preached from Ephesians VII: 'Have no fellowship with the unfruitful works of darkness, but rather reprove them.' Towards the close a woman came in, and ran wildly about the chapel with pictures in her hands. She exhibited one, which was intended to represent the crucifixion of the Saviour, and lifting up her eyes in a peculiar manner, curtsied to it. At the end of the service a scene of confusion took place. The myalists rushed into the chapel, with frantic gesticulations. They tore away ornaments from the females, and the watch-guards of the men. In the chapel-yard several people

> were seized and thrown down and had water poured on them. Some were considerably injured by these fanatics, who threatened violence to all.

The magistrate was applied to and the police arrived to arrest and charge the offenders, but the 'bad effects' of these superstitious practices were felt by the members of the chapel for a long time to come.[111] Similar events occurred in other places and the hold of the missionaries over the popular imagination seemed to be waning.

When, in 1844, James Phillippo returned to the island after a lengthy stay in England and the 'native agent' who had cared for his chapel in his absence refused to relinquish his control, with considerable popular support, Phillippo was deeply wounded. The dispute that followed – involving seven years of litigation and much financial help from England – 'greatly affected Mr Phillippo's judgement of the negro character', in the words of his biographer. It became clear to him that his bright hopes had been too bright, his expectations too high:

> If the people were free, it was also evident that long years of patient labour were yet needed to bring to maturity the seeds of truth and righteousness, purity and order, which it had been his aim and that of many other benevolent men to sow.[112]

The ascent to manhood, as the missionaries constructed it, was clearly going to be a very long business indeed. Phillippo's gloom was increased by the collapse of the prosperity of the immediate post-emancipation period and the increase in poverty and unemployment. After 1846 wages fell, sugar production declined, and between 1844 and 1854 49 per cent of plantations were abandoned, while provision prices also fell.[113] It was impossible to assert with confidence any longer the superiority of free over slave labour.[114] Meanwhile, in England anti-slavery support was lagging after the fiasco of the Niger expedition, the abolitionist-inspired venture to open Western Africa to commerce and 'civilization', and the intense divisions amongst the abolitionists as to whether the preferential duties on West Indian sugar should be maintained.[115] Phillippo wrote anxiously in his diary, 'the future is dark and gloomy. The country is increasing in poverty, and religious feeling is rapidly declining. But the Lord reigneth, therefore will I hope in Him.'[116]

Phillippo's own sense of a flawed dream must have been sharply intensified by the publication in 1847 of *Jane Eyre* with its particular and different articulation of all that was mad and bad in Jamaica, soon to be followed by Thomas Carlyle's 'Occasional Discourse on the Negro Question' (later retitled 'Nigger' in a symptomatic sign of the times), which launched a powerful and vitriolic attack on the experiment of emancipation. New voices were coming to the fore, a new colonial discourse with its own form of racism and its own polemic on England and Englishness was emerging. The missionary struggle to define blackness as both equal and not equal, whiteness as superior, but with patronage, kindness and generosity to the fore, was collapsing under the combined weight of its own contradictions, its own refusal to face the uncomfortable reality that black people might choose to be different, and a new assault from elsewhere on the mutability of racial difference. The moment of the 'poor negro' was over.

NOTES

1 Benedict Anderson, *Imagined Communities. Reflections on the Origin and Spread of Nationalism* (Verso, London, 1983).
2 The most helpful introduction to the history of 'Englishness' can be found in Robert Colls and Phillip Dodd (eds), *Englishness. Politics and Culture 1880–1920* (Croom Helm, London, 1987).
3 For a discussion of black British identities and their implications, see Stuart Hall, 'Minimal Selves', *Identity*, ICA Documents 6, London, 1987; 'New Ethnicities', *Black Film, British Cinema*, ICA Documents 7, London, 1988.
4 Paul Gilroy, 'Ethnic Absolutism', in Lawrence Grossberg, Cary Nelson, Paula Treichler (eds), *Cultural Studies* (Routledge, London, 1992).
5 On the centrality of religion to the formation of the English middle class, see Leonore Davidoff and Catherine Hall, *Family Fortunes: Men and Women of the English Middle Class 1780–1850* (Hutchinson and Chicago University Press, London and Chicago, 1987).
6 Mary Turner, *Slaves and Missionaries. The Disintegration of Jamaican Slave Society, 1787–1834* (Illinois University Press, Urbana, 1982). I am not suggesting that other groups, particularly the Wesleyans, were unimportant either to the winning of emancipation or to the construction of a particular variety of English national identity. However, I have chosen to concentrate on the Baptists and the particular effects which they had, the particular images which they constructed.

7 For a thorough survey of women's anti-slavery activities in England, see Clare Midgeley, 'Women and the Anti-Slavery Movement 1780s–1860s' (University of Kent PhD thesis, 1989).

8 For an analysis of some of the gender aspects of this debate, see Catherine Hall, 'Competing Masculinities: Thomas Carlyle, John Stuart Mill and the case of Governor Eyre' in this volume.

9 On the place of religion in the anti-slavery debates about the construction of a free-labour, capitalist world, see, for example, David Brion Davis, *The Problem of Slavery in the Age of Revolution 1770–1823* (Cornell University Press, Ithaca, 1975); Robin Blackburn, *The Overthrow of Colonial Slavery 1776–1848* (Verso, London, 1988).

10 In conceptualizing the specificity of Baptist missionary discourse I have benefited greatly from discussions with Moira Ferguson and from reading her forthcoming book, *Subject to Others: British Women Writers and Colonial Slavery 1670–1834* (Routledge, New York, 1992).

11 They are, in order of dates of publication: Joseph Sturge and Thomas Harvey, *The West Indies in 1837 being the journal of a visit to Antigua, Montserrat, Dominica, St Lucia, Barbados, and Jamaica; undertaken for the purpose of ascertaining the actual condition of the negro population of those islands* (Hamilton Adams & Co., London, 1838); Joseph John Gurney, *A Winter in the West Indies described in familiar letters to Henry Clay of Kentucky* (John Murray, London, 1840); John Candler, *Extracts from the Journal of John Candler whilst travelling in Jamaica*, 2 pts (Harvey & Darton, London, 1840–41); T. Middleditch, *The Youthful Female Missionary: A Memoir of Mary Ann Hutchins, Wife of the Rev. John Hutchins, Baptist Missionary, Savanna-la-mar, Jamaica; and Daughter of the Rev. T. Middleditch of Ipswich; compiled chiefly from her own correspondence by her father* (G. Wightman and Hamilton Adams, London, 1840); Revd F. A. Cox, *History of the Baptist Missionary Society from 1792–1842*, 2 vols (T. Ward & Co., London, 1842); James M. Phillippo, *Jamaica: its Past and Present State* (John Snow, London, 1843); John Howard Hinton, *Memoir of William Knibb, Missionary in Jamaica* (Houlston & Stoneman, London, 1847); William Fitz-er Burchell, *Memoir of Thomas Burchell, 22 years a Missionary in Jamaica* (Benjamin L. Green, London, 1849).

12 Edward Said, *Orientalism* (Penguin, Harmondsworth, 1985), p. 20. I found Lata Mani's use of Said's formulation particularly helpful in thinking about my own work. 'Contentious Traditions: the debate on "sati" in Colonial India, 1780–1833' (University of California at Santa Cruz PhD thesis, 1989).

13 'Negro' is the common usage in abolitionist writing and is, therefore, the term which I am using in exploring this historical moment.

'Black' is sometimes used, both by abolitionists and by those who were in effect pro-slavery, for example, Thomas Carlyle.

14 Richard Dyer, 'White', *Screen*, vol. 29, no. 4, 1988.

15 Parliamentary Papers, *Select Committee on the Extinction of Slavery throughout the British Dominions*, House of Commons, XX, 1832, Evidence of William Knibb, p. 254.

16 John Clark, Walter Dendy and James M. Phillippo, *The Voice of Jubilee: a Narrative of the Baptist Mission, Jamaica* (John Snow, London, 1865), p. 204

17 William Knibb, *Speech at a Public Meeting of the Friends of Christian Mission* (S. Bagster, London, 1832), p. 9.

18 William Knibb, *Speech on the Immediate Abolition of British Colonial Slavery* (J. Blackwell & Co., Newcastle, 1833), p. 13.

19 Homi Bhabha, 'The Other Question – the Stereotype and Colonial Discourse', *Screen*, vol. 24, no. 6, 1983.

20 Knibb, *Speech at a Public Meeting*, pp. 15, 16.

21 Charles Buxton (ed.), *The Memoirs of Sir Thomas Fowell Buxton* (John Murray, London, 1848), p. 295.

22 A number of works deal with the missionary presence in Jamaica: see, particularly, Turner, *Slaves and Missionaries*; Ernest A. Payne, *Freedom in Jamaica* (Carey Press, London, 1933); Philip D. Curtin, *Two Jamaicas. The Role of Ideas in a Tropical Colony 1830–65* (Harvard University Press, Cambridge, Mass., 1955); C. Duncan Rice, 'The Missionary Context of the Anti-Slavery Movement' and Michael Craton, 'Slave Culture, Resistance and the Achievement of Emancipation in the British West Indies 1783–1838', both in James Walvin (ed.), *Slavery and British Society 1776–1846* (Macmillan, London, 1982).

23 On the centrality of gender definitions to the Evangelical revival, see Davidoff and Hall, *Family Fortunes*, especially pt 1.

24 Cox, *History*, vol. 1, p. 2.

25 Cox, *History*, vol. 1, p. 2.

26 William Carey, *An Enquiry into the Obligations of Christians to use Means for the Conversion of the Heathens* (Leicester, 1792), quoted in E. Daniel Potts, *British Baptist Missionaries in India 1793–1837* (Cambridge University Press, Cambridge, 1967), p. 2.

27 Cox, *History*, vol. 2, p. 11.

28 Payne, *Freedom in Jamaica*, p. 21.

29 The figures are from Payne, *Freedom in Jamaica*, p. 26 and Cox, *History*, vol. 2, p. 231.

30 Hinton, *Knibb*, p. 45.

31 Burchell, *Thomas Burchell*, pp. 68–9.

32 Edward Bean Underhill, *Life of James Mursell Phillippo; Missionary in Jamaica* (Yates & Alexander, London, 1881).

33 Quoted in Clark, Dendy and Phillippo, *The Voice of Jubilee*, p. 147.

34 Middleditch, *Hutchins*, p. 99.
35 Burchell, *Thomas Burchell*, p. 7.
36 Hinton, *Knibb*, p. 7.
37 For a discussion of the Evangelical concept of manliness, see Davidoff and Hall, *Family Fortunes*, especially ch. 2.
38 Quoted in Clark, Dendy and Phillippo, *The Voice of Jubilee*, p. 172.
39 Hinton, *Knibb*, p. 9.
40 Martin Green, *Dreams of Adventure, Deeds of Empire* (Routledge & Kegan Paul, London, 1980), p. 3.
41 Hinton, *Knibb*, p. 276.
42 Cox, *History*, vol. 1, p. vi.
43 Burchell, *Thomas Burchell*, pp. 26, 27, 29, 33.
44 Underhill, *Phillippo*, pp. 8, 17.
45 The phrase is Underhill's, for many years secretary of the BMS, in relation to Phillippo. *Phillippo,* p. 28.
46 Jemima Thompson, *Memoirs of British Female Missionaries with a Survey of the Condition of Women in Heathen Countries* (William Smith, London, 1841).
47 Thompson, *Memoirs*, pp. 10, 13.
48 Middleditch, *Hutchins*, pp. 41, 45, 49, 60, 70.
49 Underhill, *Phillippo*, p. 12.
50 Hinton, *Knibb*, p. 371.
51 Burchell, *Thomas Burchell*, pp. 305–6.
52 The phrase is Cox's, *History*, vol. 2, p. 193.
53 Phillippo, *Jamaica*, p. 470.
54 Clark, Dendy and Phillippo, *The Voice of Jubilee*, p. 4.
55 Clark, Dendy and Phillippo, *The Voice of Jubilee*, pp. 189–90.
56 Cox, *History*, vol. 2, p. 39.
57 On the family enterprise, its place in middle-class culture and the development of capitalism, see Davidoff and Hall, *Family Fortunes*, especially pt. 2.
58 Middleditch, *Hutchins*, p. 86.
59 Hinton, *Knibb*, p. 458.
60 Name cards have been compiled for the missionaries, using a wide variety of sources, and this data is derived from them.
61 On the debates between the BMS and the missionaries in Jamaica, see Cox, *History*, vol. 2; on Phillippo's doubts about independence, Underhill, *Phillippo*; on the Serampore controversy, see Cox, *History*, vol. 1, and Potts, *British Baptist Missionaries.*
62 Burchell, *Thomas Burchell*, pp. 324–5.
63 See the account of this episode in William A. Green, *British Slave Emancipation. The Sugar Colonies and the Great Experiment 1830–65* (Oxford University Press, London, 1976). p. 342.
64 Underhill, *Phillippo*, pp. 231–2.
65 Burchell, *Thomas Burchell*, p. 150.

66 Underhill, *Phillippo*, pp. 82–3, 174.
67 Hinton, *Knibb*, p. 470.
68 William Knibb, *Jamaica*, Speech to the BMS (G. & J. Dyer, London, 1842), p. 25.
69 Phillippo, *Jamaica*, p. 218.
70 Hinton, *Knibb*, pp. 273–4, 310.
71 Phillippo, *Jamaica*, p. 284.
72 Hinton, *Knibb*, p. 480.
73 Burchell, *Thomas Burchell*, p. 332.
74 Phillippo, *Jamaica*, pp. 432, 437.
75 Middleditch, *Hutchins*, p. 97.
76 Middleditch, *Hutchins*, pp. 104, 110, 171.
77 Phillippo, *Jamaica*, pp. 151–2, 154.
78 Hinton, *Knibb*, pp. 50, 75, 210, 306.
79 Leonore Davidoff, ' "Adam spoke first and named the orders of the world": masculine and feminine domains in history and sociology', in Helen Corr and Lynn Jamieson (eds), *The Politics of Everyday Life: Continuity and Change in Work, Labour and the Family* (Macmillan, London, 1990).
80 Hinton, *Knibb*, p. 310.
81 Hinton, *Knibb*, p. 313.
82 Phillippo, *Jamaica*, p. 253.
83 Gurney, *A Winter*, p. X.
84 Sturge and Harvey, *The West Indies*, p. 346.
85 Candler, *Extracts*, p. 20.
86 Candler, *Extracts*, pp. 28–9; Gurney, *A Winter*, p. 98.
87 George Wilson Bridges, *The Annals of Jamaica*, 2 vols, 1828 (reprinted Frank Cass, London, 1968), vol. 2, p. 294.
88 S. Wilmot, 'The Peacemakers: Baptist Missionaries and Ex-Slaves in West Jamaica', *Jamaica Historical Review*, vol. 13, 1982, pp. 42–8.
89 Phillippo, *Jamaica*, p. 265.
90 Knibb, *Jamaica*, pp. 34–5.
91 Sidney Mintz, *Caribbean Transformations* (Aldine, Chicago, 1974); Alex Tyrrell, *Joseph Sturge and the Moral Radical Party in Early Victorian Britain* (Christopher Helm, London, 1987).
92 Quoted in Tyrrell, *Joseph Sturge*, p. 90.
93 Mintz, *Caribbean Transformations*, p. 160. These were figures widely discussed in England at the time.
94 Phillippo, *Jamaica*, pp. 430–31.
95 *Missionary Herald*, February 1841.
96 Gurney, *A Winter*, p. 116.
97 Phillippo, *Jamaica*, p. 235.
98 Gurney, *A Winter*, pp. 115–16.
99 Hinton, *Knibb*, p. 48.
100 Hinton, *Knibb*, p. 245.

101 Underhill, *Phillippo*, p. 159.
102 In one of his speeches in England at the height of the contest 'between slavery and Christianity', Knibb referred to the danger that if the British did not act, the slaves would. Knibb, *Speech on the Immediate Abolition*, p. 20.
103 There are rich descriptions of the end-of-apprenticeship celebrations in Phillippo, *Jamaica*, and Cox, *History*, vol. 2; of the marble memorial and the BMS jubilee in Hinton, *Knibb*; of the Jamaica jubilee in Clark, Dendy and Phillippo, *The Voice of Jubilee*.
104 Cox, *History*, vol. 2, pp. 252–6.
105 *Report of the Proceedings at Birmingham on the First and Second of August in Commemoration of the Abolition of Negro Apprenticeship in the British Colonies* (Tyler, Birmingham, 1838).
106 Quoted in Clark, Dendy and Phillippo, *The Voice of Jubilee*, p. 76.
107 Quoted in Paul Knapland, *James Stephen and the British Colonial System 1813–47* (University of Wisconsin Press, Madison, 1953), p. 171.
108 Cox, *History*, vol. 2, p. 384.
109 Hinton, *Knibb*, p. 452.
110 Clark, Dendy and Phillippo, *The Voice of Jubilee*, p. 128.
111 John Clarke, *Memorials of Baptist Missionaries in Jamaica, including a Sketch of Early Religious Instructors in Jamaica* (Yates & Alexander, London, 1869), pp. 162–3.
112 Underhill, *Phillippo*, p. 231.
113 Douglas Hall, *Free Jamaica 1836–65* (Yale University Press, New Haven, 1959).
114 Curtin, *Two Jamaicas*.
115 Howard Temperley, *British Anti-slavery 1833–70* (Longman, London, 1972).
116 Underhill, *Phillippo*, p. 245.

10 Competing Masculinities: Thomas Carlyle, John Stuart Mill and the case of Governor Eyre

In October 1865 a riot took place outside the courthouse in Morant Bay, a small town on the south-eastern side of the island of Jamaica. Crowds had gathered to protest about a disputed fine; the protest turned to violence and a number of people were killed, both by the rioters and the volunteers. There was already a high level of political tension on the island and the British Governor, Edward John Eyre, fearful of a general rising of the 350,000 blacks against the 13,000 whites, proclaimed martial law and sent in the troops. In the subsequent reprisals, 439 blacks and 'coloureds' were killed, 600 men and women were flogged and over 1,000 huts and houses were burnt. A member of the Jamaican House of Assembly, George William Gordon, was hanged.[1]

The initial response of the British government was to support Eyre but as more news filtered back to England increasing criticism was heard. A Royal Commission was set up to investigate what had happened but despite its doubts as to Eyre's conduct the government decided not to prosecute him. The debates as to the rights and wrongs of Eyre's actions raged for many months. The case became, in the words of one commentator, 'the touchstone of ultimate political convictions'.[2] Ranged on either side of this debate were the major intellectuals of the day. Thomas Carlyle led the committee established to defend Eyre while John Stuart Mill led the committee which aimed to prosecute him. Behind them were lined up many of the best-known writers, philosophers and scientists. This essay focuses on the ways in which Carlyle and

Mill, utilizing their public positions as men and as intellectuals, were able to play a crucial part in defining the agenda for debate around Governor Eyre. In this process they not only contributed to the discursive construction of the category 'black' but also to the available ethnic and gendered identities of the English middle class.

The antagonism of new class relations associated with the development of industrial capitalism in mid-nineteenth-century England had resulted in significant shifts in the balance of power and authority from the landed class to the industrial, professional and commercial classes. But the political power which the middle classes had achieved by mid-century, marked most spectacularly by the Reform Act of 1832 which gave middle-class men the vote, and the repeal of the Corn Laws in 1846 which marked an apparent defeat of the landed interest, was still seriously limited. Their formal representation at the national political level carried no guarantees as to their political effectiveness. The Cabinet, for example, remained until the end of the nineteenth century solidly dominated by the landed class. Middle-class men, however, were well used to the attempted exercise of power through influence and had perfected the art of pressure-group politics. The Utilitarians, for example, constituted themselves as a tightly organized grouping, ready to intervene with the full weight of their knowledge on whatever public issues they judged of concern. Thus the intellectual prestige of sections of the middle class was regularly mobilized to secure particular spheres of influence.

The rise of the new middle class had begun in the eighteenth century. The men of this middle class, whether professionals, manufacturers, merchants or farmers, increasingly sought independence from the paternalism and clientage relation into which they were tied with the aristocracy and gentry. Their claims for *independence* were associated with the rejection of older values linked with the gentry and aristocracy. Often scorched by the fire of religious enthusiasm, the new men of the middle class articulated a set of ideas about gentility, challenging land and wealth as the key characteristics of the gentleman. Instead, they asserted that real gentility was rooted in religious belief.[3] As that most favoured poet of the late-eighteenth-century religious revival, Willian Cowper, put it,

My boast is not that I deduce my birth
From loins enthroned or rulers of the earth
But higher far my proud pretensions rise
The son of parents passed into the skies.[4]

The middle-class challenge to the landed class was, therefore, first articulated in moral and religious terms. Their 'proud pretensions', contrary to those of the old landed class, depended on moral seriousness, expressed in daily life in their habits and demeanour. Their critique of the degeneracy and effeminacy of the aristocracy focused on its softness, sensuousness, indolence, luxuriousness, foppishness, and lack of a proper sense of purpose and direction. Central to their new and alternative set of values was the concept of the dignity of work, an old Puritan idea reworked in the smouldering flame of the dual revolutions. Men were to realize themselves in their occupations, women in the profession of wife and mother. Hard work and success in the market should be a marker of status, not something demeaning. A man's individuality, his male identity, was closely tied to independence. That independence, however, was no longer predicated on having the wherewithal not to have to work but rather on the dignity of work itself.

As Leonore Davidoff has argued, in the late eighteenth century the concept of the individual acquired new connotations. Constructed discursively as non-gendered, its meanings depended on a series of dualisms and gendered assumptions. The individual subject was central to political thought and action but that individuality was based upon difference and on 'others'. The male head of household who voted, therefore, spoke for and represented his dependants, whether wife, children or servants. 'Individuality thus implies mastery over things and people. The individual subject is both the subject who acts and the actor who acts on a subject.'[5] The individual subject, whether a captain of industry, a romantic artist, a rational intellectual or a town commissioner, was already male, whether he was active in the realm of economic activity, artistic representation, ethical responsibility or civic identity.

This conception of self reached its apotheosis in the early nineteenth century within a rich discursive formation linking Evangelical religion, romanticism and political economy. At its core was the notion of individual integrity, freedom from subjection to the will of another. 'A man must act', as the Evangelical clergyman Isaac Taylor taught his sons.[6] On the successful outcome of his actions depended his manliness, and failure in the public world could mean a loss of male identity. The Essex seed merchant, Jeremiah James Colman, a man who had experienced serious business fluctuations and had sometimes been unable to meet his creditors, expressed the fears of his generation when he noted in his diary one day, 'I may be a man one day and a mouse the next'.[7] Such a notion of individuality was premissed on the expansion of the free market which allowed individual men to break away from the clientage and paternalism of the aristocracy.

In a social world in which identity was always defined in relation to 'others', the 'others' of this manly independent individual were the dependent and the subjected – the woman, the child, the servant, the employee, the slave – all of whom were characterized by their personal dependence. Here, indeed, were the roots of the connections between the bondage of womanhood and the bondage of slavery which was richly explored both in politics and in literary and visual representations in the nineteenth century. One need only think of *Jane Eyre*, in which the heroine's search for individual freedom and independence from her subjection to men is represented as her escape from slavery, or John Stuart Mill's classic Liberal text entitled *The Subjection of Women*, with its analogy between marriage and slavery. In reality this independent man was himself dependent on those around him: his wife who managed the household and ensured his comfort, his servants who did the work within the household, tended the garden and cared for the children, his employees whose labour was essential to the running of his enterprise.

This manly middle-class subject is epitomized in Mrs Craik's most popular hero, John Halifax, Gentleman.[8] *John Halifax, Gentleman* ranked next to *Uncle Tom's Cabin* in the bestsellers of the 1850s and 1860s. It is a novel full of magical solutions which provided ideological closure within the text to the difficult and unresolvable problems associated with class and gender antagonisms.[9] It is also a novel very much of the 1850s with its optimism and its certainties about English progress. John Halifax (that 'perfectly virtuous being', in the description of Henry James), with his quintessentially English name, was the archetypical representative of that most favoured Victorian myth, the penniless orphan who by dint of hard work made his way in the world and became a public man, active not only in the market but in politics, philanthropy and civic life.[10] Even as a child John Halifax could not bear to be patronized, only wanting to receive recognition for what he had done and what he had earned. As a young boy John started working for a worthy Quaker tanner and eventually became so indispensable that he ran the business. Tanning was an extremely unpleasant process since it involved working with the skins of the animals in the various processes. The tan-pits, across which the skins were strung to be worked on, were 'deep fosses of abomination'.[11] The smell of the works, and inevitably the smell of the men who worked there, made tanning a lowly calling. Nevertheless, John was able to win for himself the epithet, *gentleman*. As John said to his friend Phineas when only a boy, 'It's a notion of mine, that whatever a man may be his trade does not make him – he makes his trade.'[12] Mrs Craik celebrates her hero's hard work and struggle for success; she represents his gentility as residing not in his birth (though in the end, in a classic twist, he turns out to be a gentleman by birth too) but in his Christian manliness, a form of manliness ritually demonstrated in a series of dramatic set pieces.

In the first episode John saves his master, who has extended his interests to a flour-mill, from the wrath of 'the mob' in a food riot. Food riots were endemic in the eighteenth and early nineteenth centuries, one of the last strongholds of that popular culture which embraced the concept of the *just price*. In Mrs Craik's fictional town the bread rioters gather in 1800, maddened by the refusal of the miller to sell or give them his flour. In a situation fraught with danger John Halifax braves the crowd and saves the mill. He addresses the rioters, who are represented as misguided but desperate with hunger, convinces them with his arguments, and gives them food:

> The rioters listened, as it were by compulsion, to the clear, manly voice that had not in it one shade of fear. 'What do you do it for?' John continued. 'All because he would not sell you, or give you, his wheat. Even so – it was *his* wheat, not yours. May not a man do what he likes with his own?' The argument seemed to strike home. There is always a lurking sense of rude justice in a mob – at least a British mob.[13]

So the rioters were convinced, reminded (as any proper crowd should be in Mrs Craik's imagination) of their deep acceptance of private property, and persuaded not with a pistol but with 'a mightier weapon still – the best weapon a man can use – his own firm indomitable will'.[14]

The second time John Halifax proved his manliness and gentility was the occasion on which he refused to fight a duel with one of the representatives of the corrupt aristocracy within the novel. This was Richard Brithwood, a man possessed of broad acres, but in Mrs Craik's terms, no gentility. He is a fox-hunting, drinking, gambling man. Brithwood was offended at having to meet a tanner socially, particularly since this tanner had ridiculous pretensions to court his cousin, a young woman of property and good family connections. Brithwood insulted John and then struck him, 'that last fatal insult, which offered from man to man, in those days, could only be wiped out with blood'.[15] John, however, fired with his Christian belief in the wickedness of the duel, refused to fight, castigating such practices as barbaric, a symbol of all that was repellant 'to the pacific, religious and commercial sense' of the provincial middle-class man.[16] John's stand was immediately welcomed by his love, Ursula, who, 'with the old impetuosity kindling anew in every feature of her noble face', cried, 'You have but showed me what I shall remember all my life – that a Christian only can be a true gentleman.'[17]

The third classic confrontation in which John Halifax decisively demonstrated both his manliness and his public-spiritedness is the occasion on which he saved the local bank. The wave of bank failures in 1825–6 had catastrophic consequences for many middle-class families and consequently lived long in the middle-class imagination. The heroes of that terrible time were those solid citizens who were prepared to risk their own capital by using it to publicly register their faith in a local bank at a time when there was public panic. The Revd William Marsh, for example, in the small town of Colchester, has taken bags of gold and silver, raised for charitable purposes, out into the market-place as the creditors gathered in fear at the news of other bank failures. By this display of confidence he had saved the bank.[18] John Halifax does just the same, risking five thousand pounds of his own money to ensure that the run on the local bank could be met and that a collapse would be avoided.

If John Halifax's manly middle-class identity was partly represented by Mrs Craik through his performances in the great theatre of public life, it was also represented by his differences from the varied 'others' within the novel. He is marked off most explicitly from the women, who occupy a smaller sphere of action than his, and from the aristocracy and gentry, who with one exception, Sir Ralph Oldtower, a true English gentleman who can boast Norman blood, are seen as less authentically gentlemen than the lowly born tanner and eventual mill-owner, John Halifax. John is distinguished from the aristocracy in numerous ways. His language was not fancy and over-elaborated, rather it was, 'a mere vehicle for thought; the garb, always chosen as simplest and fittest, in which his ideas were clothed. His conversation was never wearisome, since he only spoke when he had something to say . . .'[19] Similarly his handwriting was clear and firm, with no twirly extras. His simple clothes, always in dark colours but worn with spotless white, are compared with the 'bright nankeens, the blue coat with gold buttons, and the showiest of cambric kerchiefs swathing him up to the very chin' of Lord Luxmore, who turns out to be totally corrupt in his politics.[20] His strong working hands are contrasted with the delicate ringed hands of Lord Luxmore's son, mocked by John's children as lady's hands. His sexuality is sharply counterposed with that of Richard Brithwood in particular, who allows his wife to elope with a lover by whom she is abandoned and left, ruined and mad, to die. Lady Caroline, as she is called, is contemptuous of domesticated love and looks for what Mrs Craik describes as 'une grande passion', a concept so unlike solid English marital love that it has to be named in French.[21] John's love of domesticity and his enjoyment of a conjugal sexuality, unspoken until it is joyfully celebrated in the birth of children, is set against the laxity, immorality and double standards of the aristocracy, fictionally punished by Mrs Craik with madness, childlessness and appalling relationships between parents and children.

John Halifax is the perfect domesticated father; a fond figment of a literary imagination, perhaps, but one which was in keeping with some contemporary feminine discourses on domesticity and which finds echoes in men's diaries, journals and letters. James Luckcock, for example, the Birmingham jeweller, regarded a privatized home and garden as an ideal to be sought for, a reward which might come with the achievement of a 'modest competence' and withdrawal from business.[22] Once settled in his charming suburban home, he would be able to participate fully in the bringing-up and care of his children. In its evocation of a man's love for home and family *John Halifax* both mirrored the concerns of provincial middle-class men, such as James Luckcock, and contributed to the discursive construction of a particular masculinity, one which emphasized that men were emotional beings, capable of love, of warmth, of tears, and one which in the magical world of the novel did not produce tensions and contradictions, but straightforward happiness and satisfaction. John Halifax was always tender with his children, attentive to their education and development, ready to sit up night after night with an ill child so that 'the mother', as she was always called in the novel, would not be left alone with the anxiety. 'If I were to tell of all he did', recorded the fictional narrator, 'how, after being out all day, night after night he would sit up watching by and nursing each little fretful sufferer, patient as a woman, and pleasant as a child play-mate – perhaps those who talk loftily of the "dignity of man" would smile.'[23] John loves his home and garden, longs to be there whenever he can, and has no time for the traditional male leisure pursuits associated with the gentry. All the money he makes either goes into the business, into philanthropic pursuits, or into home improvements.

John Halifax is further marked off from the aristocracy and gentry by his commitment to labour. As a young couple, John and Ursula had very little money but John worked hard and Ursula frugally managed their little home and garden. Having made a success of the tannery John moves into flour-milling and then into cloth. He has concentration, discipline, a sharp business sense, a fascination with technical innovation and scientific enterprise, and is always willing to get his own hands dirty. He represents the perfect employer, kind and paternalistic but modern in his management.

Finally, he is the perfect public man: responsible in his civic duties, active in philanthropy, agitating on all the key issues of the day from parliamentary reform to the emancipation of the slaves. For the Halifax family, the quintessential English middle-class family, Friday, 1st August, 1834, the day when Britain 'freed her slaves', was a great day:

> many may remember that day; what a soft, gray, summer morning it was, and how it broke out into brightness; how everywhere bells were ringing, club fraternities walking with bands and banners, school-children having feasts and work-people holidays; how, in town and country, there was spread abroad a general sense of benevolent rejoicing – because honest old England had lifted up her generous voice, nay, had paid down cheerfully her twenty millions, and in all her colonies the negro was free.[24]

John Halifax, the devoted husband, the loving father, the paternalist employer, the responsible public man, generous to all his dependants whether child, servant, or apprentice, kind to animals or misguided Luddites, pleading on behalf of oppressed slaves; here is English middle-class manhood personified.

Middle-class men achieved some recognition as active economic subjects, a recognition which was promoted by such organizations as the Committees of Manufacturers, which were to become Chambers of Commerce. But this recognition was limited and their capacity to affect public economic policy, for example, left much to be desired.[25] In this context the establishment of arenas of public prestige which might enable them to build an alternative power base to that of the established aristocracy and gentry, was vital. Voluntary associations provided just such an arena and the period after 1780 was marked by the proliferation of scores of these, based initially in the towns but moving out into the countryside, with an extraordinary variety of aims and objectives. Some were focused on the defence of middle-class economic interests, such as the employers' associations. Some cultivated the arts and sciences, providing semi-public activities for the farmers, merchants, manufacturers, professionals and tradespeople who made up the middle class. Some aimed to provide for, and improve, the poor. As R. J. Morris has pointed out, the period after 1780 sees the appearance of a whole new series of words in common usage, or the alteration of existing meanings to incorporate new ones; association, society, chairman, agenda, membership, rules, constitution and annual report all enter the everyday usage of the middle class.[26] Furthermore, these words featured prominently in the burgeoning provincial press which gave extensive coverage to such societies and regularly listed the officers and subscribers of the more substantial ones.

Together, this extensive network of voluntary associations redefined civil society and created new arenas of power and prestige. This was the newly created public sphere of nineteenth-century England, bypassing traditional institutions and constructing an alternative public. For the societies were a means of extending influence for those outside established sites of power. They provided a formidable base for middle-class men; they gave opportunities for public demonstrations of weight, whether in newspaper reports, in public ceremonials or the new styles of public architecture which depended on their patronage and represented their values. The experience of such associations increased the confidence of middle-class men and contributed to their claims for political power, claims which they made as heads of households, representing wives, children and dependants.

The relation of middle-class women to this network of associations was a great deal more complicated than that of men. Excluded from the public organization of the vast majority of the early societies which were defined as men-only enterprises, they nevertheless did supportive work behind the scenes. At the same time the argument began to be made that there were spheres of philanthropic activity best suited to women, and ladies' associations began to organize work in these areas. Anti-slavery, for example, named as philanthropic rather than political, was one such arena. In the period up to mid-century, however, middle-class women rarely challenged the dominance of men organizationally and ladies' associations operated with a different public visibility from those of men.[27]

Economic power and cultural prestige were, for the middle class, the precursors of political power. In the process of struggle for authority in early-nineteenth-century England, the role of the intellectuals was crucial – those men, and indeed some women, who articulated the new concepts and claims not only at national but at provincial and local level. One of the striking features of the major political philosophers in this period is that they were concerned not only to work at a high level of abstraction but to apply their new theories to the concrete realities of their society. Such national figures were underpinned by a host of minor figures, the organic intellectuals of the middle class, the clergymen, doctors, lawyers and women writers who saw it as their task to translate new codes of behaviour into everyday life, whether they were dealing with the spheres of the economic, the political or the cultural.

Thomas Carlyle and John Stuart Mill were two of the major male middle-class intellectuals and writers of their age. Both of them came from the new middle-class world which has been described. Both had the status to intervene as significant public figures in a political debate. Both were to play a critical part in reformulating ideas about manliness and about English identity in the 1860s. Both wrote extensively about themselves in their own lifetimes as well as being written about by others. Both had their portraits painted, Carlyle many times. Neither had any problem about recognizing themselves as individuals, subjects who could speak and act for themselves, though both came, in different ways, to recognize some of the problems involved in their subjection of others.[28]

Thomas Carlyle was born in 1795 in the small town of Ecclefechan, the son of a mason. Brought up as a Calvinist, he was able to benefit from the relative openness of the Scottish educational system and go to university. Intended for the ministry, he abandoned this life scheme but an experience of spiritual rebirth, described in his book *Sartor Resartus*, after the loss of his conventional religious faith, gave him the confidence to turn increasingly to writing. At the same time he married and became one of the growing band of professional middle-class writers, relying not only on books but on periodical writing to provide a fairly modest income.

In recognition of the centrality of London to that market, the Carlyles moved to the metropolis and by the 1840s, with the publication of *Past and Present*, Carlyle had become a nationally known power with the pen. He had learned from the German Romantics a grandiose conception of the man of letters. To his mind it was writers who could claim true nobility, and make a contribution which long outlived the ephemera of political life. Indeed, in 'The Hero as Man of Letters', Carlyle was to argue that this hero must be regarded as our most important modern person. 'He, such as he may be, is the soul of all. What he teaches the whole world will do and make.'[29] This claim for respect was an intervention in the public debate over the literary profession and its status. Carlyle had been horrified after his arrival in London, as Norma Clarke has noted, by what he saw as the unmanliness of London's writers. They were not 'red-blooded *men*', but weaklings.[30] Writers in the 1830s and 1840s were preoccupied with the status of their work and with the relation between their writing and other kinds of work. They conceptualized writing as making an important public contribution, in part because of the accusations that their subjection to the world of commerce and the market interfered with their role as prophet, muse or genius. Their writing gave them potential influence but they had no institutional base or secure social position.[31] In this context, extravagant claims for the writer marked a bid for legitimation.

Fired with this sense of mission, to make the man of letters the most important modern person, Carlyle achieved a very considerable eminence amongst the educated middle class in the 1830s and 1840s. They thrived on his particular kind of writing, heavy with moral seriousness, redolent with spirituality but without the divisiveness of a particular sectarian belonging, powered by its sense of its own dignity and importance, effectively distanced from the troubling world of the market. Indeed, Carlyle's critique of mechanization was precisely the reason for his popularity in a society which had been transformed by that very process, but was simultaneously troubled by its amorality. His despair at the mechanization of man 'in head and in heart as well as in hand' fuelled his contempt for Utilitarianism, that 'dismal science', which 'reduces the duty of human governors to that of letting man alone'.[32] His bleak view of human nature drew some of its force from the Calvinist vision and this may have contributed to his insistence on the importance of government and leadership, and of prophecy, all of which became more important to him as he grew older. Carlyle had no time for the concept of rights and countered it with his belief in the necessary dependence between master and man, a mutual dependence in which each must do his duty and his work in the world. A profound believer in the dignity of labour and the power of labour to purify fallen man, Carlyle had a deep hostility to those who would not work, whether aristocrat or black. 'There is a perennial nobleness, and even sacredness, in Work', he argued: 'Were he never so benighted, forgetful of his high calling, there is always hope in a man that actually and earnestly works: in Idleness alone is there perpetual despair'.[33]

For Carlyle masculinity was associated with strength, with independence and with action for, like the Revd Isaac Taylor before him, he believed that men, to be men, must act. His rugged, craggy physique and his look of intense, frowning concentration express a particular form of male strength and seriousness. His hatred of philanthropy was associated with the ways in which it weakened men and made them depend on others. Such a notion of manhood was underpinned by an insistence on the essential difference between the sexes. Some men were made to rule over others and men must be masters in their own house. Men were born to command, women to obey. In the words of Geraldine Jewsbury, quoting Carlyle as reported to her by his wife, and her great friend, Jane Welsh,

> a woman's natural object in the world is to *go out* and find herself some sort of *man her superior* and obey him loyally and lovingly and make herself as much as possible into *a beautiful reflex of him.*[34]

John Stuart Mill occupied in some ways a very different political position to that of Carlyle but he derived his authority from the same source – his writing. For Mill, too, there was no legitimacy in the world that was not earned by the sweat of the brow. Distinction, he believed, should be won, not inherited. He himself earned the major part of his living from the East India Company, as his father had before him, a job that left him with plenty of time for his own work.

As is well known, John Stuart Mill was trained by his father and Jeremy Bentham to be a worker for the cause of rational and enlightened inquiry and improvement. His task in life was to facilitate the greatest happiness of the greatest number. One of Mill's first contributions to the success of the felicific calculus was to work on the formation of public opinion through publishing books and writing articles. Like Carlyle, Mill had a profound respect for the power of the intellect and for the capacity of intellectuals to make a difference in the world. A key weapon for Mill in the battle to win public opinion to the cause of reason was the press. Convinced that his father's influence in English society owed much to the ways in which his ideas had been aired and explored, particularly in the *Morning Chronicle*, he supported the *Westminster Review* as a conscious attempt to extend this intellectual influence through the fostering of an enlightened public. In Mill's opinion, the journal

> gave a recognised status, in the arena of opinion and discussion, to the Benthamic type of Radicalism, out of all proportion to the number of its adherents, and to the personal merits and abilities, at that time, of most of those who could be reckoned among them.[35]

After considerable dissatisfaction with the *Westminster Review*, the Philosophic Radicals abandoned their connection with it. Meanwhile, Mill had suffered a breakdown and with it the traumatic recognition that Utilitarianism perhaps did not answer all the questions. It was in the aftermath of the this crisis, when he had come to think that a true philosophical system would be more complex than anything he had yet grasped and must contain elements of the Romantic and poetic as well as the rational, that he had his first encounter with Carlyle's writing, an encounter that left him both inspired and unsatisfied. On a first reading, Carlyle's writing seemed to him

> a haze of poetry and German metaphysics, in which almost the only clear thing was a strong animosity to most of the opinions which

> were the basis of my mode of thought; religious scepticism, utilitarianism, the doctrine of circumstances, and the attaching any importance to democracy, logic, or political economy.

In time, however, he came to see the power of his writing 'not as philosophy to instruct, but as poetry to animate'.[36]

In the wake of his rethinking of Utilitarianism, Mill became the proprietor of the new *London and Westminster Review* and much of his energy and his hopes for a new Radical party went into this. Like Carlyle, he remained convinced of the importance of educating public opinion and civilizing the people. The two of them shared a manly conviction that they could be knowers and doers, teachers and improvers. Both could claim significant public power because of their writing, both had weight and recognition in the England of the 1840s. Both were profoundly public men.

Such public men would expect to take a position on the subject of slavery. The slavery issue had been a major debate in English society and the triumph of anti-slavery in the wake of the Reform Act of 1832 seemed to many to inaugurate a new era of progress. Mrs Craik represented the common sense of middle-class 'Old England' when she evoked the 'soft, gray summer morning' breaking into brightness with the dawn of emancipation. The continued influence of the planters, however, ensured that the spectre of immediate emancipation was offset by the apprenticeship scheme which tied the freed slaves in the West Indies into labour on the plantations. This system was a failure and apprenticeship was abandoned in 1838. Emancipationists had been extremely worried as to how the plantation system would work once slavery was abolished. As far as Britain was concerned, the West Indian islands were an asset because of their sugar production and it was essential to find ways of maintaining that production with a free labour system. Meanwhile the planters were convinced that they would be ruined by emancipation. Neither group had foreseen the problems which were posed not just by the need to rethink the organization of the plantations in the wake of emancipation but also by the increased competition from other sugar-cane producers and from the production of beet in Europe and elsewhere.[37] In Jamaica, the largest and most productive of the British West India islands, the period from 1838–46 saw a significant reduction in the amount of sugar exported, a disaster as far as the planters and most British commentators were concerned. Viewed from a Jamaican non-planter perspective, however, those years marked significant achievements, in particular the establishment of a healthy base in small peasant production; a development which heartily displeased the planters and which they did all in their power to discourage.

Since the West India lobby still functioned in Britain, albeit in a very modest version of their triumphant eighteenth-century years, the troubles of the planter class were well aired in the British Parliament and varied attempts made to ease their plight. The Whigs, however, were increasingly moving towards a commitment to free trade, to the dismay of the planters, who had long relied on a protectionist policy. Earl Grey, the Secretary of State for the Colonies in the administration of Lord John Russell, was entirely convinced of the desirability of abandoning protective legislation. In the case of the sugar colonies he wanted to combine the abolition of protectionist duties, which he saw as keeping wages unnaturally high and therefore encouraging idleness and obstructing the progress of civilization, with encouraging European immigration. In his view, a 'rude population' needed the example of 'civilized men' to create and foster the habits of a civilized life.[38]

The proposal from the British government in 1846 to remove the protective duties was met with panic and horror by the planters and resulted in a constitutional crisis in Jamaica where the planters held political power.[39] Their case was taken up in England by Thomas Carlyle. In the heyday of anti-slavery it would have been hard to find a respectable middle-class man willing to speak up for the planters. They had had to rely on their own propagandists to argue their case and organized public opinion had been firmly on the side of emancipation. In the 1830s and early 1840s Carlyle did not publish anti-abolitionist sentiments; he was, however, prepared to vent them in private. As Lucretia Mott (the American abolitionist and feminist who came to London in 1840 as a delegate to the International Anti-Slavery Convention, but was prevented with her female fellow delegates from taking their official places) noted in her diary when she visited the Carlyles at home, 'conversation not very satisfactory – Anti-Abolition – or rather sympathies absorbed in poor at home and own poverty and slavery . . . disappointed in him . . .'[40] By 1849, however, following a journey to Ireland, Carlyle's preoccupation with the troubles of the 'hungry forties' led him to a much harder position on the blacks. He was now willing to identify himself firmly with the planters' cause and to argue in effect for a return to slavery. This marked a significant break in the ranks of middle-class opinion on the 'negro', to adopt contemporary usage.

Carlyle published his 'Occasional Discourse on the Negro Question', as it was first called (later to be retitled with the contemptuous term 'Nigger'), anonymously in *Fraser's Magazine*, one of the most prominent periodicals, in 1849. In his words of introduction he commented on 'the strange doctrines and notions shadowed forth' in the piece and predicted that in 'these emancipated epochs of the human mind' he would probably find himself in a minority of one.[41] Carlyle's inimitable style was immediately recognizable to the discerning reading public and in speaking the words others would not speak the piece provoked reaction. The brief polemic argued that the effects of emancipation had been disastrous; it had led to the ruin of the colonies and the ruin of the blacks who would not work. Carlyle challenged the anti-slavery orthodoxy, enshrined in the motto 'Am I not a man and a brother', that blacks were potentially equal and, once civilized, would reach equality with the whites, and argued that the blacks were an inferior race.

The essay took the form of an imaginary lecture to a philanthropic association, a style of organization which Carlyle abhorred since philanthropy in his view sapped real manhood and encouraged dependence. Using a combination of characters with metaphorical names, proverbs, folk-tales, biblical references and social commentary, he held the polemic together with an acerbic humour strongly evocative of Dickens.[42] Events in the sugar colonies were held up by him as a terrifying example of what would happen more generally if natural relations were disturbed and more liberal relations allowed to dominate. In his view, blacks were born to be servants to those who were wiser than them; whites were their 'born lords'.[43] The parlous state of West Indian society, with the negroes 'all very happy and doing well' but the whites in a state of despair, had its origins for Carlyle in emancipation which had given the blacks quite false expectations and dangerous opportunities.[44] While the blacks, best compared in Carlyle's mind with horses or dogs, were 'sitting yonder with their beautiful muzzles up to their ears in pumpkins, imbibing sweet pulps and juices; the grinders and incisor teeth ready for ever-new work . . .', the British government and the British people were handing out millions to keep this lovely state of affairs going while 'doleful Whites' were without potatoes to eat.[45] The only solution was to recognize the truth, so unpalatable to sentimental abolitionists, that blacks had to be mastered by men who knew better. For Carlyle, mastership and servantship were the only conceivable deliverance from what he saw as the really dangerous forms of tyranny and slavery, when the strong, the great and the noble-minded were enslaved to the weak and the mean in the name of some foolish notion of rights. The problem of modern society was that no man reverenced another.

The place of the whites as masters in the sugar islands presented no problems to Carlyle. In his view, proprietorship must rest with those who got the best from the land – the 'Saxon-British'. When they had first arrived, the land had been jungle and swamp, producing only 'man-eating Caribs, rattle-snakes, and reeking waste and putrefaction'. It was only when the British arrived, like the prince in 'The Sleeping Beauty', that nature was awoken and brought forth her nobler elements. The islands, wrote Carlyle, 'till the European white man first saw them . . . were as if not yet created, their nobler elements of cinammon, sugar, coffee, pepper black and gray, lying all asleep, waiting the white enchanter who should say to them, Awake!'[46] It was not 'Black Quashee' who made the islands what they are. Indeed,

> Before the West Indies could grow a pumpkin for any Negro, how much European heroism had to spend itself in obscure battle; to sink, in mortal agony, before the jungles, the putrescences and waste savageries could become arable, and the Devil be in some measure chained there . . . Not a square inch of soil in those fruitful Isles, purchased by British blood, shall any Black man hold to grow pumpkins for him, except on terms that are fair towards Britain.[47]

The major source of Carlyle's hostility to the blacks was their refusal, in his eyes and those of the planters, to labour. 'He who shall not work shall not eat', inveighed Carlyle,

> no Black man who will not work according to what ability the gods have given him for working, has the smallest right to eat pumpkin . . . but has an indisputable and perpetual right to be compelled, by the real proprietors of said land, to do competent work for his living. This is the everlasting duty of all men, black or white, who are born into this world.[48]

Men who would not work of their own accord must be induced by the whip if necessary, for idleness could only lead to rottenness and putrescence, to corruption and evil. Induce him if you can, argued Carlyle, with 'beneficent whip'; the alternative was to

> let him look across to Haiti, and trace a far sterner prophecy! Let him, by his ugliness, idleness, rebellion, banish all White men from the West Indies and make it all one Haiti, – with little or no sugar growing, black Peter exterminating black Paul, and where a garden of the Hesperides might be, nothing but a tropical dog-kennel and pestiferous jungle . . .[49]

Carlyle's evocation of the whip echoed the discourse of the planters, made widely available by the efforts of the West India lobby in the struggle over abolition and its aftermath. In the fraught decade between the adoption of an official policy of amelioration by the British government in 1823 and the passing of emancipation in 1833, the Society of West India Planters and Merchants attempted to counter the very effective propaganda of the anti-slavery societies. Through their literary committee they focused on the publication and distribution of pamphlets and periodicals which were sympathetic to their cause, from Cobbett's *Political Register* to accounts of particular plantations with their happy and contended peasantries, not only selling their literature but giving it away free and paying for insertions in sympathetic newspapers such as *The Times.* For five years they published their own official organ, *The West India Reporter.*[50]

The select committees on slavery of 1831–2, established by both the Commons and the Lords, gave extended opportunities for both sides to defend their views in effect in public. While many of the missionaries and the anti-slavery advocates evoked the sound of the whip as reverberating cruelly through the plantations, an ever-present symbol of the brute physical force on which the system of slavery was based, the advocates of that system insisted that blacks would not work unless they were induced so to do. Since the planters were convinced that a very small amount of labour would produce enough for the immediate needs of any barbaric African, they insisted that without the whip the estates would break down. As John Baillie, a Jamaican planter with over thirty years experience, put it, 'The nature of the Negro is such, that, unless he is compelled, he will not work.'[51] Such sentiments were repeated again and again, combined with an assertion that the whip was necessary as a symbolic threat, rather than for use. William Shand, a Jamaican attorney for over forty years, took this optimistic view: 'The whip is not so commonly applied as is imagined in this Country. I have frequently travelled over half the Island and not heard the Sound of the Whip, except to call the Negroes to their Work.'[52] Despite such accounts, the debate as to whether blacks would or would not work without coercion simmered on, reappearing in the arguments over apprenticeship in the mid-1830s and again in the wake of the crisis over sugar duties. Carlyle's appeal to the whip, and to the assumption that only half an hour of labour a day was adequate for the barbarous needs of negroes, reworked well-established veins of thought and popular knowledge.

Carlyle's hostility to black men, who, he claimed, he did not hate, was linked to his feminization of them. They were not real men. 'I decidedly like poor Quashee,' he wrote, 'and find him a pretty kind of man. With a pennyworth of oil, you can make a handsome glossy thing of Quashee.'[53] The black men of the sugar islands, in Carlyle's rhetoric, were pretty, supple, affectionate and amenable – none of them manly epithets. His contempt for those feminine characteristics was underpinned by an underlying fear of black sexuality and its power and was linked to his contempt for women. Women should know their place and not attempt to step out of it. A man must be lord in his house just as he should be the master of his servant.

Whilst despising and blaming the blacks, Carlyle's worst ire was reserved for those he saw as responsible for maintaining this state of affairs. They were the philanthropists and Utilitarians. These were the twin horrors associated with abolition and, like the blacks, part of what was wrong with them was that they were not real men either. They were 'windy sentimentalists' and 'effeminate types' whose 'unhappy wedlock' could only lead to 'benevolent twaddle' and 'revolutionary grapeshot'. Together, wrote Carlyle, in lines redolent with perverted sexual imagery, they would 'give birth to progenies and prodigies; dark extensive mooncalves, unnamable abortions, wide-coiled monstrosities, such as the world has not seen hitherto.'[54] The combination of Utilitarianism and philanthropy was reducing the duty of human governors to that of letting men alone. 'Serious men' must take a grip of this state of affairs and realize that they have work to do in this universe.[55]

Carlyle's blast from the fastnesses of his study in Cheyne Row provoked the doyen of 'the dismal science', John Stuart Mill, to respond. Mill, with his firm belief in the right to individual fulfilment, was a fierce antagonist of slavery. This implicit defence of that abominable system could not go unanswered. 'The author issues his opinions, or rather ordinances, under imposing auspices,' wrote Mill, 'no less than those of the "immortal gods." '[56] He spoke as one with authority, assuming that one man was born lord over another. To Mill's mind, the struggle against the law of might was the struggle for human improvement. So Mill attempted to displace one voice of authority, one prestigious pen, with another. He particularly feared the effect of Carlyle's words in America:

> The words of English writers of celebrity are words of power on the other side of the ocean; and the owners of human flesh, who probably thought that they had not an honest man on their side between the Atlantic and the Vistula, will welcome such an auxiliary . . .[57]

For Mill, anti-slavery was a cause of justice, an argument based on reason, not sentiment.

In his brief response Mill attacked the planter class for their expectation of their right to live off the blacks and refuted Carlyle's gospel of work, arguing that all should take part in necessary labour but that no one could find fulfilment in labour alone. There was no evidence, he argued, that whites were born wiser than others. He was scandalized by the spectre of Carlyle, a professed moral reformer, claiming that 'one kind of human beings are born servants to another kind'. Focusing on analysis and reason, he suggested,

> It is by analytical examination that we have learned whatever we know of the laws of external nature; and if he had not disdained to apply the same mode of investigation to the laws of the formation of character, he would have escaped the vulgar error of imputing every difference which he finds among human beings to an original difference of nature.[58]

Here was the nub of Mill's argument. Just as he later refuted the notion of the differences between men and women being attributable to nature, so he argued that the races were different because of their external circumstances.[59] For Mill, both women and blacks could potentially rise to the civilization of men. His concept of equality and commitment to democracy was founded on a developmental notion of human nature. His moral vision, therefore, of a free and equal society could not be achieved without a process of education.

Mill believed that Carlyle had done great mischief by throwing his persuasive powers behind the planters and slavery and it is indeed possible to see his 'Occasional Discourse' as an extremely significant moment in the movement of public opinion away from anti-slavery as the respectable orthodoxy and towards more overt forms of racism. Carlyle's may have been the lone public voice from the intellectual establishment promulgating such opinions in 1849. *John Halifax, Gentleman* assumed a middle-class attachment to anti-slavery. By the late 1850s and 1860s no such assumptions could be made. Throughout the 1850s a more racist discourse became increasingly legitimate. The slow shift in public opinion can be registered in such arenas as the struggles over 'scientific' racism and the Indian Mutiny. It was the Mutiny which brought the term 'niggers' into common parlance.[60] This was the term that Carlyle had seen fit to use publicly in 1853.

Then came the American Civil War which was to divide English society sharply on the issue of race and slavery.[61] Carlyle was a strong supporter of the South, idealizing the conditions of the slaves, and could not understand why people should be 'cutting throats indefinitely to put the negro into a position for which all experience shows him unfit'.[62] Mill was convinced that it was the Civil War which decisively pushed the respectable into a position which implicitly, if not always explicitly, was pro-slavery. For him the war marked 'an aggressive enterprise of the slave-owners to extend the territory of slavery'. He was horrified at

> the rush of nearly the whole upper and middle classes of my own country, even those who passed for Liberals, into a furious pro-Southern partisanship: the working classes and some of the literary and scientific men, being almost the sole exceptions to the general frenzy. I have never felt so keenly how little permanent improvement had reached the minds of our influential classes, and of what small value were the Liberal opinions they had got into the habit of professing. None of the Continental Liberals made the same mistake. But the generation which had extorted negro emancipation from our West India planters had passed away; another had succeeded which had not learnt by many years of discussion and exposure to feel strongly the enormities of slavery . . .[63]

Furthermore, Mill argued, the habitual chauvinism of the English, a subject on which he could wax strong, meant that there was a profound ignorance as to what the struggles in the New World were really about. The existence of powerful pro-Southern feeling during the Civil War was, however, clearly an indicator of the shifts which had occurred in some sectors of public opinion on the subject of slavery and the rights of black peoples. It was to be the case of Governor Eyre, however, which brought these issues to the forefront of domestic politics.

The news of the riot in Morant Bay and the subsequent reprisals reached England at the end of 1865 and the press reports which started to appear galvanized humanitarian and Radical opinion. After an initially favourable response to Eyre's success in dealing with the rebels, the Liberal Government became worried about some of the apparent irregularities which had taken place, particularly around the court martial and execution of George William Gordon. Gordon had been a member of the Jamaican House of Assembly; he was the illegitimate son of a white planter by a slave-woman but had himself become a landowner and married a white woman. Under pressure from influential sections of public opinion, the government announced that a Royal Commission would investigate what had happened and Eyre was called back to London.

The Jamaica Committee had meanwhile been established, an ad hoc association to coordinate the efforts of anti-slavery groups and others who were critical of the Jamaican events. The Jamaica Committee was led in the House of Commons by Thomas Hughes, Charles Buxton, and John Stuart Mill who had been elected as Liberal MP for Westminster in the election of 1865. By April the Royal Commission was ready and its findings made public. The Commission declared that there had been a genuine danger and that Eyre had been right to react vigorously. They also argued, however, that martial law had been maintained in Jamaica for too long and that the punishment meted out had been excessive and barbarous, the burning of houses wanton and cruel.[64] Soon after the appearance of the Royal Commission the Prime Minister, John Russell, resigned when the House of Lords rejected his Reform Bill. With the Tories in power, led by Lord Derby, the Radicals were much less worried about embarrassing the government and prepared to press the issue of prosecutions hard. Mill and the activists on the committee wanted the government to prosecute Eyre. Failing this, they were prepared to proceed with a private prosecution.[65]

The increasingly militant activity of the Jamaica Committee provoked a backlash and a growing public sympathy for Eyre. This sympathy for the wronged British Governor, as he was seen, linked into the growing fears amongst the middle class of working-class activity around the issue of reform.[66] The dangers of democracy seemed all too imminent and anxieties about potential anarchy at home suffused the conservative discourses on the heroic Eyre who had saved the beleaguered whites. In this context a number of prominent public figures, led by Thomas Carlyle, organized a pro-Eyre defence group and for the next year a public debate was conducted over the events in Jamaica, with Mill and Carlyle as the two central public protagonists.

The Jamaica Committee and the Eyre Defence Committee were classic products of the time-honoured middle-class tradition of voluntary organization. In both cases a group of men got together over an issue on which they wanted to influence and orchestrate public opinion. They set up meetings, wrote to the newspapers, published pamphlets, arranged lecture tours, established committees with official positions, organized finances, sent delegations to the appropriate places, kept up pressure in Parliament and generally made themselves as publicly prominent as they could. Each organization boasted one of the doyens of the intellectual world as their leader: Carlyle, 'the universally acclaimed dean of Victorian letters'; Mill, 'the political instructor to the nation'.[67] Each of those leaders used every ounce of public influence which they possessed to maximal advantage in their search for publicity and support for their cause. But the debate between Carlyle and Mill was about more than the case of Governor Eyre or, indeed, an argument as to what kind of social and political organization there should be in Britain and her colonies. Also at issue between the two men and their followers were different notions as to what constituted a proper English manhood. In the course of the exchanges over Jamaica two different identities, two different subjectivities were being offered to English middle-class men. Both identities depended for their articulation on a sense of difference, not only from black men but also from black and white women. Both identities drew on the tradition of middle-class English manhood represented in *John Halifax, Gentleman*. But one of these identities was shown to be markedly more in favour than the other in 1866–7 and that particular vision of manhood was to contribute to the construction of popular imperialism in the late nineteenth century.

The Jamaica Committee drew its support from the cream of the Radical and scientific establishment – from Thomas Huxley, Herbert Spencer, Charles Lyall and Charles Darwin to John Bright, Leslie Stephen and Frederick Harrison. The committee was fundamentally a middle-class and urban organization with strong Unitarian representation. Their hallmarks were a commitment to dissent (in its widest meaning), rationality and scientific inquiry. The Eyre Defence Committee drew on a significantly different set of constituencies. Its members represented some of the cream of the literary establishment, including Charles Kingsley, Charles Dickens, John Ruskin and Alfred Lord Tennyson. The Defence Committee relied on support from landed society (their president was the Earl of Shrewsbury who owned land in Jamaica), from the army, and from the Church establishment. Their hallmark was a defence of what were constructed as traditional values.

John Stuart Mill and the Jamaica Committee focused their arguments around two central issues. The first was the question of the rule of law; the second the question of England's relation to her foreign dependencies. The arguments about the rule of law were provoked by what was seen as the terrible misuse of the law in Jamaica, particularly in the scandalous proceedings of the court martial which had hanged Gordon. One of the most effective propaganda weapons of the Jamaica Committee was Gordon's last letter to his wife, written on the eve of his death and very much in the manner of a Christian gentleman. Much of the public distress about the Jamaica controversy had centred on the hanging of a Christian member of the Assembly, with a trial that resembled a mockery of proper legal procedures. The use of martial law thus became a central issue. Mill and his allies maintained that this offered a threat not only to the subject-races of the Empire but to the rights of freeborn Englishmen themselves. As Mill put it in his *Autobiography*,

> there was much more at stake than only justice to the Negroes, imperative as was that consideration. The question was whether the British dependencies, and eventually, perhaps Great Britain itself, were to be under the government of law, or of military licence . . .[68]

As public meetings across the country the protagonists of the prosecution of Eyre for his violation of the law demanded that it was essential to call for 'a prompt and effective vindication of the ancient guarantees of personal liberty in this country'.[69]

The appeal to ancient laws and English constitutionalism was one of the ways of constructing a particular version of England and making a particular appeal to the British people. Both sides in the debate tried to claim the support of 'the people' and constructed 'the people' rhetorically as the arbiters of the issue. Frequent recourse was made to ideas of the honour of England and how that honour could only be saved by specific courses of action. What was at stake in the debate were particular notions of Englishness and ethnicity, notions which were publicly contested in the two narrations of the Jamaican events. Mill had been horrified from the start at the lack of response to the butcheries in Jamaica, which, if they had happened under the aegis of another government, he was sure would have been abhorred. For him, the honour of England demanded that crimes committed under English law should be adequately and justly punished.[70]

The notion was that the rule of law must stretch across the Empire for, of course, this view depended on a belief in equality between the races. Mill and his supporters insisted on the idea of formal equality between the races, equality before the law. It was necessary for the law to protect brown and black subjects because the only defence of a state in Liberal theory was as the protector of individual freedom. No individual should be forced into subordination to another and the state should ensure that this was not the case. One of the main worries of the abolitionists who had concerned themselves with conditions in Jamaica after emancipation was that they could not be confident that the Jamaican legal system was being used impartially. There were constant complaints that the magistrates were also the planters and that they misused their power. For Liberals, the issue of the impartiality of the law irrespective of race was clearly crucial. Indeed John Stuart Mill's classic defence of the rights of the female sex, *The Subjection of Women*, relied on a similar argument in relation to gender. Laws of marriage and inheritance which prevented women from achieving their full development as individuals must be bad laws.

The analogy between slavery and women's subordination was central to Mill and, as has already been pointed out, a commonplace for some nineteenth-century thinkers. Mill's *Subjection* is suffused with the comparison between the bondage of slavery and the bondage of womanhood. His better knowledge of the second leads him to regard it as in some ways more complete a form of dependence since men demand emotional support from women as well as obedience. 'I am far from pretending,' he writes, 'that wives are in general no better treated than slaves, but no slave is a slave to the same lengths, and in so full a sense of the word, as a wife is.'[71] Both slavery and the subordination of women were defended as *natural*, but both were rooted in the social practices of savage societies and the ways of barbarism could be civilized. Civilization, for Mill, was a key concept, and civilization meant the possibility of individuals acting together with a common purpose, the recognition of community, the development of a collective will (made possible by the immense advances of the middle classes) and a movement of power from individuals to the masses. One of the dangers of civilization, to his mind, was that it could lead to individuals becoming too dependent on society in general and this was something which must be struggled against.[72]

For Mill, *dependence*, whether of grown men who should know better, of slaves or of women, is a primitive state, uncivilized. Unlike many men of his period he believed that if full personhood could be achieved by both women and blacks, they could become independent. He accepted the particular form of individuality, associated with masculinity, that was the common sense of mid-nineteenth-century middle-class men, as being the norm to which all should aspire. But he built on the myth of independence which lay at the heart of masculinity and believed that others could achieve it, thus challenging the gender and ethnic specificity of the common-sense view of the individual.

The assumption that peoples should be subject to the laws in the same way, and able to develop their potential to the highest possible point, did not mean that Mill and his supporters believed the races were entirely equal. They emphasized the *potential* for equality rather than an equality which was yet fully realized. Women, blacks and browns, having been denied opportunities, must now have access to them but it would be necessary for them to learn civilization, just as working-class men would have to learn that civilization. This faith in the civilizing power of education, a characteristically nineteenth-century faith, was shared by missionaries and improvers of many kinds and one of the most common representations of the freed slave was as the child who needed help, guidance and support in the transition from freedom to manhood.[73]

The analogy between race and gender and the assumption that different groups were differently positioned on the ladder of full personhood informed the organizational practice of the Jamaica Committee as well as the public declarations of its leaders and supporters.[74] The committee itself was entirely male in the time-honoured tradition of voluntary organizations, especially when they required a high public profile. The national committee boasted MPs and numerous well-known provincial figures as well as intellectuals. The auxiliary committees, set up in provincial towns, had a similar structure with exclusively male committees composed of local bigwigs and dignitaries. Publishing their names in the newspaper, registering their activities in the public sphere, was itself part of the politics of prestige.

Women had no public profile in any of this, but undoubtedly, as in every similar organization, they did much of the backstage work and were crucial to the financial well-being of the campaign. However, their role was not simply to support the men in their more public endeavours. In organizations such as the Edinburgh Ladies' Emancipation Society the women were concerned to establish their special, and feminine, contribution. No one could deny, they argued,

> that Governor Eyre has been accessory to great cruelty and loss of life, flogging and slaughter of women as well as men, and a part of this after he had declared any fancied necessity at an end. It is disgusting to find English men, and especially English women, applauding the hero of such deeds as these.[75]

The reason, of course, for finding it particularly horrifying that Englishwomen should be supporting Eyre was that it challenged the ideal of woman as more sensitive and more open to morality than men. A special relation with religion and morality had long informed the practice of those middle-class women who were involved in anti-slavery and related issues.[76] In the late eighteenth and early nineteenth centuries the issue that had especially engaged women was the attack on the slave family and the maternal relation.[77] By mid-century, increasing involvement with the American movement was one of the reasons for the more explicit focus on questions of sexuality, which for the Edinburgh ladies, for example, was part of their thinking about Jamaica. For them, 'the deepest shame of womanhood' associated with slavery was the subjection of female slaves to the potential abuse of their masters.[78] Their horror at the hanging of Gordon was compounded by the fact that he had had a very close relationship with his mother and that he had bought his sisters out of slavery as soon as he could, thus demonstrating the depth of his familial affections.

For the Jamaica Committee and their allies the negroes belonged to the same human family as the whites, but for Carlyle and the Eyre Defence Committee, whites and negroes were not the same species. As Carlyle had argued in 1849, blacks were a lower order and should be treated as such. Eyre, in his evidence to the Royal Commission, had stated,

> That the negroes form a low state of civilization and being under the influence of superstitious feelings could not properly be dealt with in the same manner as might the peasantry of a European country . . . That as a race the negroes are most excitable and impulsive, and any seditious or rebellious action was sure to be taken up by and extend amongst the large majority of those with whom it came in contact.[79]

Carlyle's view of the negroes as 'an ignorant, uncivilized, and grossly superstitious people', 'creatures' of 'impulse and imitation, easily misled, very excitable', full of 'evil passions' and 'little removed in many respects from absolute savages' became the orthodoxy of the campaign. The blacks, in other words, were not up to freedom. Nothing, then, could 'be more absurd than to compare a negro insurrection with a rebellion in England' and the Jamaica Committee's claim that negroes should be subject to the same laws as the English could not possibly be defended.[80]

The main efforts of Carlyle and the Defence Committee were focused on celebrating Eyre, his character and his actions. For Carlyle, Eyre was the man who had saved Jamaica from anarchy and horror and should be profoundly congratulated for it. As the narrator of heroism, he placed Eyre firmly in the great tradition of Cromwell and Frederick the Great. As a white man and an Englishman, with the memory of Haiti and the Indian Mutiny in the forefront of his mind, Eyre had been absolutely right to act resolutely and to use force. The double spectres of Haiti (when the blacks had driven out all the whites), and of the Indian Mutiny (when, according to the collective English myth, the Indians had brutally massacred, in the most treacherous circumstances, English men, women and children) were ever present in both the Jamaican and the English consciousness, shaping expectations and raising hopes and fears.[81]

In Carlyle's view, Eyre had quenched a savage insurrection by prompt and skilful conduct. He had shown 'some of the very highest qualities that ever in a man ... have been considered meritorious'.[82] Furthermore, Carlyle argued that far from Eyre transgressing the laws of England he had maintained the real and natural laws against the lawlessness of the black rebels.[83] Carlyle called on the English to be grateful to Eyre for his actions. 'The English nation,' he trumpeted, 'never loved anarchy; nor was wont to spend its sympathy on miserable mad seditions, especially of this inhuman and half-brutish type; but always loved order, and the prompt suppression of sedition.'[84]

After he met Eyre, Carlyle commented that he was 'visibly a brave, gentle, chivalrous and clear man, whom I would make dictator of Jamaica for the next twenty-five years were I now king of it . . .'[85] For Carlyle, the death of a few hundred 'niggers' was not something to get agitated about. 'If Eyre had shot the whole Nigger population and flung them into the sea, would it probably have been much harm to them, not to speak of us,' he wrote.[86]

Carlyle's appeal to the English, for despite his Scottish origins he persisted in this usage, was pinned on the conviction that the English both valued order over anarchy and believed that strong men provided the best route to ensure this. He depended on the practical sense of the English. They were doers not talkers. 'Commend me to the silent English,' he wrote, 'to the silent Romans.' Their epic poems were written on the earth's surface. How much preferable to the 'ever-talking, ever-gesticulating French'.[87] Ask Mr Bull his spoken opinion of any matter, thought Carlyle, and there would be little benefit, but

> set him once to work, – respectable man! His spoken sense is next to nothing, nine-tenths of it palpable *non*sense: but his unspoken sense, his inner silent feeling of what is true, what does agree with fact, what is doable and what is not doable, – this seeks its fellow in the world. A terrible worker; irresistible against marshes, mountains, impediments, disorder, incivilisation; everywhere vanquishing disorder, leaving it behind him as method and order.[88]

Here was Governor Eyre, the true Englishman, impregnable against savagery and black barbarism. Here also were echoes of John Halifax, the man who did not mince words but acted.

Carlyle's celebration of Eyre rested in part on his notion of English 'doers' who knew what was 'doable' and did it. His critique of the effeminate moaners who complained about such action, who would allow the fire to utterly destroy rather than risk pouring on the water, drew on his long-established contempt for the groaning philanthropists who thought that the world could survive without pain. In 'Occasional Discourse' the ostensible setting was a meeting of the 'UNIVERSAL ABOLITION-OF-PAIN ASSOCIATION', a bitter Dickensian touch from Carlyle.[89] For the prophet of the heroic, the Jamaica Committee were likened to 'a group or knot of rabid Nigger-Philanthropists barking furiously in the gutter'.[90] The barking, yapping little dogs lacked passion, feeling and humanity. Real manhood meant a capacity to act with authority and power.

The commitment to a particular variety of English masculinity and the denunciation of alternative forms as effeminate, was linked with a specific set of ideas about sexual difference as well as about the fundamental nature of racial inequality. A profound believer in the proper spheres of men and women, Carlyle was convinced that mastery in the household meant mastery over wife as well as over servants. A properly hierarchical social order was infinitely preferable to the dangers of democracy. It was the collapse of hierarchy, the enfranchisement of large sections of the male working class, the spectre of feminism and the grotesque ambitions of the blacks in the wake of abolition, that threatened to engulf right thinking and doing. Eyre was not only the hero who had saved Englishmen from a gruesome death, he had also protected Englishwomen and shielding 'the weaker sex' was, of course, a crucial aspect of independence and manliness.

As John Tyndall, the only major scientist to support the Defence Committee, argued, the negroes were lazy, profligate and savage. Eyre had the duty not only to preserve the lives of seven thousand British men, but also to preserve the honour of seven thousand British women from the murder and lust of black savages. Evoking the horrors of Haiti and Cawnpore, he approved:

> the conduct of those British officers in India who shot their wives before blowing themselves to pieces, rather than allow what they loved and honoured to fall into the hands of the Sepoys . . . the women of England ought to have a voice in this matter, and to them I confidently appeal . . . there is something in the soul of man to lift him to the level of death, and to enable him to look it in the face. But there is nothing in the soul of woman to lift her to the level of that which I dare not do more than glance at here . . .[91]

The reference was to the well-known horror stories of rape associated with the Haitian revolution. Such matters could not be discussed on public platforms in the 1860s. Eyre's own 'proudest recollection' of Morant Bay, he claimed, was that he had saved the ladies of Jamaica.[92] In fact, the terrifying stories that gathered, and were repeated in the British press, about the brutalities done to women were shown in the evidence collected by the Royal Commission to be grossly overstated, but such empirical detail had little to do with the mythic qualities of the tales.

Englishmen's fears of black male sexuality and the threat it posed to 'their' women were linked with fears about the powers of black women unleashed. Eyre's reports to the Colonial Office had, from the start, stressed the atrocities committed by the rebels, which in his view justified his response. He, together with many others, commented on the women who were even more brutal and barbarous than the men.[93] Such an image was harshly at odds with a Carlyle or a Ruskin view of the proper nature of womanhood.[94] Large numbers of individual Englishwomen were, indeed, involved in the activities of the Eyre Defence Committee, apparently fully supporting the manly ideal of the hero who would protect them from danger. As W. F. Finlason, a major protagonist of Eyre commented, they were delighted to count amongst their number some of the most distinguished of the women of England:

> Their sex – whose perceptions of the *right* are, it has been observed, far more rapid than those of the other sex – and, in this respect, more resemble the rapid intuitions of genius than the slower processes of judgement – were, from the first, strongly in favour of the unfortunate ex-Governor.[95]

In the first months after the news of Morant Bay broke in England, public opinion was on the side of the critics. After the report of the Royal Commission and the decision by the Jamaica Committee to prosecute Eyre, a backlash formed, fuelled by Carlyle and his allies. There is little doubt that domestic political issues played a large part in the shift of the upper and middle classes away from a critique of a defender of order. The famous events in Hyde Park, when working-class reformers imposed their will by occupying the park, and the passage of the 1867 Reform Act, together with the alarms over the Fenians, frightened many. The connections between events in Jamaica and events in London began to appear much more dangerous. The Jamaica Committee had to rely increasingly on hard-core Radical and working-class support, but this did not enable them to prosecute successfully since no jury would agree that there was a charge to answer. Their pressure did stop the Government from reinstating Eyre, however, and it was not until the Tories were back in power in 1873 that he received a pension.

It was quite apparent to Mill that the failure of middle-class support was central to their lack of success. As he wrote in his *Autobiography*,

> It was clear that to bring English functionaries to the bar of a criminal court for abuses of power committed against negroes and mulattoes was not a popular proceeding with the English middle classes.[96]

Similarly *The Spectator*, in an article in June 1868 analysing why the middle classes had supported Eyre, noted that they were 'positively enraged at the demand of negroes for equal consideration with Irishmen, Scotchmen and Englishmen'.[97] The acute irony at the heart of this judgement, in a period when the English were beginning to reconstruct the meanings of Englishness in such a way as to effectively marginalize yet again the Irish and the Scots, was unfortunately lost on the author.[98]

Carlyle, the Grand Old Man of English Letters, had played a significant part in articulating this rage and legitimating with Englishmen and Englishwomen the notion that negroes could not, and should not, expect equal consideration. In 1849 he had been a lone voice speaking in the wilderness, denouncing the hegemony of abolitionist and emancipatory discourses. By 1866 a new hegemony was in the making, not to emerge fully for quite some time. The optimism that had informed the Radical Liberal vision with its conviction that the great free market of the world would spread benevolence, civilization and happiness; that slavery was immoral and economically unnecessary; and that a free market economy would allow the negroes to rise to the heights of Englishness, was on the wane. It was Disraeli and Joseph Chamberlain who discursively constructed a new popular imperialism in the decades to follow, and who secured a base for a politics rooted in that imperialism. They could build on the legacy of Carlyle who, like Enoch Powell at a much later political moment, was central to the articulation of a new racism.

Mill and Carlyle both drew on the tradition of *John Halifax, Gentleman*. Both had a profound belief in the centrality of individual action and individual responsibility. Both had a deeply rooted sense of themselves as individual subjects, active in the world and able to act on others. Both were strong believers in the glory of work. Both were convinced that they must speak out when necessary and risk public unpopularity. Both had a deep conviction of their own public importance as writers and thinkers, doers in the prestigious world of letters. Both Carlyle and Mill were, like John Halifax, men of the middle class who saw themselves as effective actors in the great public theatre of life. But they built on that myth of individuality in significantly different ways, utilizing the same term but accenting and articulating it differently within Liberal and conservative discourses.

Both appealed strongly to an idea of England and a particular notion of Englishness, but they offered significantly different meanings to their ethnicities. Carlyle's Englishness was complacent and deeply chauvinistic. The England he evoked was unmitigatingly English. It was a nation which hated anarchy and loved order. Its epitome was to be found in John Bull, who might not be clever with words but who knew what was what when it came to deeds. The English people were born conservatives, but then 'All great Peoples are conservative; slow to believe in novelties', a noble, silent, peaceable people but one that could be roused to terrible rage.[99] Mill's view of his country was far more critical, his appeal to the English nation more to do with his profound belief in rationality than with a grasp of popular consciousness. As the child of an Enlightenment tradition he was deeply hostile to little Englishness, to the common English problem of 'judging universal questions by a merely English standard'.[100] Far from despising the French, he appreciated their less narrow-minded culture. He stood for the brotherhood of the free world, for England as the potential seat of reason and justice rather than custom, tradition and prejudice.

English manhood, in the eyes of Carlyle and Mill, had significantly different meanings. Carlyle's heroes were Cromwell and Hampden, men of action who could be roused to great emotion. Eyre, in Carlyle's narrative, was cast in this same mould. A man of passion rather than a man of reason. A man who acted first and sorted out the effects afterwards. A man of feeling. In the eyes of Carlyle, Mill was seriously lacking in such feeling. He described Mill's *Autobiography* as the 'Autobiography of a steam-engine', or 'the life of a logic-chopping engine'.[101] It showed, he felt, a chilling absence of humanity. Carlyle was not alone in this. Late-nineteenth-century critics of Mill were repelled by his account of his own relationship with Harriet Taylor and his insistence that a truly rational relation between a man and a woman could transcend mere sensuality. Mill's first biographer, echoing Carlyle's attack on the lack of manliness of abolitionists, commented that he was 'not singular in the opinion that in the so-called sensual feelings, he [Mill] was below average'.[102] Carlyle, then, was the man of passion, Mill the man of reason, a difference which can be traced in their very physiques; the one craggy and rugged, the other with the aquiline features of the classical.

Finally, the different views of manhood of Carlyle and Mill were to do with the different conceptions of authority and power associated with masculinity. While Carlyle clung to a notion of hierarchy and order, with white Englishmen as the ultimate arbiters in the interests of all, Mill dreamed of a more egalitarian society in the future in which all individuals, whether black or white, male or female, would have achieved 'civilization'. His relationship with Harriet Taylor provided his prefiguring of the potential between men and women, yet in the *Subjection* he still falls back on a notion of the natural division of labour between the sexes. Whether there were similar limitations on his conceptions of relations between the races, whether there would be in the end, whatever the degree of education achieved by the blacks, a *natural* division of labour between the races, remains a problem.

The debate over Eyre became a site of struggle over the dignity, sexual identity, hierarchic and legal status of whole categories of people – blacks as opposed to whites, Jamaican whites as opposed to the English, the middle class as opposed to the working class, men as opposed to women. In the process of that political struggle a particular definition of English manhood was triumphant, with consequences for all those defined as outside of, and alien to, it.

In December 1874 Disraeli, as Prime Minister, wrote to Carlyle. He offered him the Grand Cross of the Bath and a yearly income, saying, 'A Government should recognize intellect. It elevates and sustains the tone of a nation.'[103] This recognition, from the most powerful politician in the land, and one who was in the process of reconstructing the meanings of conservatism, marks one of the ways in which intellectual power is sustained and reproduces itself. Public distinction had been offered and even though Carlyle refused it, he was of course highly gratified. Carlyle's intervention, with the full weight of his literary and political prestige, in the debate over the conduct of the authorities in Jamaica in 1865, could only be judged as elevating and sustaining the tone of the nation in a conservative, ethnocentric and racist conception of Englishness.

NOTES

1 Some of the major sources for the Eyre controversy are: Hamilton Hume, *The Life of Edward John Eyre, late Governor of Jamaica* (Richard Bentley, London, 1867); William F. Finlason, *The History of the Jamaica Case: being an account founded upon official documents of the rebellion of the negroes in Jamaica* (Chapman & Hall, London, 1869); Edward Bean Underhill, *The Tragedy of Morant Bay: a narrative of the disturbances in the island of Jamaica in 1865* (Alexander & Shepheard, London, 1895); Sydney S. Olivier, *The Myth of Governor Eyre* (Leonard and Virginia Woolf, London, 1933); Philip D. Curtin, *Two Jamaicas: The Role of Ideas in a Tropical Colony, 1830–1865* (Harvard University Press, Cambridge, Mass., 1955); Douglas Hall, *Free Jamaica, 1836–65; an Economic History* (Yale University Press, New Haven, 1959); Bernard Semmel, *The Governor Eyre Controversy* (Macgibbon & Kee, London, 1962); Douglas Lorimer, *Colour, Class and the Victorians: English Attitudes to the Negroes in the Mid-Nineteenth Century* (Leicester University Press, Leicester, 1978); Geoffrey Dutton, *The Hero as Murderer: The Life of Edward John Eyre, Australian Explorer and Governor of Jamaica, 1815–1901* (Collins, London, 1967); Gad J. Heuman, *Between Black and White. Race, Politics and the Free Coloreds in Jamaica 1792–1865* (Greenwood, Conn., 1981); Abigail B. Bakan, *Ideology and Class Conflict in Jamaica. The Politics of Rebellion* (McGill–Queen's University Press, London, 1990).

2 Leonard Huxley, quoted in Semmel, *Governor Eyre Controversy*, p. 14.

3 For a longer version of this argument, see Leonore Davidoff and Catherine Hall, *Family Fortunes: Men and Women of the English Middle Class 1780–1850* (Hutchinson and Chicago University Press, London and Chicago, 1987).

4 Quoted in Davidoff and Hall, *Family Fortunes*, p. 76.

5 Leonore Davidoff, ' "Adam Spoke First and Named the Orders of the World": masculine and feminine domains in history and sociology', in Helen Corr and Lynne Jamieson (eds), *The Politics of Everyday Life: Continuity and Change in Work, Labour and the Family* (Macmillan, London, 1990).

6 Revd Isaac Taylor, *Self Cultivation Recommended; or, Hints to a Youth Leaving School* (T. Cadell & Son, London, 1817), p. 17.

7 Quoted in Davidoff and Hall, *Family Fortunes*, p. 229.

8 As Sally Mitchell points out in her book on Mrs Craik, *Diana Mulock Craik* (Twayne, Boston, 1983), p. 50: '*John Halifax, Gentleman* was an enormously successful book. Hurst & Blackett were kept busy resetting the type; four sets of plates had been used by 1858. The first cheap edition was illustrated with a steel engraving by Pre-Raphaelite painter J. E. Millais. An 1863 listing of the era's most popular books put *John Halifax, Gentleman* just behind *Uncle Tom's Cabin.*' The edition that I have used, picked up in a second-hand bookshop for thirty pence (with coloured illustrations), is the 'Bordesley Edition' with no date and no place of publication.

Utilizing the novel as a form of historical evidence has clearly become more problematic for historians influenced by critical theory for we have learned that we must be attentive to the relation between form and content, to questions of genre, of narrative structure, of textual contradiction and ambiguity. Nevertheless, provided we are attentive to these formal questions and do not read literary sources naively, critical theory has also shown us how different forms of writing give access to different ideological and discursive formations. As a historian I use multiple forms of historical evidence, from Parliamentary Papers to the jottings of a commonplace book, from sermons to census, from maps to visual representations. The range of sources precludes the kind of elaborated textual work on each source essential to the art historian or the deconstructionist critic with their different projects. As historians, we need to be sensitive to the new questions opened up by the post-structuralist critique. This does not, however, mean that we have to abandon the specificity of the historical project – the construction of narratives which deal with change over time, with process, with agency and determination, with particularities situated in their wider social context.

9 Raymond Williams, *The Long Revolution* (Chatto & Windus, London, 1961). See particularly his analysis of the 1840s in ch. 2.

10 James continued, 'He is infinite; he outlasts time; he is enshrined in a million innocent breasts; and before his awful perfection and his eternal durability we respectfully lower our lance.' Quoted in Mitchell, *Craik*, p. 51.

11 Craik, *John Halifax*, p. 25.

12 Craik, *John Halifax*, p. 28.

13 Craik, *John Halifax*, p. 79.

14 Craik, *John Halifax*, p. 81.

15 Craik, *John Halifax*, p. 162.

16 Davidoff and Hall, *Family Fortunes*, p. 21.

17 Craik, *John Halifax*, p. 163.

18 Catherine Marsh, *The Life of the Rev. William Marsh* (James Nisbet & Co., London, 1868), pp. 102–3.

19 Craik, *John Halifax*, p. 117.

20 Craik, *John Halifax*, p. 234.

21 Craik, *John Halifax*, p. 227.
22 James Luckcock, 'My house and garden', Birmingham Reference Library, no. 375948.
23 Craik, *John Halifax*, p. 290.
24 Craik, *John Halifax*, p. 415.
25 John Money points out how in the West Midlands, for example, the traditional route for putting pressure on the House of Commons through the county MPs became increasingly unsatisfactory in the late eighteenth century. *Experience and Identity: Birmingham and the West Midlands, 1760–1800* (Manchester University Press, Manchester, 1977), especially pt 3.
26 Robert J. Morris, 'Voluntary Societies and British Urban Elites, 1780–1850: An Analysis', *The Historical Journal*, vol. 26, no. 1, 1983; *Class, Sect and Party. The Making of the British Middle Class, 1820–50* (Manchester University Press, Manchester, 1990).
27 F. K. Prochaska, *Women and Philanthropy in Nineteenth-Century England* (Oxford University Press, 1980); Davidoff and Hall, *Family Fortunes*; Mary P. Ryan, *Women in Public. Between Banners and Ballots, 1825–1880* (Johns Hopkins University Press, Baltimore, 1990).
28 See, for example, Thomas Carlyle, *Reminiscences*, (ed.) James Anthony Froude (Longmans, Green & Co., London, 1881); James Anthony Froude, *Thomas Carlyle: A History of His Life in London* (Longmans, Green & Co., London, 1882); John Stuart Mill, *Autobiography* (Oxford University Press, London, 1924); Alexander Bain, *John Stuart Mill. A Criticism with Personal Recollections* (Longmans, Green & Co., London, 1882).
29 Thomas Carlyle, 'The Hero as Man of Letters', in *Selected Writings* (Penguin, Harmondsworth, 1971), p. 236.
30 Quoted in Norma Clarke, 'Shock Heroic', *Times Higher Educational Supplement*, 4 May 1990.
31 See the fascinating discussion of Dickens' contribution to this debate in Mary Poovey, *Uneven Developments. The Ideological Work of Gender in Mid-Victorian England* (Virago, London, 1989), especially ch. 4.
32 Thomas Carlyle, 'Occasional Discourse on the Negro Question', *Fraser's Magazine*, vol. 41, January 1850, p. 672. The piece was republished in a revised version as a pamphlet in 1853. That version, titled 'Occasional Discourse on the Nigger Question', appears in *English and Other Critical Essays* (Dent, London, 1964). I owe the point about the significant change in the title to Thomas Holt who first pointed this out to me.
33 Thomas Carlyle, *Past and Present* (Dent, London, 1960), p. 189.
34 Quoted in Norma Clarke, *Ambitious Heights. Writing, Friendship, Love. The Jewsbury Sisters, Felicia Hemans and Jane Carlyle* (Routledge, London, 1990), p. 99. See also Phyllis Rose, *Parallel*

Lives: Five Victorian Marriages (Penguin, Harmondsworth, 1983) on the marriage of Thomas Carlyle and Jane Welsh.

35 Mill, *Autobiography*, p. 82.

36 Mill, *Autobiography*, p. 148.

37 On Jamaica post-emancipation, see Curtin, *Two Jamaicas*, Hall, *Free Jamaica*, and William A. Green, *British Slave Emancipation. The Sugar Colonies and the Great Experiment 1830–65* (Oxford University Press, London, 1976).

38 Earl Henry G. Grey, *The Colonial Policy of Lord John Russell's Administration* (Richard Bentley, London, 1853), vol. 1, pp. 60, 63.

39 Hall, *Free Jamaica.*

40 Lucretia Mott, *Lucretia Mott's Diary of her visit to Great Britain to attend the World's Anti-Slavery Convention of 1840*, (ed.) F. B. Tolles (Friends' Historical Society, London, 1952), p. 54.

41 Carlyle, 'Occasional Discourse', p. 670.

42 My comments on 'Occasional Discourse' benefited greatly from the discussions with the third-year seminar group working with me on Governor Eyre in the Cultural Studies Dept, Polytechnic of East London, in the spring of 1988. I am particularly grateful to Lynn Clegg for letting me use some of her ideas.

43 Carlyle, 'Occasional Discourse', p. 677.

44 Carlyle, 'Occasional Discourse', p. 671.

45 Carlyle, 'Occasional Discourse', p. 671.

46 Carlyle, 'Occasional Discourse', pp. 674–5.

47 Carlyle, 'Occasional Discourse' (1853 edn), p. 327.

48 Carlyle, 'Occasional Discourse', p. 673.

49 Carlyle, 'Occasional Discourse', p. 675.

50 Lowell Joseph Ragatz, *The Fall of the Planter Class in the British Caribbean 1763–1833* (The Century Co., London, 1928), pp. 427–9.

51 Parliamentary Papers, *Select Committee of the House of Lords on the State of the West India Colonies*, 1831–2, vol. 11, p. 60.

52 Parliamentary Papers, *Select Committee*, 1831–2, vol. 11, p. 218.

53 The emphasis on the feminization of blacks is sharper in the 1853 edition than in the 1849 edition of the essay. Carlyle, 'Occasional Discourse' (1853 edn), p. 311.

54 Carlyle, 'Occasional Discourse', pp. 672–3.

55 Carlyle, 'Occasional Discourse', pp. 672.

56 John Stuart Mill, 'The Negro Question', *Fraser's Magazine*, vol. 41, January 1850, p. 25.

57 Mill, 'The Negro Question', p. 31.

58 Mill, 'The Negro Question', p. 29.

59 John Stuart Mill, *The Subjection of Women* (Virago, London, 1983).

60 Lorimer, *Colour, Class and the Victorians*; Nancy Stepan, *The Idea of Race in Science: Great Britain 1800–1960* (Macmillan, London, 1982); George Dangerfield, *Bengal Mutiny: The Story of the Sepoy*

Rebellion (Hutchinson, London, 1933); Patrick Brantlinger, *Rule of Darkness. British Literature and Imperialism 1830–1914* (Cornell University Press, Ithaca, 1988); Victor G. Kiernan, *The Lords of Human Kind: European Attitudes to the Outside World in the Imperial Age* (Weidenfeld & Nicolson, London, 1969), pp. 48–9.

61 Christine Bolt, *The Anti-Slavery Movement and Reconstruction: A Study in Anglo-American Cooperation* (Oxford University Press, London, 1969).

62 Quoted in Semmel, *Governor Eyre Controversy*, p. 105.

63 Mill, *Autobiography*, p. 226.

64 Parliamentary Papers, *Report of the Jamaica Royal Commission 1866.*

65 Jamaica Committee, 'Jamaica Committee Papers, 1–3'. I am grateful to Janice Wells for the work she did in locating the papers.

66 Semmel, *Governor Eyre Controversy*, focuses on the connections between class issues in Britain and the Jamaica debate.

67 Semmel, *Governor Eyre Controversy*, p. 103; John Vincent, *The Formation of the Liberal Party, 1857–68* (Constable, London, 1966), p. 150. It is, of course, important to note that not everyone involved in the campaign shared the views of the two leaders. Indeed, it would seem a fruitful line of inquiry to look at the differences within the two groups and the politics of alliance that was constructed in each case.

68 Mill, *Autobiography*, p. 252.

69 Birmingham Jamaica Committee, *Jamaica Question* (Hudson & Son, Birmingham, 1866), p. 7.

70 It is noticeable that the term 'Britain' is scarcely used. The English were confident in their assumption of dominance.

71 Mill, *Subjection of Women*, p. 57.

72 John Stuart Mill, 'Civilization', in *Dissertations and Discussions, Political, Philosophical and Historical* (J. W. Parker & Son, London, 1859), vol. 1.

73 See, for example, the Edinburgh Ladies' Emancipation Society, *Annual Report and Sketch of Anti-Slavery events and the Condition of the Freedmen* (H. Armour & Co., Edinburgh, 1867), pp. 3–4.

74 Again, it would of course be dangerous to suggest that all members thought alike. For the purposes of this paper, Mill and Carlyle are being taken as representative figures, with all the problems that raises.

75 Edinburgh Ladies' Emancipation Society, *Annual Report*, p. 3.

76 On women and anti-slavery, see Louis Billington and Rosamund Billington, '"A Burning Zeal for Righteousness": Women in the British Anti-Slavery Movement, 1820–1860', in Jane Rendall (ed.), *Equal or Different: Women's Politics 1800–1914* (Blackwell, Oxford, 1987); Kenneth Corfield, 'Elizabeth Heyrick: Radical Quaker', in *Religion in the Lives of English Women, 1760–1930* Gail Malmgreen

(ed.), (Indiana University Press, Bloomington, 1986); Clare Midgeley, 'Women and the Anti-Slavery Movement 1780s–1860s' (unpublished PhD thesis, University of Kent, 1989).

77 See, for example, Hannah More's famous poem, 'The Black Slave Trade', in *The Works of Hannah More* (T. Cadell & Son, London, 1830), vol. 2.

78 Edinburgh Ladies' Emancipation Society, *Annual Report*, Appendix, p. 19.

79 Parliamentary Papers, *Royal Commission on Jamaica*, vol. 1, pp. 1–3. For an example of the way in which Eyre's views were popularized, see Hume, *Edward John Eyre*.

80 John Tyndall, quoted in Hume, *Edward John Eyre*, App. C, p. 281.

81 On Haiti, see C. L. R. James, *The Black Jacobins: Toussaint L'Ouverture and the San Domingo Revolution* (Vintage, New York, 1963). On the impact of the Indian Mutiny on popular writing in England, see Brantlinger, *Rule of Darkness*. The Royal Commission quotes many examples of witnesses who refer both to Haiti and the Mutiny.

82 Quoted in Olivier, *Myth of Governor Eyre*, pp. 336–8.

83 Thomas Carlyle, 'Shooting Niagara: and After?', in *Critical and Miscellaneous Essays* (Chapman & Hall, London, 1899), vol. 5.

84 Hume, *Edward John Eyre*, App. D, p. 290.

85 Finlason, *History of the Jamaica Case*, p. 369.

86 Jane Welsh Carlyle, *Letters and Memorials of Jane Welsh Carlyle*, (ed.) James Anthony Froude (Longmans, Green & Co., London, 1883), p. 381. I owe this reference to Sophia A. Rosenfeld, 'Fear of Anarchy among the Victorian Literary Elite: The Anti-Democratic Social Thought of the Eyre Defense Committee (1865–67)' (unpublished paper, junior independent work, History Dept, Princeton University, May 1987).

87 Carlyle, *Past and Present*, pp. 151–6.

88 Carlyle, *Past and Present*, pp. 155–6.

89 Carlyle, 'Occasional Discourse', p. 304.

90 Carlyle, 'Shooting Niagara', p. 12.

91 Quoted in Hume, *Edward John Eyre*, App. C, p. 283.

92 Parliamentary Papers, *Royal Commission on Jamaica*, pp. 30, 478.

93 For an example of a typical comment on the brutality of the women rioters, see Parliamentary Papers, *Royal Commission on Jamaica*, pp. 34–5.

94 For Ruskin on women, see John Ruskin, *Sesame and Lilies* (George Allen & Sons, London, 1907).

95 Finlason, *History of the Jamaica Case*, p. 386 fn.

96 Mill, *Autobiography*, p. 253.

97 Quoted in Semmel, *Governor Eyre Controversy*, p. 171.

98 Richard Colls and Philip Dodd (eds), *Englishness: Politics and Culture, 1880–1920* (Croom Helm, London, 1987).

99 Carlyle, *Past and Present*, p. 156.
100 Mill, *Autobiography*, p. 50.
101 Quoted in Emery E. Neff, *Carlyle and Mill. An Introduction to Victorian Thought*, (Columbia University Press, Norwood, Mass., 1926) p. 52.
102 Bain, *John Stuart Mill*, p. 149.
103 Disraeli to Carlyle, December 1874, preserved in Carlyle's house.

Index